DARK LORE

VOLUME I

DAILY GRAIL PUBLISHING

CONTENTS

INTRODUCTION.   I

HUNGRY GHOSTS • *Michael Prescott*   3

HER SWEET MURMUR • *Greg Taylor*   15

LIFE WITH THE GREAT SPHINX • *Robert Schoch*   39

WHO IS FLYING THE TRIANGLES • *Nick Redfern*   57

A PSYCHEDELIC APOCALYPSE • *Daniel Pinchbeck*   69

THE AUTHORS ARE IN ETERNITY • *Susan B. Martinez*   83

BIGFOOT'S BOGUS BURIAL • *Loren Coleman*   95

THE HIGH PRIEST AND THE GREAT BEAST • *John Higgs*   111

MULTILINGUAL MEDIUMSHIP • *Michael E. Tymn*   121

HELLFIRE AND DAMNATION • *Philip Coppens*   129

EYE SPIRITS • *Paul Devereux*   145

INCREDIBLE AS IT MAY SEEM • *Blair Mackenzie Blake*   153

TEMPLAR REVELATIONS • *Lynn Picknett & Clive Prince*   183

OUIJA! • *Mitch Horowitz*   199

THE UNBELIEVABLE STRANGENESS OF BIGFOOT • *The Emperor*   217

ENTER THE JAGUAR • *Mike Jay*   237

THE BEATIFIC VISION • *Michael Grosso*   255

WERE THE UFO CONTACTEES RITUAL MAGICIANS? • *Adam Gorightly*   269

ENDNOTES AND SOURCES   289

Round about the accredited and orderly facts of every science there ever floats a sort of dust-cloud of exceptional observations, of occurrences minute and irregular and seldom met with, which it always proves more easy to ignore than to attend to.

- William James

If you would like to be notified of future releases of *Darklore*, please send an email to darklore@dailygrail.com. Please be assured your contact details will not be used for any other purpose.

EDITOR'S INTRODUCTION

elcome to the first issue of *Darklore*, a journal of exceptional observations, hidden history, the paranormal and esoteric science. Bringing together some of the top researchers and writers on topics from outside of mainstream science and history, *Darklore* will challenge your preconceptions by revealing the strange dimensions veiled by consensus reality. Featuring contributions from Daniel Pinchbeck, Loren Coleman, Nick Redfern, Robert Schoch, Blair Blake, Michael Grosso, Lynn Picknett & Clive Prince and many others, Volume 1 of *Darklore* offers only the best writing and research from the most respected individuals in their fields. We are extremely proud of the end result, and are sure you will find the contents to your liking.

Please note that we don't claim to be offering scientific or academic papers on these topics. *Darklore* is meant as a fun read, for those interested in these topics – the kind of material that is just perfect for a late night read, passing some time on the train, or during that relaxing weekend you needed. If you *are* looking for scholarly comment on these subjects, you should look no further than the *Journal of Scientific Exploration* (www.scientificexploration.org). We recognize that there is an abundance of bad writing and terrible research out there on the topics we cover – which is why we feel that *Darklore* stands out from the crowd. We are very careful in choosing our contributors, and the content – while out on the very edges of science – is presented with common sense and a questioning, critical mind. We hope you agree.

The other thing that sets *Darklore* apart is that any profits are funneled directly back to the contributors – those who deserve it the most. By purchasing *Darklore*, you are actively supporting the 'good guys' out there. Please keep your eye out for future issues (to be notified, send an email to darklore@dailygrail.com) and spread the word – the more support we have, the better our ability to attract the best content. Happy reading!

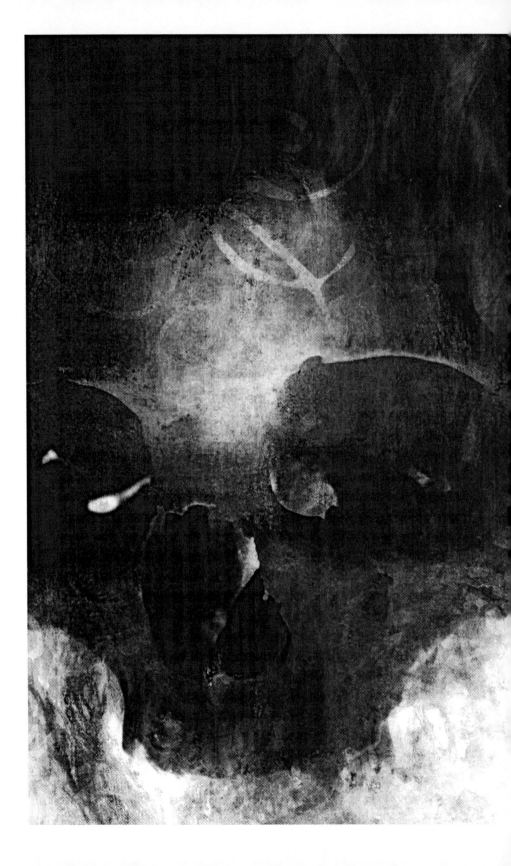

the dark side
of the PARANORMAL

by *Michael Prescott*

ears ago, on a whim, a friend led me into a New Age bookstore in Los Angeles. At the time I was a committed rationalist and knew nothing about paranormal phenomena except what I'd read in skeptical, debunking books. Unlike my friend, who found the bookstore's atmosphere amusing, and who enjoyed pointing out the bizarre titles and covers, I felt distinctly ill at ease. There was something disturbing about being immersed in all that occult literature. I felt as if I'd ventured into unknown territory – dangerous territory. And I was glad to leave.

Later, as I became interested in the paranormal and began to grasp the extent of the evidence for such phenomena, I chalked up my earlier reaction to a form of culture shock. There I was, a rather repressed rationalist, coming into close contact with ideas I found threatening to my worldview. After all, there was nothing actually dangerous about that little bookstore – was there?

Maybe there was. Over the years, as I've studied this subject, I've encountered a fair number of cautionary tales. People who become unduly interested in psychic phenomena – interested to the point of obsession – can find their mental health deteriorating, their relationships fragmenting, and their social status undermined. Of course, obsession is a bad thing regardless of its focus, but I suspect that it's easier to become obsessed with the paranormal than with, say, stamp collecting. Something about this field of inquiry tends to draw people in and make them vulnerable to harm.

THE CURIOUS CASE OF SIR ARTHUR CONAN DOYLE

Since I'm a writer, I take particular interest in the case of Arthur Conan Doyle. Doyle was one of the most popular writers of his day, and his Sherlock Holmes stories are still widely read and dramatized. Fairly late in life he became convinced that it was possible to communicate with the dead through mediums. As his interest grew, he neglected his fiction writing and spent most of his time traveling the world to attend séances and deliver lectures on spiritualism. His reputation suffered, and he was the target of ridicule from some quarters. He had a widely publicized feud with the debunking magician Houdini. Editors began to dread getting Doyle's manuscripts in the mail, for fear that his latest contribution would be yet another essay on the talkative dead. Doyle's fame was such that his essays were invariably published, but his editors weren't always happy about that fact.

With the passage of time, Doyle's critical faculties suffered. He became more credulous, more willing to vouch for even the most dubious phenomena. Many of the mediums he endorsed were later exposed as fakes. Doyle refused to accept some of these exposures. Famously, he even accused Houdini himself of using psychic powers, since – he felt – there was no way the escape artist could have carried out some of his stunts without paranormal gifts.

Most embarrassing was the often retold affair of the Cottingley fairies. Two girls, ages 16 and 10, shot some photos of "fairies" they'd allegedly found in their garden. The fairies were paper cut-outs, and the photos were obvious fakes. Nevertheless, Doyle endorsed the photos as genuine, even publishing an article in *The Strand Magazine* with the regrettable title "Fairies photographed – an epoch-making event." Later he put out an entire book devoted to the subject, *The Coming of the Fairies*. Skeptics have enjoyed skewering him for his gullibility and foolishness ever since. James Randi devotes a chapter of his debunking book *Flim-Flam* to a detailed dissection of the Cottingley case. And yes, there is something funny about a presumably worldly and sophisticated man, rich and internationally famous, falling for a rather inept hoax perpetrated by two young girls. At the same time, there is something about it that's both sad and troubling.

The Cottingley 'Fairies'

How could Doyle's rational faculty deteriorate so badly? Critics suggest that he was never much of a thinker, but I've read a great deal of his work, as well as Daniel Stashower's excellent biography, and my impression is that Doyle had a more penetrating intellect than his detractors admit. Trained in medicine, he traveled around the world as a ship's doctor, acquiring a range of knowledge and experiences that made him far more intellectually interesting than his closed-minded Victorian colleagues. He resisted prejudices – women and minorities are generally treated with respect in his work – and had an appreciation of exotic cultures and variant points of view. In short, Doyle was a sensible, astute observer of the world around him – until he got caught up in his obsession with mediums. At that point his mental and emotional stability began to suffer, and he became increasingly fanatical, blind to any interpretation of the evidence but his own.

THE HUNGRY GHOSTS

If this were an isolated case, it would not be very important, but it is far from isolated. Some cases, in fact, have much worse consequences. One of these is described in anguished, agonizing detail in Joe Fisher's *Hungry Ghosts*. Fisher joined an amateur circle that met regularly to "channel" information from spirits. Initially skeptical, Fisher was soon won over by the information that came through. He and his friends became increasingly obsessed with the meetings, while the woman who ran the circle began to exercise an unhealthy degree of control over some group members, exploiting them and attempting to coerce them into sexual liaisons. As Fisher became convinced that he was in contact with a female spirit guide who'd been his lover in a previous lifetime, he lost interest in his real-life relationships, an attitude that led to the break-up of his marriage. Eventually he went to Europe, intending to verify the information he'd been given. Instead, to his shock, he discovered that much of it was false. Shattered, he returned to America and shared his findings with the group – only to be met with hostility and denial. The group members were so caught up in their shared fantasy that they could not tolerate the intrusion of facts and evidence. Fisher left the group and eventually concluded that he had been victimized by what the Tibetan Book of the Dead calls *pretas*, or 'hungry ghosts' – malign spirits who deceive and corrupt their human interlocutors. He warns his readers to be wary of involvement in the supernatural, and on this note of caution the book ends.

But this was not the end of Joe Fisher's story. He continued to obsess on his experience. Eleven years after the publication of *Hungry Ghosts*, he confided to a friend that he believed the spirits were out to get him for publicizing their activities. They would not leave him alone. In 2001, at age 53, he made his escape. He threw himself off a cliff, ending his life.

There are at least two ways of interpreting this bizarre story. Either Fisher became unhinged as a result of his participation in the séances, and eventually fell victim to his own paranoia; or he actually did come into contact with malevolent spirit entities, against which he had no protection.

Fisher wasn't the only person in the medium's circle to suffer psychological damage. Everyone in the group was affected to some extent. This is not uncommon. Immersion in the occult can have unpredictable effects on the dynamics and psychology of a group. An example that comes to mind are the ITC experiments described by Mark Macy in *Miracles in the Storm*.

ITC is an acronym for Instrumental Transcommunication. This activity, which has gained a surprising number of adherents, involves using technology to contact the dead. It evolved out of EVP, or Electronic Voice Phenomena, a field of amateur research in which "spirit voices" are supposedly picked up on tape recorders. ITC is more high-tech, employing video cameras, TV sets, fax machines, and computers. Enthusiasts claim they have received images and messages from another dimension, and that they are in regular contact with like-minded "experimenters" from beyond.

Macy's book details a group effort to establish and maintain contact with these forces. Such contact is said to require harmony among members of the experimenting groups on both sides of the veil. Unfortunately, harmony proved difficult to come by, at least on the earthly side, and much of *Miracles in the Storm* concerns the in-fighting and mutual suspicion that led to the group's downfall. Organizational chaos is remarkably common among those who explore the paranormal, and the fate of Macy's group is unsurprising.

Although the experiments documented in Macy's book have ended, Macy and some of his colleagues have attempted to renew their work. He reports that his team has made contact with a group of spirits who live on the extradimensional planet Marduk. According to these spirits, "Marduk is watered by only one large stream flowing with many bends across a great part of the planet," a watercourse called the River of Eternity. "We live here together with other forms of life," they explain, "with men [who had] lived on other planets before their bodily death, with dwarfs, giants and gnomes, and with bodiless entities, too."[1] The spirits have what seem to be physical bodies, all in the prime of youth and health.

Among the spirits inhabiting Marduk is Sir Richard Francis Burton, the 19th century explorer and linguist. Burton and his spirit colleagues, calling themselves the Timestream group, established a transmission station on Marduk, by means of which they were able to send video images and text messages to their earthly counterparts. At one point, a rival group of spirits with evil intentions seized control of the transmission station, but the Timestream faction mounted a daring counterattack and regained control.

If all this sounds like science-fiction, there's a good reason. It *is* science-fiction, or at least it was – in Philip Jose Farmer's Riverworld series. Beginning with *To Your Scattered Bodies Go* in 1971, the

Riverworld books feature an intriguing premise: When we die, we are resurrected on an earthlike planet bisected by a single vast river. Both good and evil individuals – human, prehuman, and nonhuman – abide in this land, restored to youth and vigor. As we make our way along the river, we must form alliances and ward off enemies, sometimes in physical combat. And our hero in this adventure? None other than Sir Richard Francis Burton!

I will admit that there are differences between the ITC messages and Riverworld. Farmer's story provided a technological, rather than supernatural, explanation for humanity's resurrection, and dealt extensively with a super-advanced race of humans dubbed the Ethicals who were controlling this vast experiment. None of this relates to the ITC communiqués. And other famous figures who appear in Farmer's saga – Mark Twain, Hermann Goering, and King John of England, among others – have not made any appearance in the messages from Marduk, as far as I know. Nevertheless, the vast river, the physical resurrection in youthful form, the rival alliances and mortal combats, and the presence of Burton himself all combine to create the strong suspicion that the ITC messages are only fiction. Indeed, the whole situation seems reminiscent of role-playing games like *Dungeons & Dragons*, in which the players submerge themselves in a virtual world based on science-fiction archetypes – a world that can begin to seem very real.

A couple of years ago I emailed Mark Macy to ask him about the parallels between Riverworld and his group's findings. I received brief replies from both Macy and one of his colleagues. Neither of them was interested in pursuing the issue, and neither saw any problem in the similarities I'd mentioned.

No problem? Suppose I were to tell you that, by paranormal means, I'd established contact with the crew of an interstellar starship in the 23rd century. Excitedly I report that the ship's captain is James Tiberius Kirk, his first mate is an alien named Spock, and the ship's doctor is McCoy. You point out to me that these characters are all found in the 1960s TV series *Star Trek*. "So what?" I say. "I don't see a problem with that." I'll bet you'd decide that my critical faculties are not quite what they should be.

How can presumably serious people be willing to overlook such an obvious difficulty? I suggest that wholesale immersion in the paranormal can gradually erode one's capacity for appropriate skepticism. Arthur Conan Doyle came to believe in fairies; Joe Fisher's marriage collapsed because he fell in love with his "spirit guide"; Macy and his co-workers are caught up in what appears to be a replay of a science-fiction saga from the 1970s.

ENTER THE TRICKSTER

A wealth of similar cases can be found in George P. Hansen's authoritative study *The Trickster and the Paranormal*, which takes a highly original interdisciplinary approach to the question of why psychic phenomena – and people associated with such things – tend to be marginalized in society. Hansen's book is too complex and densely argued to be summarized in its entirety, but one of his major themes is that long-term, active involvement in the paranormal often produces personal or collective dissociation from reality.

Hansen identifies a constellation of attributes that folklorists call "the trickster" – a mythical figure found in most ethnic traditions, whether as Coyote in Native American lore or the god Hermes in Greek mythology. The trickster is deceitful, playful, disruptive, irrational, unpredictable, often sexually adventurous or perverse, sometimes malevolent, and always to be approached with caution. He is a marginal figure among the other deities, and those humans who are associated with him – shamans, mediums – typically occupy a marginal place in society. He resists institutionalization. He hovers outside the establishment, functioning as both an escape valve and a threat.

While not going so far
as to say that the trickster
actually exists, Hansen uses
the archetype to stand for a
collection of disparate qualities.
And he makes the point
that paranormal phenomena
not only exhibit these same
qualities but often induce them in persons who immerse themselves
in the field.

Like the trickster, psychic phenomena are playful and
maddeningly elusive. They are irrational, in the sense that they fall
outside the purview of rationalist thinking. They are disruptive –
sometimes overtly so, as in the case of poltergeist outbreaks. They
are unpredictable, a fact that has led many a legitimate psychic to
supplement his talents with trickery. They are sometimes malevolent
– as with Fisher's hungry ghosts, not to mention the rich tradition
of malign spirits in every culture, including the devils of Judeo-
Christian theology. They are sometimes associated with bizarre or
coercive sexual practices, as witnessed in many rituals and in the
strange private lives of many mediums and psychics. They resist
institutionalization; despite widespread public interest in psychic
phenomena, no large institutions exist to study the field, and the only
major institutional studies of psychic powers were undertaken by spy
agencies, which are themselves immersed in a culture of ambiguity
and deceit.

Hansen observes that people who directly engage the paranormal,
or try to, sometimes fall into the role-playing trap mentioned above.
A role-playing game, he writes…

> "can become a shared fantasy, wherein the players voluntarily
> suspend normal, rational considerations…The games give more
> direct contact with supernatural ideas than does literature alone.

Live people are involved; they participate in a drama; props may be used, and some physical action is required...Cheating is frequent despite there being no winners or losers in the game...Players can identify with their characters, and sometimes they prefer not to separate themselves from those roles...[O]ccasionally the 'game' becomes obsessive and interferes with real-world pursuits.[2]

Reading these words, I find it hard not to think of the purported messages from Marduk.

There is, then, a dark side to the paranormal. It is not all benevolent angels and comforting words from deceased relatives. There can be obsession, deterioration of rational thought, shared fantasy, even a descent into madness. There can be hungry ghosts. There can be channelers who sexually exploit their followers. There is always the risk that inquiring too deeply into these matters will lead to one's own marginalization – a fate that has befallen even prominent researchers in the field, who have seen their reputations suffer and their prestige stripped away.

Much in the paranormal is worthy of study. But if you choose to examine it, proceed with caution. And if you run into trouble, don't hesitate to turn back. After all, I felt a lot better when I'd left that bookstore...

Michael Prescott is a fiction writer with approximately three million books in print worldwide under various pen names. He has authored nine thrillers, the most recent of which is *Final Sins*. More information about Michael and his books can be found at his website (www.michaelprescott.net). He writes often on the topics of survival research and the paranormal at his blog (michaelprescott.typepad.com).

Exploring the
aural phenomenology
of border experiences.

by *Greg Taylor*

here are many exceedingly strange experiences which happen to people, from interactions with paranormal entities and unidentified objects in the sky, right through to anomalous encounters at the time of death. These are often grouped together under the title of 'boundary experiences,' sometimes 'Forteana,' and sometimes simply as 'the paranormal.' But this grouping is generally one of convenience, and each element of this group is, for the most part, considered to be a separate area. However, this may not necessarily be the case, as a scan of the literature, and individual experiences, will attest.

In order to explore the topic with some precision, I would like to concentrate on one particular aspect of boundary experiences – the sounds heard by experiencers which accompany the phenomenon. Cross-referencing these seemingly disparate experiences via their aural aspects yields surprising results, with implications that are quite staggering for our modern conception of reality.

What Dreams May Come...

I will begin at the end, so to speak, with the near-death experience (NDE). Perhaps the man most responsible for the modern fascination with NDEs is George Ritchie, whose experience inspired Raymond Moody to write his seminal book *Life After Life* in the mid-1970s. Ritchie begins his account by telling of a sound:

> I heard a click and a whirr. The whirr went on and on. It was getting louder. The whirr was inside my head and my knees were made of rubber. They were bending and I was falling and all the time the whirr grew louder. I sat up with a start. What time was it? I looked at the bedside table but they'd taken the clock away. In fact, where was any of my stuff? I jumped out of bed in alarm, looking for my clothes. My uniform wasn't on the chair. I turned around, then froze. Someone was lying in that bed.[1]

In surveying others who had undergone strange experiences when flirting with death, Raymond Moody found that certain elements were recounted over and over. From these accounts, he constructed an 'archetypal NDE' which contained all of these common elements – one of which was the sound component:

> A man is dying and, as he reaches the point of greatest physical distress, he hears himself pronounced dead by his doctor. He begins to hear an uncomfortable noise, a loud ringing or buzzing,

and at the same time feels himself moving very rapidly through a long dark tunnel.[2]

A survey of experiences shows Moody to be correct in including this as part of the NDE (though not ever-present, it certainly is prevalent). Beyond the whir/buzz/hum mentioned above though, there are also other sounds reported. Consider the following two examples:

> I heard what seemed like millions of little golden bells ringing, tinkling; they rang and rang. Many times since, I've heard those bells in the middle of the night. Next I heard humming and then a choir singing. The singing got louder and louder, and it was in a minor key. It was beautiful and in perfect harmony. I also heard stringed instruments.[3]

and…

> Vicki Umipeg also began to hear sublimely beautiful and exquisitely harmonious music akin to the sound of wind chimes. With scarcely a noticeable transition, she then discovered she had been sucked head first into a tube and felt that she was being pulled up into it. The enclosure itself was dark, Vicki said, yet she was aware that she was moving toward light. As she reached the opening of the tube, the music that she had heard earlier seemed to be transformed into hymns and she then "rolled out" to find herself lying on grass.[4]

Similarly, the phenomenon of 'astral projection', often termed 'out-of-body experiences' (OBEs), is said to be heralded by sounds such as buzzing, roaring, humming, music, singing and voices. Any suggestion that these sounds have become associated with NDEs or OBEs through the spreading of modern NDE folklore (ie. via suggestion) can be discounted, as there are historical accounts of this experience, such as in the Tibetan Book of the Dead, which explains that after the soul of the deceased separates from the physical body, it is likely that roaring, thundering and whistling sounds will be heard. The 'practical' exploration of the transition into the state of death was not peculiar to the Tibetans though, and we find another example in a passage from a Graeco-Egyptian magical papyrus, in which the dying subject is attempting to ensure immortality or regeneration:

> When you have spoken in this wise [magical names], you will hear thunder and rushing of the air-space all around; and you yourself will feel that you are shaken to your depths. Then say again: 'Silence...'; thereupon open your eyes and you will see the gates open and the world of the gods within the gates; and your spirit, gladdened by the sight, will feel itself drawn onwards and upwards. Now remain standing still and draw the divine essence into yourself, regarding it fixedly. And when your soul has come to itself again, then speak: 'Approach Lord!' [magic words]. After these words, the rays will turn towards you; and you, focus your gaze on the center. If you do that, you will see a god, very young, beautifully formed, with flame-like hair, in a white tunic with a red mantle and a fiery wreath. [5]

This passage obviously follows the archetype of the NDE – the hearing of strange noises, the feeling of the spirit being drawn upwards, and an experience with a divine light or being. However, the magical schema in which the above passage is rooted begs the question: is the NDE an experience unto itself, or part of a much wider catalogue of mystical journeys, available via other methods such as magical ritual, shamanic journey and even unwanted 'intrusions' from an external source?

To an explorer, a ship

To recap the sounds of the near-death/out-of-body state, we have specific, repeated accounts of:

· Buzzing/Humming
· Bells Tinkling/Chimes
· Thunder/Rushing of wind
· Stringed instruments
· Choir/hymns

Any person that has studied border experiences in general should recognize these sounds as being common to multiple phenomena. Turning to shamanism, we readily find a number of examples. For example, consider Terence and Dennis McKenna's description of the onset of a 'magic mushroom trip', from the book *True Hallucinations*:

> But it was definitely at some point in time near to that conversation that I first heard the sound, immeasurably distant and faint, in the region between the ears, not outside, but definitely, incredibly there, perfectly distinct on the absolute edge of audible perception. A sound almost like a signal or very, very faint transmissions of radio buzzing from somewhere, something like tingling chimes at first, but gradually becoming amplified into a snapping, popping, gurgling, crackling electrical sound.[6]

Terence McKenna also made much of 'the Logos': what appears to be an external voice, sometimes heard while under the influence of psilocybin mushrooms. It is interesting to note some research done on the prevalence of this phenomenon, conducted by Horace Beach, Ph.D. In his paper titled "Listening for the Logos," Beach notes that "one of the most interesting findings of this study is that in over 45% of participants' total experiences with a voice(s) and psilocybin,

sounds other than voices were present." He
goes on to list the words used by participants
in describing these sounds: "high pitch,
high tone, humming, buzzing, whirring,
ringing, rustling, rushing water, howling,
vibrations, whooshing, crinkling, insect-
like, drumming, whirling-circular."

Dr Rick Strassman, in his research
into the potent hallucinogen DMT
(dimethyltryptamine), catalogued repeated
instances of 'entrance' sounds. "There was this loud intense hum,"
said one research volunteer. Another, 'Sara' – who claimed to have
been visited by an 'angel' once when she had a high fever as a child
– said "there was a sound, like a hum that turned into a whoosh, and
then I was blasted out of my body at such speed, with such force…
there are sounds: high-pitched singing, like angel voices."[7]

Anthropologist Michael Harner described the onset of a shamanic
journey via the DMT-containing brew ayahuasca with these words:
"the sound of rushing water filled his ears, and listening to its roar, he
knew he possessed the power of Tsungi, the first shaman. He could
now see…"[8] Cognitive psychologist Benny Shanon, recognized as one
of the world authorities on ayahuasca, notes Harner's description in
his book *The Antipodes of the Mind*, and also relays his own insights
about the archetypal nature of these sounds:

> There are also specific auditory effects that drinkers of Ayahuasca
> commonly report. One effect, usually described as most annoying,
> is the hearing of a continuous buzzing sound inside the ears.
> Another effect is that described by many as 'the sound of running
> water.' This very phrase has been articulated by several of my
> informants and is also used by Harner; curiously, the 'noise of great
> water' is also mentioned in the most spectacular vision described in
> the Bible, the Divine vision opening the book of Ezekiel (1:24).

It should also be noted that Shanon cites Goldman in saying that during the ayahuasca trip one may hear "music, the sound of people singing, and the sound of flowing water." Shanon points out that the hymns of the ayahuasca-using Santo Daime Church are 'received' music – either via the intoxicated individual spontaneously composing, or alternatively actually copying music heard during the experience. He even relates a personal experience in which he was accompanied by "a grand choir of angels."

Reichel-Dolmatoff [9] says of the *yage* (ayahuasca) experience: "The hallucination has several phases, and during the first the person feels and hears a violent current of air, as if a strong wind were pulling him along." Usage of *Heimia salicifolia* (sinicuiche), a plant that appears to have been used in Aztec rituals and which contains the alkaloid cryogenine, is reported to sometimes be accompanied by a ringing in the ears which turns into orchestrated music[10] – two sounds that are common to our investigation. Meanwhile, Paul Devereux, in his book *The Long Trip*, tells how during opium intoxication Reverend Walter Colton heard "harps and choral symphonies." Interestingly, Devereux also relates that "the locations of oracles were often "hallucinogenic" in that they had roaring water or wind at them."

PROPHETS, MYSTICS AND VISIONARIES

Returning to Shanon's off-hand comment regarding Ezekiel's Biblical vision, we encounter yet another area to explore – the sacred ground of religious visions. This topic is often left out of paranormal investigations, though we are left to wonder why when there are so many parallels (Ezekiel and the 'UFO' is perhaps one of the more popular). Turning to the New Testament, we find this narrative during Pentecost (from Acts 2:1):

And when the day of Pentecost was fully come, they were all with one accord in one place. And suddenly there came a sound from heaven as of a rushing mighty wind, and it filled all the house where they were sitting. And there appeared unto them cloven tongues like as of fire, and it sat upon each of them. And they were all filled with the Holy Ghost, and began to speak with other tongues, as the Spirit gave them utterance.

Enoch also notes sounds during his shaman-like transformation:

As soon as the Holy One, blessed be He, took me to serve the throne of glory, the wheels of the chariot, and all the needs of the Shekhinah, at once my flesh was changed into flame, my tendons into a fire of glowing heat, my bones to glowing juniper coals, my eyelids to radiance of lightning bolts, my eyeballs to torches of fire, the hair of my head to glowing heat and flame, all my limbs to wings of burning fire, and my bodily frame to scorching fire. On my right were hewers of fiery flames, on my left torches were burning. There blew around me wind, storm, and tempest, and the noise of earthquake upon earthquake was in front of me and behind me.

Interestingly, considering the prevalence of the buzzing sound in multiple experiences, esoteric scholar Manly P. Hall cites Thomas Inman as saying that Beelzebub, "…which the Jews ridiculed as My Lord of Flies, really means My Lord Who Hums or Murmurs" (in the Bible, Beelzebub was an oracular deity of the Philistines).

Turning to Islam, we find the traces of these sounds in the very inspiration behind the faith, in the revelations to Mohammed from the Archangel Gabriel:

The Prophet heard at times the noise of the tinkling of a bell. To him alone was known the meaning of the sound. He alone could distinguish in, and through it, the words which Gabriel wished him to understand.[11]

This is interesting – Mohammed hears the tinkling of a bell, but he "knew the meaning of the sounds"…distinguishing "in, and through it" the revelations from Gabriel. There may be a curious parallel here with the 'Virgin Mary apparitions' (and I use the term very loosely) of Fatima. In their book *Heavenly Lights*, Joaquim Fernandes and Fina D'Armada devote a chapter to the buzzing sounds heard by witnesses to the event. In particular, witness Maria Carreira relates that the buzzing seems to have coincided with the conversations between Lucia and the 'Lady':

> We would follow the children and kneel in the middle of the field. Lucia would raise her hands and say, 'You bade me come here, what do you wish of me?' And then could be heard a buzzing that seemed to be that of a bee. I took care to discern whether it was the Lady speaking.

Maria subsequently described this phenomenon, from the June apparition, to another investigator with these words: "Then we began to hear something like this, in the manner of a very fine voice, but what it said could not be comprehended or put into words, for it was like the buzzing of a bee." A month after the first event (the Fatima apparitions occurred on the 13th of each month from May to October 1917), another person witnessed the same effect:

> After this question, she (Lucia) waited in silence for a short period of time, the time of a brief response. And during this silence, he (the witness) heard, as if coming from the oak tree, a faint voice, similar, he says, to the humming of a bee, but without distinguishing a single word.

Another witness described it as "the buzzing of a fly inside an empty barrel, but without articulation of words," and on another occasion as an indefinable sound, heard throughout the duration of the experience, like that which is heard next to a hive, but altogether more harmonious. And another witness: "I thought I heard at that moment, a little wind, a zoa-zoa sound. While Lucia was listening to a response, it seemed there was a buzzing sound like that of a cicada."

Buzzing was not the only sound heard at Fatima though. Fernandes and D'Armada point out that witnesses likened the sounds "to thunder, to rumors, to rumbling, to the clapping of hands, to the detonation of bombs, to the hiss of rockets." For instance, one witness recounted that "when Lucia said, 'There She goes,' I heard a roaring in the air that seemed like the beginning of thunder."

So what of other 'Blessed Virgin Mary (BVM) apparitions'? Consider the the case of the 'Virgin of Guadeloupe':

> ...the apparition took place on December 9th 1531 in Mexico. it began with the 'sweet sound of singing birds' followed by a voice which came from the top of the hill. The source of the voice was hidden by 'a frosty mist, a brightening cloud'. The technology of the BVM was at work![12]

And while speaking of Virgin Mary apparitions, perhaps the best known case is that of Lourdes. The seer who experienced the visitation in that case – the young girl Bernadette – mentions these sounds in her own testimony:

> Hardly had I taken off my first stocking, when I heard a sound as though there had been a rush of wind. I looked around towards

the meadow. I saw the trees quite still. So I continued to take off my shoes. Again I heard the same noise. I looked upward towards the grotto. I beheld a lady dressed in white. She wore a white dress a blue sash and a yellow rose on each foot..."[13]

It is interesting to note, in regards to this common 'rush of wind' sound, that there was an instance of this in the Fatima case also. In 1915, two years before the more famous sequence of apparitions, Lucia and her two cousins were said to have been taking shelter from rain in a small cave when they heard the rumble of a powerful wind and then saw a "youth of admirable beauty" who called himself the 'Angel of Peace'. Jacques Vallee has pointed out the similarity of this particular apparition (and other 'entity' visitations) with the description in the Biblical Apocrypha of a young child appearing from a 'bright cloud' within a cave.[14]

Before moving on to the next section, there is one final aspect worth noting. Both the Pentecost account, and the Fatima event, yielded 'group' hearing...that is, more than one person present 'heard' the sounds. This is suggestive of some objective source, and is something we will return to.

THERE'S NOTHING NEW...

The phenomena discussed so far – NDEs, entheogenic experiences, magical ritual – largely suggest that these sounds herald the onset of an altered state of consciousness. This appears to be confirmed when we survey mystical traditions from around the world, most especially those from the East, which are already well ahead of us in describing these sounds in connection with altered states.[15]

Beginning with the literature on kundalini, according to *Sat Chakranirupana*, written more than five hundred years ago by the Bengali yogi Purnanada:

The sleeping kundalini is extremely fine, like the fiber of a lotus stalk. She is the world-bewilderer, gently covering the "door" to the central Great Axis. Like the spiral of a conch shell, her shiny snake-like form is coiled around three and a half times; her luster is like a strong flash of lightning; her sweet murmur is like an indistinct hum of swarms of love-mad bees.

From the classic treatise on Hatha Yoga, *Shiva Samhita*, we learn of the 'sounds' that a practitioner is likely to experience:

The first sound is like the hum of the honey-intoxicated bee, next that of a flute, then of a harp; after this, by the gradual practice of Yoga, the destroyer of the darkness of the world, he hears the sounds of the ringing bells, then sounds like roars of thunder.

Another of the classic yoga texts, *Hatha Yoga Pradapika*, also describes sounds:

In the beginning, the sounds resemble those of the ocean, the clouds, the kettledrum and Zarzara (a sort of drum cymbal); in the middle they resemble those arising from the Maradala, the conch, the bell and the horn. In the end they resemble those of the tinkling bells, the flutes, the vina, and the bees.

Moving from Hinduism to Sufism, we find this extremely accurate description of sounds heard during the induced altered states of that particular mystical tradition, as described by the Sufi master Hazrat Inayat Khan:

An adept who practices Shaghal, after some time will have an experience of that Shaghal during times when he is not practicing. He will hear sounds of the sphere in ten forms: in the form of the buzzing of the bees, in the form of the bells ringing in the ears, in the form of whistles blowing, in the form of the fluttering of the leaves, in the form of the running of the water, in the form of the sound of Vina, in the form of the cooing of the wind, in the form of the crashing of the thunder, in the form of the music of the spheres, in the form of the song of the angels.

It pays to revisit this final passage after reading the complete essay – Hazrat Inayat Khan obviously knew his topic!

UFOs and Aliens, Oh My!

Surveying the topic of UFO sightings in regards to the sounds heard is problematic, not least because many UFO proponents will argue that the phenomenon has nothing to do with the paranormal, and that genuine (ie. unexplainable) UFOs are of extraterrestrial origin. Beyond that point, there is also no doubt many UFO sightings are actually of conventional or 'secret' (Earthly) craft. Therefore, roaring, buzzing and humming sounds could well be due to the propulsion systems of these craft (whether Earthly or otherwise). However, it is still worth surveying some of these sounds, especially considering the 'high strangeness' aspect of many sightings, which do suggest a paranormal origin. Researcher James McCampbell identified five distinct types of sounds emanating from UFOs in his survey of close encounters[16], which are strikingly familiar to the sounds we have been discussing:

- · Violent (roar, explosion)
- · Low Pitch (hum, buzz)
- · Rush of Air (whoosh, swish)
- · High Pitch (shrill, whistle)
- · Signals (beeps, pulses)

One such encounter, which featured two of the above sounds, is the UFO sighting of Charles Early. Early was raking leaves at his home in Greenfield Massachusetts, under a clear sky, when he heard a "swishing noise" as if a wind storm was coming. He looked up and saw two rings parallel to each other, one on top of the other separated by a distance of about 4 feet. He estimated the diameter to be about 30 feet and described them as "bright, like polished chrome" and tubular…Early said that when the double ring was directly over him it made a "humming" sound similar to the hum heard when standing under electrical wires.

In his book *Forbidden Science*, Jacques Vallee discusses the well-known 'Affa' case of 1954: A 'contactee', Mrs Frances Swan, told how she was in telepathic communication (via automatic writing) from the commanders of two alien spaceships (Affa and Ponnar). Vallee recounts that whenever Mrs Swan was in contact with the 'aliens', she would get a buzzing sound in her left ear "to indicate that they were 'on the line'." While this is interesting enough in itself, there was also apparent confirmation from the CIA and Naval Intelligence officers who interviewed Mrs Swan, who told of hearing these same buzzing sounds in their ears (though they did not receive any actual communication).[17] Furthermore, when the officers asked to see one of these alien spaceships, Affa (through Mrs Swan) told them to look outside – and when they went to the window, saw a circular object in the sky.

John Keel recounts the tale of Mrs Malley, who was driving home along Route 34 to Ithaca, New York, at around 7pm, when she saw a red light following her – "a disk about the size of a boxcar, with a domed top and square red and green windows… and it made a humming sound, something like the vibration of a television antenna in the wind." Describing the experience in more detail, Mrs Malley says "a white twirling beam of light flashed down from the object…and I heard the humming sound. Then I began to hear voices. They didn't sound like male or female voices but were weird, the words broken and jerky…it was like a weird chorus of several voices."

In a UFO and humanoid sighting report from 1914…

> …the witness was at a local trash dump looking for old discards when he suddenly heard a "musical" humming sound. Turning around he then saw a strange craft hovering above a fence and partially above the street in front of a church. The object was gray in color with a high dome on top and a slight dome on the bottom. An opening, like two sliding doors, then appeared. Then two short figures emerged and took positions each on one side of the object, more came out until there were eight abreast.[18]

Introductory sounds are especially the case with alleged 'alien abductions', an area which has already been associated with what Dr John Mack called "intrusions from the subtle realms." Respected ufologist Karl Pflock described one of the original 'abduction' cases, that of Betty and Barney Hill, as being preceded by a sound described as a "buzzing vibration." Brad Steiger too has mentioned the prevalence of buzzing and 'rushing' sounds in both UFO sightings and 'entity' encounters. He also compares the sound to that heard in poltergeist activity:

> A number of revelators and UFO contactees have since mentioned to me that just before the appearance of an entity they were aware of a strange buzzing sound. Witnesses of unexplained aerial phenomenon have also referred to a buzzing or rushing sound shortly before the 'flying saucer' appeared over them. I am also reminded that great deal of poltergeist activity produces a preparatory 'signal' of a buzzing, rasping, or winding noise.[19]

In their book *The Unidentified*, Jerome Clark and Loren Coleman also say that many contactees have reported a bee-buzzing sound that introduced and ended their encounters.

In the aforementioned book on Fatima, *Heavenly Lights*, Fernandes and D'Armada also recount a number of UFO/alien sightings which were preceded by a buzzing sound (often explicitly described, as at Fatima, as the 'buzzing of bees'.) John Keel also notes the variety of noises heard in his book *Operation Trojan Horse*. He points out that the well-known 'high strangeness' case of Joe Simonton consisted of 'humming' sounds and the sound of "wet tyres on pavement."

Jacques Vallee has been perhaps the most instrumental in focusing ufological research on the fact that there are significant parallels with UFO/paranormal events and folkloric tales from around the globe – suggesting that this is a phenomena intrinsically linked to human experience through the ages. We also find more examples of these same sounds...

The Good (Bad, and Ugly) Folk

Entity 'contact' experiences certainly come with their share of paranormal sounds. For instance, consider this Mothman report. Journalist Rick Moran tells how he interviewed...

> ...an older woman who said she had encountered Mothman in her backyard. Her property was close to the boundaries of the TNT area and, hearing a buzzing or humming sound coming from the back of her home, she went out to investigate. It was mid-afternoon, and when she opened the back door she found herself face to face with Mothman, hovering about 10 feet in front of her. Her description was detailed, suggesting something more like a machine than an animal.[20]

Consider too these other reports of entity contact: Near Croton Falls, New York, it was reported that "dwarf-like hooded beings" emerged from a shimmering circle of blue that appeared in an outcrop of rock "following a buzzing sound."[21] In a humanoid entity report from 1975, "Angelica Barrigon Varela and co-worker Remedios Diez were on their way to work at a local factory along the wall that divided the railroad tracks and the street when they heard a loud buzzing sound coming from the area of the tracks. Looking in that direction they beheld a bizarre creature floating and balancing itself above the railroad tracks. It appeared to be wearing a monk-like smock or coat, dark green in color that emitted intermediate flashes of light under the light rain."[22]

Another strange phenomenon which features 'entity contact' is 'Old Hag' syndrome (also known as 'Night Terrors' and by other names around the world). These reports, in which an experiencer feels that someone is in the room with them, perhaps even on them, and has a terrible feeling of dread, have been related to the condition of 'recurrent sleep paralysis.' This too is introduced by the same certain sounds:

> A buzzing / ringing / roaring / whistling / hissing / high-pitched screeching sound in the ears sets in and becomes louder and louder to the point of becoming unbearable.[23]

In the 17th century writings of the demonologist Fr. Sinistrari, we find this example of entity contact which happened to a young lady:

> During the following night, while she was in bed with her husband and both were asleep, she found herself awakened by an extremely fine voice, somewhat like a high-pitched whistling sound. It was softly saying in her ear some very clear words: 'How did you like the cake?' In fear, our good lady began to use the sign of the cross and to invoke in succession the names of Jesus and Mary. [24]

Turning our attention to the British Isles, there are a number of similar cases, and one particular (relatively) modern tale which may have profound significance for our investigation.

In *Fortean Times # 31,* we find the curious case of the "Wollaton Park Fairies," which occurred in Nottingham at the end of October in 1979:

> Several children returning home after playing, heard a sound like a bell and saw coming out of the wooded area about 60 little gnome like men with wrinkled faces and long white beards, they were about 2-foot tall and were riding small bubble-like vehicles. The beings rode over the swamps near the lake and some chased the children towards the gate of the park. Some of the humanoids wore red hats and green pants and seemed to be laughing in a peculiar way. The children ran from the area.

Furthermore, in describing the Wollaton fairy event, Janet Bord adds this seemingly innocuous footnote, based on its similarities to the sighting:

> Over six years before the Wollaton fairies were reported in the media, I had corresponded with Marina Fry of Cornwall, who wrote to me giving details of her own fairy sighting when she was nearly four years old, around 1940. One night she and her older sisters, all sleeping in one bedroom, awoke to hear a buzzing noise (one sister said 'music and bells'). Looking out of the window they saw a little man in a tiny red car driving around in circles'. He was about 18 inches tall and had a white beard and a 'droopy pointed hat'…he just disappeared after a while.[25]

This sighting stands out particularly because of the detail that one sister heard a different sound. Different, but still part of the subset which we have been examining (and in view of this, adds some legitimacy to the story). This has the curious effect of making the sounds a 'subjective' experience (due to different perceptions of it), while seemingly coming from an objective source (as a number of people all heard a sound). Further to that, why did the sisters see the same thing, if it was a subjective experience? Interestingly, there are other accounts of groups of people subjectively hearing 'paranormal' noises, which are not to do with 'entity' contact. They are to do with death.

THE CIRCLE IS COMPLETE

In his books *A Casebook of Otherworldly Music* and *A Psychic Study of the Music of the Spheres* [26], D. Scott Rogo recounts a number of situations which have a similarity to the fairy story above – in that the sound (in this case, music), is heard subjectively. Perhaps one of the most interesting is the tale of the final hours of the German philosopher, Wolfgang Goethe.

Rogo tells how two hours before Goethe's death, the great German writer was visited for the final time by a 'Countess V.', who upon entering the house was dismayed to hear music being played at such a somber time. However, the music was not actually coming from anyone in the house:

> "So you have heard it too?" replied Frau von Goethe. "It's inexplicable! Since dawn yesterday, a mysterious music has resounded from time to time, getting into our ears, our hearts, our bones." At this very instant there resounded from above, as if they came from a higher world, sweet and prolonged chords of music which weakened little by little until they faded away."

However, the account tells how each person hearing the music disagreed with another on what it consisted of. The Countess described it as "a quartet playing fragments of music some way off," Frau von Goethe "the sound of a piano, clear and close by," while others heard "an organ, for the other a choral chant" and another a concertina.

There is a similar account in Sir William Barrett's *Death-Bed Visions*, in which a husband and wife heard music/singing at the time of death (of the wife's brother):

> Mrs. Allen says the sounds she heard resembled singing – sweet music without distinguishable words – that she went upstairs directly she heard the music, which continued until she reached the bedroom. Mr. Allen's impression is that the sound resembled the full notes of an organ or of an aeolian harp.

Rogo's keen eye also recognized another similar example, though this time in the annals of mediumship. D.D. Home, one of the first mediums to be scientifically tested – and one of the 'stars' of the history of mediumship – was said to have encountered 'psychic music' throughout his life. One case in particular parallels the anecdotes we have mentioned above, and is recorded in Lord Adair's book *Experiences in Spiritualism with D.D. Home*:

> Almost immediately after we had gone to bed and put the lights out, we both heard the music…Home said that the music formed words; that, in fact, it was a voice speaking and not instrumental music. I could hear nothing but the chords like an organ or harmonium played at a distance.

Lord Adair's account sounds extremely similar to the accounts of Mohammed, and Lucia at Fatima. Mohammed heard Gabriel's words 'through' the tinkling of bells, while Lucia appears to hear the Virgin Mary 'through' a buzzing sound. It is almost as if the strength of 'signal' varies from person to person, and only those with the strongest signal get the intended message…the others get the psychic equivalent of static.

Accounts of Home's séances also mention the 'rushing of wind', with almost exactly the same results as those of the Pentecost (which I mentioned earlier):

> Lindsay and Charlie saw tongues or jets of flame proceeding from Home's head. We then all distinctly heard, as it were, a bird flying round the room, whistling and chirping, but saw nothing, except Lindsay, who perceived an indistinct form resembling a bird. There then came a sound as of a great wind rushing through the room, we also felt the wind strongly; the moaning rushing sound was the most weird thing I have ever heard. Home then got up, being in a trance, and spoke something in a language that none of us understood; it may have been nonsense, but it sounded like a sentence in a foreign tongue.[27]

THE MYSTERY REMAINS

What are we to make of this? We have numerous 'boundary' or paranormal experiences, all of which appear to consist of definite sounds (enumerated previously in mystical literature, as above). What's more, these 'sounds' appear to be subjectively perceived, but sometimes originate from some objective source, as evidenced by the group experiences.

There is some evidence to suggest that these sounds are caused by stimulation of certain parts of the brain. For instance, it is known that sufferers of Temporal Lobe Epilepsy (TLE) also experience a remarkably similar set of sounds:

> Simple auditory phenomena such as humming, buzzing, hissing, and roaring may occur if the discharges arise in the superior

> temporal gyrus; and olfactory sensations, which are usually
> unpleasant and difficult to define, can signal the start of seizures in
> the Sylvian region or ento-rhinal cortex.[28]

The comment about olfactory sensations should not go unnoticed
either, considering many paranormal encounters also involve smells
(from sulphorous to the sweet smell of roses). Most readers will also
be familiar with the research of Dr Michael Persinger, who claims to
have elicited 'entity contact'-like experiences via magnetic stimulation
of the temporal lobes – in fact, Persinger's modified motorcycle
helmet, fitted with magnetic induction devices, has been nicknamed
'The God Helmet'.

At face value then, it might be surmised that all of the experiences
listed in this essay are simply hallucinations, created by a malfunction
of the brain. But a closer examination prompts more questions.
How do we explain the the 'group hearing', such as that of Fatima?
Persinger would have it that some electromagnetic field was present,
affecting the brains of all those within a certain radius from the EM
source, and varying depending on the exposure. But then how do
we explain the Wollaton fairy report, or the tale of Marina Fry, who
with her sisters saw the little man in the tiny red car. In both events,
the sound was heard by a group, but *the same thing was also seen* – and
in the case of Marina Fry, we have the added complication that the
sound was heard differently.

Furthermore, the reports of celestial music at the time of death
– again, heard subjectively – confound the hallucination explanation,
and also Persinger's EMF theory. Apart from some over-construed
physicalist explanation (describing a state of group catalepsy or similar),
there is a real possibility here that the explanation we must face is
that there is another facet to the time of death (and also, obviously,
to paranormal events in life) which is thus far unexplainable.

Such experiences lend weight to the idea that the brain is certainly
involved in these border phenomena, but that it is mediating or receiving

the experience, rather than creating it (as a hallucination). If so, we are faced with a real mystery – the true origin of these various phenomena. Whatever it is, it appears to be connected to everything from UFOs and mystical experiences, right through to our fate after death. We would do well to pay more attention to the crossovers between the various branches of paranormal research in future.

Greg Taylor is the owner/editor of the online alternative news portal, *The Daily Grail* (www.dailygrail.com), and is also the editor of *Sub Rosa Magazine* and this journal, *Darklore*. He is widely read in topics that challenge the orthodox worldview, from alternative history to the mysteries of human consciousness. Greg currently resides in Brisbane, Australia. His first book. *The Guide To The Solomon Key,* is a guidebook to the esoteric history and locations likely to be included in Dan Brown's next book.

Life
with the

Some Personal Reflections

By **Robert M. Schoch**

first met the Great Sphinx face-to-face on 17th June 1990. She (yes, I consider the Great Sphinx a female) has influenced and in many ways defined my life ever since. It has been apparent to me that many a person knows me, or believes they know me, or more accurately knows of me, due to the controversy over the age of the Sphinx that my research has engendered.

For those not familiar with my research on the Great Sphinx, I will summarize it very briefly. For more extended discussions, I refer the reader to my books (listed in the notes to this article).

History of an Enigma

The Great Sphinx, carved out of solid bedrock limestone, sits on the eastern edge of the Giza Plateau, the area famous for containing the Great Pyramid attributed to the Fourth Dynasty pharaoh Khufu (Cheops), on the west bank of the Nile across from Cairo. The Sphinx sits due east of the second pyramid, the pyramid generally attributed to the pharaoh Khafre (Chephren, Khephren), possibly the son or brother of Khufu. The second pyramid is just slightly smaller than the Great Pyramid. A third major pyramid, though considerably smaller than the other two, is also located on the Giza Plateau; it is attributed to the pharaoh Menkaura (Menkaure, Mycerinus), possibly a grandson or son of Khufu. It is these three pyramids that various researchers, most notably Robert Bauval, have correlated with the belt of the constellation Orion (representative of, in some guises, the Egyptian god Osiris).

The traditional academics of the late twentieth century attributed the Great Sphinx to the pharaoh Khafre, builder of the second pyramid, circa 2500 B.C. In contrast, some classical Egyptologists of the nineteenth and early twentieth centuries dated the Great Sphinx to an earlier, pre-dynastic, period, foreshadowing my own work. There are no definitive ancient records of who originally carved the Sphinx, when, or why. We do not even know the name that the Old Kingdom Egyptians gave to the Sphinx.

A granite stela erected between the paws of the Sphinx by Thutmose IV, circa 1400 B.C., when first excavated was reported to include in its inscription the name, or at least part of the name, of Khafre (this portion of the inscription has since flaked away). This has been variously interpreted to indicate that either Khafre ordered the Sphinx carved, or that Khafre ordered the Sphinx renovated, as Thutmose IV did over a millennium later. In reality, however, it is unclear if indeed it was the Fourth Dynasty pharaoh Khafre being named on the stela, or what relationship the stela may have suggested that Khafre had to the Sphinx: builder, restorer, supplicant, or something else. Bottom line: The Thutmose IV stela provides no definitive evidence of when, or by whom, the Sphinx was constructed. Also possibly bearing on the origins of the Great Sphinx is the so-called Inventory Stela, alternatively known as the Stela of Cheops' (Khufu's) Daughter. Although the actual stela dates to the seventh or sixth century B.C., it purports to be a copy of an Old Kingdom text. According to the Inventory Stela, the Great Sphinx was already in existence during the reign of Khufu. Indeed, Khufu is credited with repairing the Sphinx after it was struck by lightning. Modern Egyptologists generally dismiss the Inventory Stela as a late period fabrication.

In New Kingdom times (circa 1550 to 1070 B.C. or so) the Great Sphinx was sometimes referred to as *Horemakhet* (*Hor-em-akhet*, *Harmakhet*, *Harmachis*), which can be translated as 'Horus of the Horizon' or 'Horus in the Horizon', or as *Ra-horakhty*, translated as 'Ra of the Two Horizons'. In medieval Arabic times one appellation given to the Great Sphinx was *Abu el-Hol* (*Abu al-Hol*, *Abou el Hôl*), or '*Father of Terror(s)*'. The name 'Sphinx' may come from a Greek word meaning "to strangle" as, according to one legend, the Greek sphinx, often depicted as a winged lion with the head of a woman, had the habit of strangling and devouring those who could not answer her riddles. Another interpretation is that the word sphinx was derived, possibly through Greeks visiting Egypt, from the ancient Egyptian *Shesep-ankh*, sometimes translated as "living statue" or "living image," a term used to refer to royal statues during the Old Kingdom.

I have extensively studied the nature and extent of the weathering and erosional features found on the Great Sphinx directly, under the numerous repairs to the Sphinx (some of which date back to Old Kingdom times), in the so-called Sphinx enclosure (the Sphinx sits in a hole or quarry, with its body below the level of the plateau behind it), and in the subsurface under and around the Sphinx.

Based on my geological analyses, I have calculated that the oldest portions of the Sphinx date back to the period of approximately 7000 to 5000 B.C. I arrived at this conclusion through a variety of independent means, such as correlating the nature of the weathering with the climatic history of the area, calculating the amount of rock eroded away on the surface and estimating how long this may have taken, and calibrating the depth of subsurface weathering around and below the Sphinx.

Key to my redating of the Sphinx is the interpretation that the weathering observed on the body and the walls of the Sphinx enclosure is not due to the arid desert conditions found in the region during the last four to five thousand years. Rather, the observed weathering resulted from rain, precipitation, and water runoff – and sufficient precipitation was available only during pre-Sahara conditions, prior to circa 3000 B.C. Other geologists, such as Colin Reader and David Coxill (each working independently of me, and also independently of each other), have corroborated my analyses of the nature of the weathering and erosion, concluding that the causative agent was water and not wind and sand. I must note, however, that while Reader, Coxill, and I agree that the Sphinx is weathered by water and must date to an earlier period than the traditional attribution, we do not all agree on the same age estimate. In particular, Reader has argued that the Sphinx can still be accommodated into a very early dynastic timeframe and thus is perhaps only a few hundred years older than the traditional date of circa 2500 B.C. However, I firmly believe that the extent of the erosion and weathering firmly push the core body of the Sphinx into a much more remote period. Furthermore, Reader does not take into adequate account the subsurface data that Thomas Dobecki and I collected (see discussion below), which allows me to calibrate the rate of subsurface weathering and arrive at my age estimate for the Sphinx. My dating places the Sphinx well back into pre-dynastic times, a period when many suppose that the technology and social organization did not exist to create such a monument.

Even though the Sphinx exhibits water erosion, this erosion was clearly from precipitation and rain runoff, not from flooding or the rising of the Nile. I want to be clear about this, since some people have misrepresented my data as supporting the notion that the Sphinx witnessed "Noah's Flood" or a worldwide deluge. Furthermore, fossil shells, sea urchins, and so forth can be found on the Giza Plateau, but these have nothing to do with the water erosion seen on the Sphinx. Rather, the fossil sea organisms are millions of years old and have weathered out of the limestone rocks from which the Sphinx, pyramids, and many other structures are built.

Concerning my redating of the Sphinx, I emphasize that I am comfortable attributing it to the period of circa 5000 B.C. or a bit earlier. Could it be considerably older? Based on the geological data, and depending on how one interprets the data, possibly. However, I have never claimed an age for the Great Sphinx prior to the 7000 B.C. to 5000 B.C. period. It is simply false when people state that I have confirmed the age of the Sphinx as being on the order of 10,500 B.C. It is also sometimes suggested that the leonine aspect of the Sphinx connects it to the constellation Leo, and thus with the precessional Age of Leo, placing the Sphinx in the period of circa 10,500 B.C. (if it was carved at the beginning of that age). I question this association, however, as I am not certain that the constellation of Leo as such was recognized some 12,000 or more years ago, and even if the Great Sphinx does represent or commemorate, in some aspect, the Age of Leo, that does not necessarily imply that it was sculpted during that age. Even more widely speculative is the idea that the Great Sphinx was carved not in the last Age of Leo, but in the preceding Age of Leo some 36,000 or so years ago. Another widespread notion is to view the leonine-human hybrid aspect of the Sphinx as a representation of Leo and Virgo combined, the masculine and feminine, the animal or beastly vitality and the human intellect united.

While most of the focus of, and controversy surrounding, my work has been on the Great Sphinx, to my mind the so-called Sphinx

Temple – sitting directly in front of (east of) the Sphinx – is in many ways even more significant than the Sphinx itself from a construction and dating point of view. The Sphinx Temple is built of megalithic limestone blocks, many weighing tens of tons, assembled in a tightly enclosed space. How these blocks were maneuvered is difficult to fathom. Pertinent to our current theme, however, is the fact that the Sphinx Temple (or at least the original parts of the temple, as it too, like the Sphinx, was reworked and repaired in dynastic times) was built contemporaneously with the oldest portions of the Great Sphinx. The blocks from which the temple was constructed were removed from around the body of the Sphinx as the statue was carved. The sculptors of the Sphinx did not simply chisel, pound, and shovel out the excess rock they needed to remove; rather, they meticulously quarried it as huge blocks used to construct the Sphinx Temple. Although in ruins today, I consider the building of the Sphinx Temple to be an engineering feat even more incredible than the carving of the Great Sphinx, and this occurred in circa 5000 B.C. or earlier.

We Never Forget a Face?

I must stress that in my assessment, the Great Sphinx of pre-dynastic times did not look like the Sphinx we see today. It is only what I refer to as the core body (the torso or trunk) of the Sphinx that dates back to that much earlier period. The front paws have been heavily reworked and repaired (today they are mostly covered with modern blocks of limestone), and the head is surely not the original head. I have always contended that the head of the Great Sphinx is out of proportion relative to the size of the body. It is too small. In my opinion, the head was originally larger, but it was damaged by weathering and erosion, and to "repair" it the ancients recarved the head, resulting in its relatively small size today. Originally the head may not have been that of a human. Although I have no hard evidence, my speculation is that the head was originally that of a lion, to fit the leonine body. As an aside, some years ago noted Egyptologist refused to believe my observation that the current head of the Great Sphinx is too small for the body.

Sphinx's Head (© Robert Schoch)

He subsequently undertook an analysis of the proportions of many ancient Egyptian sphinxes, only to find that virtually all had similar head to body ratios, except for the Great Sphinx, in which case the head was proportionally smaller.

In my opinion, based on analyses of the weathering and chisel marks, as well as on stylistic considerations and the ethnicity of the head (clearly a "black African" or "Nubian" in my opinion), the current head of the Sphinx is a dynastic recarving, but probably older than the Fourth Dynasty. Some researchers have claimed that the current face of the Great Sphinx resembles the face found on statues of the pharaoh Khafre (builder of the second pyramid on the Giza Plateau), and have used this supposed evidence to support the attribution of the Sphinx to the period of Khafre, circa 2500 B.C. However, in the early 1990s forensic expert Frank Domingo (formerly with the New York City Police Department) undertook a detailed comparison of the face of the Sphinx and the face of Khafre, concluding that they certainly do not represent the same individual (and indeed, they do not appear to represent persons of the same race or ethnicity). In recent years some researchers have suggested that the face of the Sphinx represents that of Khufu (builder of the Great Pyramid), and either the Great Sphinx was ordered built by Khufu himself, or by his son Djedefre (Ra'djedef, who reigned for a short period between Khufu and Khafre) in the image of Khufu. Personally, I am not convinced that the current face of the Sphinx

represents Khufu. As an aside, when Domingo first came out with
the results of his analysis, I was teaching an evening college course
in a local Massachusetts prison. I mentioned Domingo's conclusions
to the class and immediately one of the students commented (here I
paraphrase, after all these years), without any apparent bitterness or
sarcasm, "Oh, I know about Domingo. He's good. His reconstructions
resulted in my cousin being convicted of murder."

I suspect the head of the Great Sphinx was recarved during the
period of the First to Third dynasties (circa 2920 to 2575 B.C.).
Stylistically, to my eye, it might fit this early dynastic period. And
the African or Nubian ethnicity of the Sphinx might fit an earlier
period when the southern element of Egypt had greater sway than
during certain later periods of Egyptian history. One must also
remember that the head may have been further altered in later
dynastic times. For instance, the entire Great Sphinx may have
been modified, repaired, and brightly painted at various periods
in its history, including during the New Kingdom. The current
head as we view it today has been damaged, apparently both by
weathering and by vandalism over the ages, and is incomplete.
Researcher Colette Dowell has suggested that the Sphinx appears
to be missing the uppermost part of its skull, the region of the
crown, or top of the head, chakra. Is this simply coincidental? Or
was the crown purposefully removed for symbolic purposes? Also,
to my eye the face of the Great Sphinx has always appeared to be
either androgynous or female, and my personal intuition is that in
fact it is a female face. Admittedly this is a subjective impression.
Yes, parts of the Sphinx's 'beard' (actually a ceremonial false beard)
have been found and now reside in various museums, but that
proves nothing. The beard was added much later, and subsequently
removed or lost again. At any rate, a beard on the Sphinx would be
a symbol, such as of royal power and authority, and not indicative
of the gender of the statue. I have seen more than one living African
woman whose face strongly resembled that of the Great Sphinx.

SECRET CHAMBERS?

As part of our research on the Sphinx, geophysicist Thomas Dobecki and I undertook low-energy seismic studies around the Sphinx and elsewhere on the plateau. My primary concern with these studies was not to search for "buried treasure," but to gather good data on the nature, degree, and depth of subsurface weathering, both around the Sphinx and in areas of confidently dated dynastic structures. Indeed, we acquired excellent data supporting my attribution of the Sphinx to 5000 B.C. or earlier. However, we also discovered clear evidence of a cavity or chamber under the left paw of the Sphinx. Additionally, we found some lesser (and previously known) cavities under and around the Sphinx, and the data also indicated that there may be a tunnel-like structure running the length of the body under the Sphinx.

A chamber in the vicinity of the paws of the Sphinx was certainly interesting to me, but I did not put that much emphasis on it. However, upon publication of our data, I soon found that a number of parties considered the chamber to be of extreme interest and importance. I still remember well the day, sitting in my office between teaching classes, that I received a phone call from the Virginia Beach headquarters of the A.R.E. (Association for Research and Enlightenment, informally known as the Edgar Cayce Foundation). Unbeknownst to me, the American psychic Edgar Cayce (1877-1945) had predicted that a "Hall of Records" would be found in the general area where we had discovered the chamber. According to Cayce, the ancient continent of Atlantis had been destroyed circa 10,500 B.C. The survivors dispersed to the far corners of Earth, founding new offshoot civilizations, including what in time would come to be recognized as ancient Egypt. In several locations they had secreted libraries recording their history, science, and accomplishments, including in the region of the Great Sphinx. Furthermore, the representative of the A.R.E. informed me that my research on redating the Great Sphinx went a long way toward confirming the Cayce chronology of Atlantis and the building of structures on the Giza Plateau well before dynastic times. I found myself formally interviewed for the A.R.E.'s magazine, and I have spoken at their conferences in Virginia Beach. (To their credit, I would note that the A.R.E. has a history of attracting top-notch researchers to speak at some of their conferences, researchers who in some cases are clearly antithetical to the main tenets and interests of the organization. I have always found the leaders and members of the A.R.E. to be warm, friendly, open, and honest.)

It turns out that not only the members of the A.R.E. have a special interest in the discovery of chambers and tunnels under the Sphinx, but many other groups as well, such as various Rosicrucian and Masonic groups, who believe (with some good basis) that there is a complex network of tunnels and chambers below the surface of the Giza Plateau.

Questions I am often asked include: Where is the entrance to the chamber under the left paw of the Sphinx? Have the Egyptian authorities allowed you to explore the chamber, and if not, why not?

In answer to the first question, I have not located any entrance to the chamber on the surface. However, based on the seismic data and analyses, we found that just in front of (just east of) the Sphinx Temple, buried under the sand, there is a substantial drop in the bedrock. That is, if the sand and debris were removed from in front of the Sphinx Temple, it would be found that the temple sits atop a cliff with the Great Sphinx itself looming behind the temple. This must have been a very dramatic sight. I speculate that the entrance to the chamber under the paw of the Sphinx may be found in the cliff face.

To this date, the Egyptian authorities have not allowed me to explore the chamber that we found. Certainly, they are well aware that I would like to, and for the record, I have never been denied permission to do so outright; I have simply not yet been granted permission. I have some understanding of the complex intricacies and highly sensitive nature of exploring and excavating new archaeological finds in Egypt. I am not surprised that the authorities do not want to open more "cans of worms" at this time, and I am not an advocate of conspiracy theories – I am not aware of any credible evidence that the chamber has already been entered, as certain persons have contended. The area of the Sphinx is very open and public and it would be incredibly difficult to successfully hide such surreptitious activities. Even drilling into the chamber and inserting a miniature camera, as many have suggested, could risk damaging any artifacts that may be contained therein. In recent years, however, the Egyptians have begun, ever so slowly, to excavate the area in front of the Sphinx Temple. If they persist in their endeavors, at some point they should uncover the cliff we discovered using geophysics, and I will not be surprised if a door or opening, leading to a passage under the Sphinx Temple and thus into the chamber under the Sphinx, is eventually found. Something I have learned while working in Egypt is patience.

MEETING THE SPHINX

How did I ever become involved with the Great Sphinx? I was first introduced to the problem of the age of the Sphinx in the late 1980s by the "independent Egyptologist" John Anthony West, perhaps best known for his studies and popularization of the Egyptological work of the philosopher and mathematician R. A. Schwaller de Lubicz (1887-1961), and for his guidebook titled *The Traveler's Key to Ancient Egypt*. The way I met West was through a colleague then teaching in the same college as I; he had met West while teaching in Cairo. I quickly became interested in the problem of the age of the Sphinx, realizing that my own expertise in geology might shed light on the issue.

Even before I met West, however, I had given some thought to the Great Sphinx. As a teenager I loved ancient history, read profusely

on the subject, and even acquired a few minor Egyptian antiquities
from an aged fellow whose family had brought them out of Egypt
when it was still legal to do so. But more directly applicable to my
later research, I remember as a graduate student reading a couple of
articles on the geology of the Great Sphinx.

In particular, a certain Egyptian researcher, now living and
teaching in America, promulgated the notion that the Great Sphinx
began as a yardang, that is, a natural hill or rock outcropping that
had been weathered and shaped by the elements, primarily wind
in the case of desert yardangs as found in Egypt. The ancient
Egyptians, so the hypothesis went, saw in the yardang the crude
shape of a Sphinx (sort of like seeing the shapes of animals or
people in clouds), and decided to start chiseling and carving the
yardang to turn it into an actual Sphinx. I remember sitting in the
geology department graduate student lounge at Yale laughing over
this crazy notion with my peers. Remember, to free the body of the
Sphinx from the bedrock, large blocks of limestone were quarried

The Sphinx Buried in Sand

and removed. We thought it was hilarious that someone would think that wind could somehow carve out multi-ton blocks from around the body of the Sphinx and reassemble them as a temple in front of the statue. Furthermore, the weathering features on the Sphinx (and mind you, we were basing this just on photos, as none of us had actually been to Egypt) did not appear to fit the yardang hypothesis. At most, perhaps the head of the Sphinx, which does sit above the level of the plateau, was once a yardang, but it has now been too heavily carved and recarved to tell for sure. We had our own theory: the author of the yardang hypothesis grew up in Egypt and as a small child visited the Great Sphinx. He was impressed by its size and majesty, and also noted the heavy weathering to the statue, but did not at that time pay attention to the details of the geological and cultural context. Years later, without revisiting the Sphinx to check the geology and location, he based his theory on those formative impressions from childhood.

Once I had traveled to Egypt to study the Great Sphinx firsthand, I reinvestigated the yardang hypothesis. As we had discussed in graduate school, it made absolutely no sense (except, perhaps, for the head), but there was one important aspect to it. The author of the yardang theory observed, and acknowledged, the very ancient weathering features still preserved on the body of the Sphinx. Indeed, one way to view the yardang theory is that it provides a way to explain how such incredibly ancient weathering can be found on a dynastic structure. According to the yardang theory, the weathering came first, followed by the carving of the Sphinx. But given the context, this is patently impossible. The body of the Sphinx and the walls of the Sphinx enclosure were clearly weathered after being carved, and the weathering bears on the age of the Sphinx.

My work researching the Sphinx was done on my own time without remuneration, and the travel expenses to Egypt were funded by a group, spearheaded by West, intent upon producing a documentary on the subject. The immediate result was *The Mystery of the Sphinx* (hosted by 'Moses' – Charlton Heston, who played the role in the famous 1956 Cecil DeMille movie *The Ten Commandments*), which aired on NBC in the United States the evening of 10th November 1993, and is now available on DVD.

Not long after I became "notorious" for my work on the Sphinx, a senior faculty member at my college (College of General Studies, Boston University; I have taught there full-time since 1984), now deceased, told me that I had managed to immortalize myself by connecting my name to what is arguably the greatest and most recognizable sculpture on Earth – though this was certainly never my intention.

An Unsuspecting Heretic

I first presented my analyses of the data on the Great Sphinx – coming to the conclusion that the core body dates well back to pre-dynastic times – at the 1991 annual meeting of the Geological Society of America (GSA). Before the formal presentation I happened to run into a colleague of mine, a very talented geologist whose specialty was stratigraphy, the exact field that pertained to my data and analyses of the Great Sphinx. I showed him my data and explained my conclusions. His response? He began to laugh. My heart sank to the pit of my stomach. I was sure I must have made some fundamental mistake to induce such laughter from him, and in the next hour I was scheduled to present my work in the public forum. I asked hesitantly what was wrong. He answered (again, a paraphrase after all these years), "Nothing, nothing at all. It is just so obvious. Hasn't anyone ever looked at the Sphinx before? Where have all the Egyptologists been? Why didn't they see this long ago?"

Some weeks after the 1991 GSA presentation, I heard from one of my former undergraduate professors, a man I had always respected, though never known well. He was scathing in his comments regarding my work on the Sphinx, vehemently contending that I was quite wrong in recasting the age as anything other than circa 2500 B.C. But, his arguments against me made no logical or scientific sense, as far as I could determine. Then it came out that he was a devout, and apparently somewhat fundamentalist, Christian (although by no means a creationist or a proponent of a young Earth), and basically he somehow viewed the implications of my redating of the Sphinx as questioning his religious faith (how, I am not exactly sure). Scientists are humans too, and their deep beliefs and long-held assumptions can certainly cloud their ability to think clearly.

At one Egyptological conference to which I was invited to speak, I gave a nice, stolid, presentation on the evidence for an older Sphinx. I did not get many comments from the audience, but afterwards I was approached by a very senior, elderly, and rather grandfatherly, Egyptologist. His comment to me, and I can only paraphrase it now as it was many years ago, was to the effect "I do not understand geology, and I cannot refute your evidence, but I know you are wrong. Now there are lots of rocks other than at Giza and in Egypt; I suggest you go study the rocks somewhere else." By his demeanor and the tone of his voice, I took this as more than just a friendly suggestion. It was clear that he did not want me studying the Sphinx, and he was not beyond gently threatening me that there could be untold consequences if I persisted in my endeavors along such lines.

At another conference, to which I was invited to debate the age of the Great Sphinx, prior to the public discussions I was sharing some of my data with a member of the "opposition." It was not that I was required to do so, but I shared my data of my own free will. I have never treated the controversy over the age of the Sphinx as a situation where I am determined to "win" and "prove" my hypothesis for an older Sphinx. Rather, my concern as a scientist and researcher is to gather data, share the data, and honestly follow the data to wherever it should lead. Anyway, I was showing this professional "geoarchaeologist" some of the seismic data that we had collected around and under the Sphinx. He was having a difficult time interpreting it; looking down at the table, I saw a potential problem. Gently, and trying not to embarrass him, I said "You might want to look at it this way" and I turned the charts around, as he had been trying to read them upside down. Even when viewing them in their correct orientation, he seemed not to be able to follow them. I quickly realized that despite his position at a major university, and a Ph.D. in a relevant field, this man had absolutely no clue as to what he was looking at or how to interpret the data, and he was too proud to ask for help. The rest of the so-called debate was not very illuminating from my point of view. I attempted to present and discuss real data while my opponents at best skirted the issues and at worst lowered themselves to *ad hominem* attacks and insults against me personally.

At the same conference, I ran into one of my "opponents" in a back hall, a man hailed as one of the world's experts on the Great Sphinx. We were alone and standing face-to-face, eye-to-eye. He said to me something like, "You can't really believe that the Sphinx is older than the Fourth Dynasty. You must know that is nonsense." Clearly, he was attempting to appeal to my academic, orthodox side. I almost felt like he was trying to "save" me from the unholy alternative theorists and "New Age" camp. He then asked me some question about my analyses of the Sphinx data. I honestly no longer remember the question, but I remember that the tone of his voice was rather bitter and sarcastic. I proceeded to answer in detail as he just stared at me with a blank look on his face, saying nothing. Then, as I was in mid-sentence, he simply turned around and walked away. I realized afterwards that his "question" was meant as a rhetorical comment, and he had neither expected me to be able to answer it, nor dare try to answer it. When I did answer him, he was caught off-guard and apparently felt he had no other choice but to ignore me and walk away.

I have often felt that I am misunderstood when it comes to my work on the Sphinx. I am trained as a staid, traditional academic, with a Ph.D. from an Ivy League school (Ph.D. in geology and geophysics from Yale University, 1983) and a tenured teaching position. I think of myself as quite conventional, not as the radical alternative thinker that some have cast me. But, I believe in following the data to wherever it may lead, and my hypotheses and conclusions have not always gone over well with my traditional academic colleagues. For some years after first becoming involved with the Sphinx, realizing that the implications of an older Sphinx suggest – at least to some – a lost civilization as epitomized in Plato's concept of Atlantis, I refused to actually say the word "Atlantis" in public for fear of being ridiculed and condemned by my more traditional colleagues in academia. Rather, I referred to the "A-word." Sometimes I feel I straddle a tenuous existence between two worlds. I am not "normal" and "conventional" enough for the traditionalists, but I am not sufficiently "radical" and "far-out" for some members of the alternative camp. The Sphinx has taught me to live in my own world.

Robert Schoch has a Ph.D. in Geology and Geophysics from Yale and has been working in Egypt focusing on the Great Sphinx and Great Pyramid, since 1990. He is a tenured full-time faculty member at the College of General Studies of Boston University where he has taught a variety of science courses since 1984. His books include *Voyages of the Pyramid Builders*, *Pyramid Quest*, and *Voices of the Rocks*.

DRAFT

Directive Regarding Project ENVIRONMENT

When conditions become non-conducive for growth in our environment and Washington cannot be influenced any further, the weather is lacking any precipitation...it should be wet.

? WHO IS FLYING THE TRIANGLES

EARLY ENCOUNTERS WITH ANOMALOUS CRAFT

By *Nick Redfern*

For more than two decades, sightings of large triangular-shaped UFOs, usually described as being black in color, making a low humming noise, and very often with rounded rather than angled corners, have been reported throughout the world. The sheer proliferation of such reports has led some ufological commentators to strongly suspect that the Flying Triangles (as they have now come to be known) are prime examples of still-classified aircraft, the development of which was secretly begun in the 1980s by elements of the United States' Department of Defense and Air Force. And while it would, of course, be foolish to completely rule out such a scenario, the stark fact is that when placed under scrutiny, this argument completely and utterly collapses. As my extensive research into – predominantly – British-based UFO reports clearly demonstrates, the Flying Triangles have been with us for a very long time. Indeed, far longer than perhaps anyone has ever realized – until now...

MISSISSIPPI DELTA, AND TRIANGLES AHOY!

One exception to my discoveries of a strictly British nature is an investigation of a Flying Triangle-style UFO described in officially-declassified U.S. Air Force documents of May 26th, 1949 that originated with the Air Force Office of Special Investigations (AFOSI) at Barksdale Air Force Base, Louisiana. According to Special Agent Bernard A. Price: "Investigation at Vicksburg, Mississippi regarding an unidentified aerial phenomena described as being a flying triangle, failed to verify definitely just what type of object was sighted."

In this particular case the object, which was seen on the night of April 22nd, 1949, was relatively small in size when compared to its present-day equivalent; but was described by the witness to Special Agent Price as moving "faster than mail planes, or National Guard planes, but slower than a jet type aircraft." Also, the object reportedly did not exhibit "any kind of propulsion," nor "stabilizers or antenna."[1]

In September 1952, the North Atlantic Treaty Organization (NATO) coordinated a huge military exercise in the North Sea and North Atlantic. Dubbed Mainbrace, the exercise utilized the armed forces of Britain, the United States, Canada, Norway, Denmark, France, the Netherlands, and Belgium. Approximately 85000 personnel took part; the purpose of which was to demonstrate to the then-Soviet Union that NATO was fully prepared to withstand, and counter, any possible assault on Western Europe.

Only twenty-four-hours into the exercise, two reports of encounters with unidentified flying objects were filed with British,

American and NATO authorities by naval personnel on board ships in the Atlantic between Ireland and Iceland. The first involved a "blue-green triangle" that was observed flying high over the sea shortly after dawn broke, at a speed estimated to have been no less than 1500 miles-per-hour. Later that same day, a similar-shaped craft – but this time emitting a "white light exhaust" – was reported to the U.S. Air Force's UFO investigative body known as Project Blue Book.[2]

CIRCLING TRIANGLES

Four years later, the Flying Triangles were back in force. In his self-published report *Flying Triangle UFOs - The Continuing Story*, British UFO researcher Omar Fowler wrote: "On 19th April 1956 at 11am, Robin Gibbard and a colleague were working on a house roof at Allestree, Derby [England], when their attention was drawn to an approaching Avro Anson aircraft. They saw a triangular craft circle the aircraft twice, before speeding skyward."[3]

Then, on the night of September 9, 1960, an unidentified flying object – described as a "triangular formation of lights with a red light in the center" – was viewed by various people in the Consett, South Shields, Fawdon, and Fenham areas of the British city of Newcastle. Leslie Otley said that his wife and two neighbors saw the UFO circling over Fenham between 9.15 p.m. and 9.40 p.m. "A friend of mine, Mr. A. Miller, telephoned to say he saw them too, over Consett at 8.30 p.m.," added Otley, who telephoned a local Royal Air Force base – RAF Acklington – to report the encounters.

After having been firmly pressed by the *Newcastle Evening Chronicle* newspaper for a comment, a spokesman at RAF Acklington admitted that he had indeed received two independent reports of the mystery object, and said that these were duly being forwarded to the Air Ministry at London for examination.

He also added, somewhat cryptically, that: "I have no further information about this, and even if I had, we are not allowed to release information."[4]

For the most convincing evidence that exists to support the notion that Flying Triangles – identical to those seen today - were being viewed much earlier than many students of the mystery would have us believe, we have to turn our attention, once again, to the British Isles – but this time to early 1965. While digging through a whole host of formerly classified UFO files at the National Archive at Kew, England in 1996, I uncovered a one-page document that revealed some truly startling data.

As the relevant Ministry of Defense paperwork stated, on March 28th, 1965, at around 9:30 p.m. near the town of Richmond, North Yorkshire, a man saw, "Nine or ten objects...in close triangular formation each about 100ft long...orange illumination below...each triangular in shape with rounded corners, making low humming noise." The "rounded corners" and "low humming noise" are *precisely* what many witnesses to Flying Triangle-style UFO encounters reported throughout the late 1980s and 1990s, and continue to report to this day. Recognizing the significance of this, I began a search to locate the witness...

Moor UFOs

Upon ultimately finding the man, named Jeffrey Brown, I introduced myself, and explained that I had located at the National Archive a copy of the original report that dealt with his sighting of all those years ago.

"Yes, I did send in a report all those years ago, but I didn't think they would have kept it all this time," Brown said to me. As he explained, he had been driving at night through the remote North Yorkshire moors of England, when, on approaching the village of

Skeeby, near Richmond, the engine of his car suddenly began to fail: "It was a 1951 Ford, and it was a good car but a bit unpredictable at times. I didn't want to break down on the moor because it was icy cold. I got out of the car to have a look at the engine and that's when I saw this light."

Brown continued thus: "At first, because it was so dark, I wondered if it might be a weather balloon. But then I had a good look at it over the hedge and realized how big it was and how low down it was. It was about one hundred feet from end-to-end, about one hundred feet above the moors and shaped like a huge triangle and white, milky-white in color. It kept coming towards me and then stopped about two hundred yards from me over the moors. It hovered for a while – nothing came out of it, but there was a light below it that just pulsated like a light bulb. There could have been quite a few lights on it but from a distance the light just looked like a glow. Then without a warning, it just took off at a speed that isn't recognized. Good gracious, I thought, it must be a UFO.

"It shot up, not vertically but at an angle, [and] it joined a group of others that were identical and that were in a triangular or V-formation. The others were very, very high – a whole fleet of them. They all then headed south, I think, at a tremendous speed and disappeared over the horizon. I saw the main one for no more than a couple of minutes, but after they had gone I was still stood by the moor watching this fleet disappear. I waited in case something else exciting happened, but of course it didn't."

Not long after he had reported the events in question to the Ministry of Defense, Brown noticed: "…awful red marks on my skin which were like a stretch mark, but they were like a deep salmon red and they kept coming and going. But I didn't have them before."

He continued: "For about eighteen months after the sighting, I would get strange telephone calls from people. These would be every two or three months. They just phoned out of the blue but didn't introduce themselves. They just said they were from some bureau or other. They didn't mention the name of the bureau but kept mentioning 'sightings' and asked whether I had seen anything else strange. Had any men come to interview me?"

Brown was never visited by anyone with regard to his memorable Flying Triangle encounter, nor did the MoD ever offer him a satisfactory explanation for what had taken place on that fateful night back in March 1965. But Brown's welcome recollections raise three important questions: Why was someone so carefully determined to find out if he had received any strange visits with regard to the event at issue? Why the interest in knowing if he had undergone any other unusual encounters of a specific UFO nature? And who indeed were his mysterious phone-callers? Today, more than four decades after Jeffrey Brown's remarkable sighting, those questions still remain intriguingly unanswered.[5]

Police Lights and MoD Secrets

Shortly after midnight on Sunday, August 28, 1977, a large object – that fits the description of those discussed thus far – was seen by more than ten police officers and several members of the public in and around the Windermere area of Cumbria, England.

Sergeant James Trohear described the "triangular or slightly diamond-shaped" nature of the craft; while another officer commented that it "resembled the shape of a stingray fish." Meanwhile, Constable David Wild added that it appeared to be "kite-shaped, or like a skate fish," adding that it was "very large and solid in construction." It, like so many other sightings of a similar nature, was classified as unexplained.[6]

I have been granted permission to relate the following account on the understanding that I do not divulge any compromising information concerning the source. For a period of months in 1981, my source was employed as a radar operator at a particular British military facility on the island of Cyprus. On August 16 of that year, an object – described as being "vast" – was tracked on radar approaching the island at a height in excess of 30000 feet, and at a speed of 900mph.

It was initially believed that this was a conventional aircraft, albeit certainly one of unusual and profound dimensions. This theory quickly evaporated, however, when the object reportedly came to a sudden stop and hovered over the base for around three-quarters of an hour. To the complete and utter astonishment of those who witnessed the object, it was triangular in shape, sparkling white in color, and, most incredible of all, over 700 feet in length.

My source also stated that prior to the sighting, an encrypted message was sent to the base from the British Ministry of Defense in London, ordering a "complete stand-down" of aircraft in the event that any strange "aerial phenomena" were sighted in the vicinity of the base airfield.

Numerous photographs were reportedly taken of the object and were held under lock and key, along with the relevant radar tapes and log reports. On the following day, two people – one a middle-aged woman and the other an elderly man, both rumored to be from the Ministry of Defense – arrived at the base and, after six hours, left with all of the available evidence concerning the event. Needless to say, those involved were sworn to complete secrecy and strongly reminded of their obligations to the British Government.

My source also learned, via a colleague with intimate knowledge of the encounter, that a meeting to discuss the case was held at RAF Lakenheath in the English county of Suffolk, at some point during August 1981. Present were representatives of the Ministry of Defense and the United States' Air Force Office of Special Investigations.

I was advised that other UFO incidents had occurred within the vicinity of the base throughout the summer of 1981, but the precise details were not imparted to me. I should stress that my source was most uneasy about breaking his security oath, but was of the firm opinion that there was no justification for the British Government withholding such information if, as is officially maintained, UFOs present no threat to the security of the British Isles.

Perhaps the most puzzling aspect of this affair, however, is the fact that the Ministry of Defense appeared to have prior knowledge that something unusual was afoot. In light of this, I inquired of my source if he had considered the possibility that the object had been some form of experimental aircraft – despite its incredible size and ability to hover in one position for close on an hour. If this was the case, I reasoned, it would have gone a long way towards explaining the MoD's order that all military aircraft should be stood down at the time that the UFO appeared. This brought forth the following reply to me:

"Whatever we saw, it was not man-made; I can guarantee that. This thing was seven hundred feet long, and was over the base for three-quarters of an hour. I'm pretty sure we don't have the technology to build something like this, nor the Americans [sic]. And if it was Russian, why weren't we allowed to intercept it?"

He continued: "Plus, you've got to remember that it isn't easy to hide a seven hundred foot long aircraft on the ground. You'd think

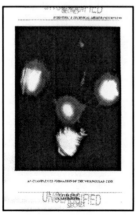

Triangle in British MoD Report

that it would have been seen taking off and landing if it was something of ours that was being regularly tested. Now, I know that we do test-fly some weird things now and again, but no, this was something else."

The man concluded: "Then there's the Lakenheath meeting: I know that they were really bothered about it. I don't really have much else other than what I've already told you, but you can take it from me, this thing was really alien. How did the MoD know that it was going to arrive? Well, your guess is as good as mine. Maybe it's not a good idea to ask questions like that. Don't forget: it was all graded Top Secret."

SEEKING ANSWERS

Some people, however, did ask questions. Notably, a letter contained within declassified British Ministry of Defense files of 1984 reveals the details of what seems to be a very similar case; and one which also occurred on the island of Cyprus, just months before the astounding Flying Triangle event cited above.[7]

Found in the released records of a now-defunct Ministry of Defense office known as Defense Secretariat 8 is a photo-copy of a long letter written by Mark Birdsall – the brother of the late Graham Birdsall, of *UFO Magazine*, who was heavily active in UFO research in the late 1970s and subsequent decades. Dated March 27th 1984, the letter from Mark Birdsall requested access to any and all official data pertaining to a certain UFO incident – the details of which, Birdsall explained, were known to "a high ranking RAF [Royal Air Force] officer and thirteen others," and which had occurred in early 1981.

Birdsall added to the Ministry of Defense that his informant had advised him that "the incident" involved the sighting of a huge, triangular-shaped object over a military base on Cyprus, and one that was described as being "silver [and] hanging motionless in the sky at 60,000 feet." The Flying Triangle, Birdsall elaborated, was "100m in length by 50m," and, according to his sources, was apparently tracked on radar as well as having been sighted visually.

On April 24, 1984, declassified Ministry of Defense files reveal, a DS8 representative replied to Mark Birdsall's letter and advised him that they had "no record" of any such incident on file. To this day, the case remains unresolved.[8]

An Extraterrestrial Conclusion?

As the reader will have clearly noted, the reports that I have cited above span a period of time that covers almost sixty years. Contrary to the popular belief perpetuated by elements of the worldwide UFO research community, we now know that sightings of the mysterious Flying Triangles have proliferated for, quite literally, decades. They are most assuredly *not* a relatively recent development.

Had we – and by "we" I mean the collective Human Race – been designing, building and flying huge triangular-shaped, high-performance aircraft in the 1950s and 1960s, then surely they would not still be subject to an overwhelming blanket of secrecy to this very day.

More likely, they would either have been put to regular use in a battlefield environment, or the projects would have been canceled as not being seen as ultimately viable. Either way, we would by now have widespread awareness of their existence, in much the same way that the existence of the famous U-2 spy-plane of the Cold War, and today's F-117 Stealth Fighter and the B-2 Stealth bomber has been acknowledged. The fact that we do not have such awareness, however – and the fact that the UFO research community is still scratching its collective head as it seeks to resolve the puzzle – suggests strongly that the ubiquitous Flying Triangle has a far stranger point of origin.

Those that seek a definitive answer to the conundrum of the Flying Triangle might be very wise to turn their attentions away from restricted military bases and firmly towards the distant heavens...

Nick Redfern is the author of many books on unexplained phenomena, including *A Covert Agenda*, *Body Snatchers in the Desert*, *On the Trail of the Saucer Spies*, and *Memoirs of a Monster Hunter*. More information about Nick and his research can be found at his website, www.nickredfern.com, and at his blog, www.ufomystic.com.

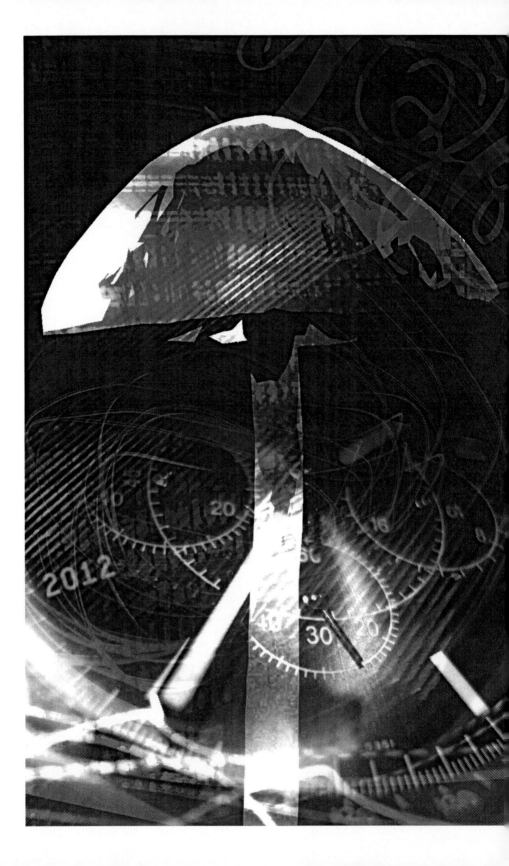

A PSYCHEDELIC APOCALYPSE

@

TRAVELING THROUGH TIME WITH THE

BROTHERS MCKENNA

By *Daniel Pinchbeck*

originally encountered the idea of an approaching global mind-shift, related to the year 2012, in the works of Terence McKenna – who proclaimed that, while tripping on mushrooms in the Colombian Amazon in the early 1970s, he had discovered the "timewave," a spiraling involution or concrescence of time that would bring history to an end on the winter solstice of 2012. During that time, he also believed he had interacted with an alien intelligence and been visited by flying saucers. "My story is a peculiar one," he admitted. "It is hard to know what to make of it." McKenna sometimes approached this bizarre idea playfully, yet at other times seemed sincerely convinced of his prophetic role.

McKenna was the most loquacious and entertaining proponent of shamanic exploration to appear on the scene since Timothy Leary. Before his death from a brain tumor in 1999, he promoted the idea of an "archaic revival," defining a new context for use of psychedelics among a global counterculture of ravers, hackers, slackers, and futurists. He was capable of speaking for ten hours straight, mesmerizing audiences with his deadpan delivery of hermetic ideas and alchemical possibilities. "We are like coral animals embedded in a technological reef of extruded psychic objects," he wrote in a 1983 essay. "All our tool making implies our belief in an ultimate tool." He saw the archetypal apparition of the UFO or flying saucer as a foreshadowing of this tool awaiting us at the end of history, that would exteriorize the human soul and interiorize the body, releasing the psyche into the infinite realm of the Imagination —"a kind of Islamic paradise in which one is free to experience all the pleasures of the flesh provided one realizes that one is a projection of a holographic solid-state matrix."

Exploring the 'Spirit Molecule'

One of McKenna's achievements was to popularize, and glamorize, the short-acting but revelatory DMT trip. He was fascinated with "the rose window topologies of the galacterian beehives of the dimethyltryptamine flash, that nexus of cheap talk and formal mathematics where wishes become horses and everybody got to ride." Made illegal by the U.S. government under the Controlled Substances Act of 1970, DMT is a naturally occurring chemical in the human body, found in the brain and spinal column, and produced by many plants. The DMT molecule is similar to serotonin and melatonin, tryptamines involved in the modulation of conscious states and rhythms of sleep and dream.

Dr. Rick Strassman, the researcher who conducted a 1990 study on the effects of DMT through the University of New Mexico, advanced the thesis that DMT could be the "spirit molecule," linking the physical brain to as-of-yet unknown domains of the afterlife. A practicing Buddhist, Strassman made this proposition based on an intriguing correspondence between fetal development and Buddhist scripture. According to Buddhism, the soul reincarnates seven weeks after death. The pineal gland – that singular organ in the brain that Descartes had considered the seat of the soul – develops in the embryo forty-nine days after conception. Strassman hypothesized that the pineal gland might act as a receiver for the soul, and that DMT could function as the conducting medium. "The pineal gland of evolutionarily older animals, such as lizards and amphibians, is also called the 'third eye,'" Strassman wrote. "Just like the two seeing eyes, the third eye possesses a lens, cornea, and retina." In the event of a cataclysmic shock or at death, the pineal gland might release a flood of DMT into the brain, causing the "life review" and the intense visionary phenomena reported in numerous near-death experiences.

When McKenna smoked DMT – a wrenching event accompanied by a sound similar to the ripping of cellophane – he described "bursting into a space inhabited by merry elfin, self-transforming, machine creatures…friendly fractal entities, looking like self-dribbling Faberge eggs on the rebound." His explorations led him to propose that the afterlife may be "more Celtic fairyland than existential nonentity." However, he also recognized the threatening nature of the experience, which forces anyone who dares it to undergo "a mini-apocalypse, a mini-entry and mapping into hyperspace." The greatest danger one encounters is the possibility of "death by astonishment."

In my own explorations of smoked DMT – the psychedelic equivalent of bungee jumping – I did not encounter any merry "elfin entelochies." I felt I was rocketing out of my body, through some intermediary tunnel of symbols and mystical geometries, vibrating and incandescent around me, then reaching a kind of vast vaulted cavernous space, some infradimensional fusion of quartz crystal and Silly Putty, mutable and fast-changing. Immense Cyclopean guardians seemed to preside over this realm, like giant stalagmites, chattering wildly, projecting toward me what I interpreted as a terrifying impartiality. During my second DMT trip – although only seven or so minutes, the subjective experience seems far longer – I found myself making alarming insect-like vocalizations, an example of the "glossalia-like linguistic phenomena" McKenna explored during tryptamine trance, and defensive gestures. Recovering my ability to speak, I turned to the supramental samurai or bardo wardens looming above me, and said, as politely as possible, "Thank you very much – I really appreciate this. And now I would like to go back to my reality."

Soon I found myself rematerializing in the musty Haight-Ashbury attic from which I had launched. Coming out of my trance, I looked down at my arm. Standing on my sleeve was an intricate metropolis, a science-fiction city of glittering spires and emerald skyscrapers in which I could almost see the movements of an infinitesimal transport grid. I looked around at my friends sitting in a circle around me, and all of them appeared radically transformed. They were themselves, but patina'd with complex multicolored tattoos, sporting celestial headdresses, prismatic auras, and elaborate comic-book-superhero armatures. The thought occurred to me that we were actually space aliens or cosmic deities who had projected ourselves backward into this time, prearranging this crude but amusing encounter in "meat-space" from our holographic homeland. "Everyone is God," I muttered, as the vision faded away. Back in conventional space-time, I hugged the woman sitting next to me, feeling I had never known anything as comforting as the solid warmth of her flesh, soft sweater, and patchouli-perfumed scent.

Nietzsche proposed, "Something might be true while being harmful and dangerous in the highest degree. Indeed, it might be a basic characteristic of existence that those who know it completely would perish, in which case the strength of a spirit should be measured according to how much of the 'truth' one could still barely endure – or to put it more clearly, to what degree one would *require* it to be thinned down, shrouded, sweetened, blunted, falsified." DMT, as well as my DPT experience and other hallucinatory forays, suggest that "truth" is not only dangerous but neither singular nor definitive – that "reality" is a dynamic and daimonic process, closer to the multi-latticed meanings implied by music or art than the confident postulates of science, which often supports conventional psychology and the antiquated mechanistic paradigm under its suspect cloak of objectivity. Like a quick bath in the quantum foam of seething "perhapsness" described by quantum physics, such trips help to undermine any cosmological or ontological framework that one might like to hold, accentuating the "curious literary quality running across the surface of existence," noted by McKenna, who thought language, or "the logos," had a crucial role in shaping reality.

The Psychonautical Wright Brothers

McKenna first stumbled upon the notion of an approaching end point to human history in 1971, when he and his younger brother Dennis, along with some friends, went to the village of La Chorrera, deep in the Colombian Amazon, hoping to find *oo-koo-he*, a DMT-containing snuff, used by the Witoto tribe – a kind of Hardy Boys investigation into the far antipodes of the psyche. The snuff was only a small part of their quest; they were interested in exploring particular aspects of the DMT trance, its relationship to language – "under the influence of DMT, language was transmuted from a thing heard to a thing seen" – and to alien forms of consciousness, as well as, perhaps, UFOs. They had great dreams. "I could feel the golden chain of adepts reaching back into the distant Hellenistic past, the Hermetic

Opus, a project vaster than empires and centuries; nothing less than the redemption of fallen humanity through the respiritualization of matter," he wrote in his 1993 memoir, *True Hallucinations*.

The McKennas never found *oo-koo-he*. In fact, McKenna spent the rest of his life puzzling out exactly what they did or didn't find in the Amazon. The brothers and their friends discovered psilocybin instead, bushels of plump *Stropharia cubensis* that weren't even on their original menu. "We are closing distance with the most profound event a planetary ecology can encounter: the emergence of life from the dark chrysalis of matter," McKenna jotted after his first mushroom munch. Drawn in by the fungus, as if it were calling to them, they proceeded to ingest the *Stropharia* in vast quantities over the next weeks. The mushroom became the focus of their quest to combine the experiential techniques of shamanism with the empirical methods of science in order to investigate the invisible landscape, "the simultaneous coexistence of an alien dimension all around us," which they had first accessed through DMT.

Although McKenna was only twenty-four, he had been fascinated with fringe matters since early adolescence. "My interest in drugs, magic, and the more obscure backwaters of natural history and theology gave me the interest profile of an eccentric Florentine prince rather than a kid growing up in the heartland of the United States in the late fifties." His brother, a few years younger, shared his enthusiasms. McKenna had participated in 1960s campus politics at Berkeley, discovering DMT "at the apex of the summer of love," watched the radical counterculture collapse, traveled in the Far East, studying Sanskrit in Nepal and trafficking hash. As he had proposed it to one of his fellow travelers, DMT was "some kind of outrage" that, properly understood, could have "tremendous importance for the historical crisis everybody is in."

The McKennas dreamed of becoming the psychonautical Wright Brothers of the New Age, making charter flights through new realities, garnering Nobel Prizes for melding science and shamanism. "If the world beyond the doorway can be given consensual validation of the sort extended to the electron and the black hole – in other words, if the world beyond the doorway is found to be a necessary part of scientifically mature thinking about the world – then our own circumscribed historical struggle will be subject to whole new worlds of possibility," they wrote in *The Invisible Landscape* (1975), their book on the adventure, a precocious and inscrutable blend of scientific hypothesis and psychedelic philosophy. They proposed that the existence of these realms required scrupulous – and courageous – exploration.

It was Dennis who provided the impetus for what the McKennas would later dub the "La Chorrera experiment." When McKenna described the glossolalia he sometimes explored during DMT trips, Dennis activated the same phenomenon while under the influence of the mushrooms, emitting "a very machine-like, loud, dry buzz," threateningly insectile, which suggested to him the development "of a shamanic power of some sort." Inspired by this new ability, Dennis developed the thesis that this nonsensical sound-stream – accessible only during tryptamine trance – could be directed in some way that would result in "a molecular aggregate of hyperdimensional, superconducting matter that receives and sends messages transmitted by thought." Despite the patent absurdity of this idea, the McKennas took it seriously, and created the conditions in their rain forest shack for a test. They had read accounts of Amazonian shamanism that referred to a "violet or deep blue" magical liquid produced from the body during ayahuasca sessions, used for divination and sorcery – Terence believed he had once encountered this "psychofluid" during a confused and orgiastic night on a rooftop in Katmandu, involving LSD, datura, DMT, and UFOs. The seemingly impossible goal of their La Chorrera experiment was to produce and stabilize this extradimensional liquid in the three-dimensional world. "And end history. And go to the stars."

An Ancient Galactic Intelligence

It didn't happen, it would seem – to the McKennas' chagrin, history refused to fold up its tent on March 4, 1971. The omega point did not arrive. But something happened, or at least McKenna continued to believe something had. For the next weeks, he found himself in telepathic rapport with some alien other that downloaded ideas and information into his mind, speaking to him like a teacher to a student. For nine days and nights he claims he did not sleep, as a deep cognitive reorganization took place. "The overwhelming impression was that something possibly from outer space or from another dimension was contacting us," he recalled. "It was doing so through the peculiar means of using every thought in our heads to lead us into telepathically induced scenarios of extravagant imaginings, or deep theoretical understandings, or in-depth scannings of strange times, places, and worlds." As McKenna received these flows, Dennis retreated further and further from consensual reality, into a temporary state of schizophrenia. While their friends worried, McKenna remained unconcerned, certain that everything was proceeding according to plan. "I used no psychoanalytical jargon in thinking about it, but I noted a reaction in myself that included the idea that he might be unfolding into a mythopoetic reality, or as I thought of it then, 'going bananas.'"

During the time in La Chorrera, McKenna noted an amassing of tiny episodes that seemed to abort, momentarily, the Newtonian constraints of space and time. Clouds formed into lenticular saucers; mysterious lights roved across the fields; the rushing waters on part of the lake suddenly appeared to stop their flow. When McKenna awoke one night and lit a candle, he saw "an intense, triple-layered corona of light," shimmering out for four feet, resembling the aura around Christ's body in a painting by Matthias Grünewald. In the aftermath of the adventure, although lacking the "consensual validation" he had hoped to establish, he continued to believe "under certain conditions the manipulative power of consciousness moves beyond the body and into the world." In particular non-ordinary states, at particular times, the mind can determine "the outcome of the normally random, micro-physical events."

The culmination, in McKenna's account, occurred on his last night in the village. Sitting by the lake in the gray predawn, he watched clouds coalesce in the distance, forming odd symmetries. One cloud seemed to swirl inward "like a tornado or waterspout," take particular form, and rush toward him. As it flew directly overhead, McKenna looked up. "It was a saucer-shaped machine rotating slowly, with unobtrusive, soft, blue and orange lights," he recalled. "It was making the whee, whee, whee sound of science fiction flying saucers."

To increase the effect of this "cosmic giggle," McKenna realized the saucer was identical to an infamous photograph of a UFO by George Adamski, widely believed to be a hoax, "a rigged up end-cap of a Hoover vacuum cleaner." The Mystery had unveiled itself to him as a cheesy stereotype, already debunked. "By appearing in a form that casts doubt on itself, it achieves a more complete cognitive dissonance than if its seeming alienness were completely convincing," he theorized. When McKenna read ufologist Jacques Vallée's *The Invisible College* several years after the adventure, he learned that "an absurd element is invariably a part of the situation in which contact with an alien occurs." Decades later, he felt he had witnessed "a manifestation of a humorous something's omniscient control over the world of form and matter," choosing to take the shape of a saucer in this instance, but capable of taking any form.

The alien "other" that continued to speak in McKenna's mind long after the event seemed to be the mushroom itself, which represented itself as an ancient galactic intelligence interested in making a productive symbiosis with modern humanity. "It is far more likely that an alien intelligence would be barely recognizable to us than that it should overwhelm us with such similarities as humanoid form and an intimate knowledge of our gross industrial capacity," he suggested, proposing, "the *Stropharia cubensis* mushroom is a memory bank of galactic history." As McKenna related, this fungal consciousness told him that it distributed itself through the galaxies as spores, traveling on meteorites, awaiting contact with the nervous system of a higher animal capable of conscious evolution.

"The mushroom which you see is the part of my body given to sex thrills and sun bathing," the fungus informed him. "My true body is a fine network of fibers growing through the soil." These mycelial networks "may cover acres and have far more connections than the number in a human brain." Psilocybin and psilocyn were compounds produced to open the psychophysical gateway to a galactic community of mind. "You as an individual and humanity as a species are on the brink of a formation of a symbiotic relationship with my genetic material that will eventually carry humanity and earth into the galactic mainstream of the higher civilizations" – thus spake the fungus.

A New Conception of Time

The other part of the message the mycelial intelligence conveyed to McKenna, as he formalized it over the next years, was a revelatory new conception of the nature of time. "Quite unexpectedly, what I now propose, based on those initial experiences, is a revision of the mathematical description of time used in physics," he wrote in *True Hallucinations*. "According to this theory, the old notion of time as pure duration, visualized as a smooth plane or straight line, is to be replaced by the idea that time is a very complex fractal phenomenon with many ups and downs of many sizes over which the probabilistic universe of becoming must flow like water over a boulder-strewn riverbed." The ancient Chinese divinatory system of the I Ching, the Taoist "Book of Changes," and the bioenergetic matrix of the DNA code seemed to be keys to unlocking a deeper pattern or underlying structure of temporality.

Far more than a divination system, the sixty-four hexagrams of the I Ching could be seen as a description or map of the processes of evolution, development, decay, and transformation as they are experienced by any organism, species, individual, or civilization. "The Logos taught me how to do something with the I Ching that perhaps no one knew how to do before," he wrote. "Perhaps the Chinese knew how to do it once and then lost it thousands of years ago. It taught me a hyper-temporal way of seeing." It was McKenna's inspiration to take the most august arrangement of these hexagrams, the King Wen sequence, and utilize mathematical postulates to transform it into a graph or wave that represented "the ingression of novelty into history." He dubbed the result "timewave zero," proposing that time was not an unvarying extension but "a medium of variables in flux," where no two instants are alike, and where new possibilities can enter the frame at certain propitious moments. The timewave revealed an "ocean of resonances," linking every moment "through a scheme of connection that knew nothing of randomness or causality."

The fractal or holographic vision of time that McKenna discovered, or that his hyperspatial ally proposed to him, contained the inherent idea that there exist different "time orders," various forms or structures of temporality. "And these kinds of time come and go in cyclical progression on many levels; situations evolve as matter responds to the conditioning of time and space." Such an understanding helped to free the individual from the burden of time: "If you know what is contained in time from its beginning to its end you are somehow no longer in time," he wrote. "Even though you still have a body and still eat and do what you do, you have discovered something that liberates you into a satisfying all-at-onceness."

The timewave also implied an imminent rupture, an end to our linear time that would be a movement into a new temporal structure. "Because we suggest a model of time whose mathematics dictate a built-in spiral structure, events keep gathering themselves into tighter and tighter spirals that lead inevitably to a final time. Like the center of a black hole, the final time is a necessary singularity, a domain or an event in which the ordinary laws of physics do not function." Such an event would mean "passing out of one set of laws that are conditioning existence and into another radically different set of laws. The universe is seen as a series of compartmentalized eras or epochs whose laws are quite different from one another, with transitions from one epoch to another occurring with unexpected suddenness."

Back in California, after La Chorrera, McKenna found himself "in the grip of a creative mania more extreme than any I had thought possible." Prodded by his ally and his own intuitions, McKenna conjectured that the concrescence of the "final time" would occur during a rare astronomical conjunction: the eclipse of the galactic center by the solstice sun, an event that occurred approximately once every twenty-six thousand years. Utilizing software, he discovered that this would next occur on December 21st, 2012. According to McKenna, he arrived at this date without knowledge of the Mayan calendar, "and it was only after we noticed that the historical data seemed to fit best with the wave if this end date was chosen that we were informed that the end date that we had deduced was in fact the end of the Mayan Calendar." He theorized that the Eschaton, strange attractor, or merkhaba-like object awaiting us at that final time has in a sense already appeared, and what we experience as history are the shockwaves sent backward from this culmination.

"What is it that gives both a twentieth-century individual and an ancient Mesoamerican civilization the same date upon which to peg the transformation of the world?" he asked. "Is it that both used psychedelic mushrooms? Could the answer be so simple? I don't think so. Rather, I suspect that when we inspect the structure of our deep unconscious we will make the unexpected discovery that we are ordered on the same principle as the larger universe in which we arose. This notion, surprising at first, quickly comes to be seen as obvious, natural, and inevitable."

By opening their psyches to the Unknown at La Chorrera, had the McKennas retrieved some deep-buried archetypal complex, a psychophysical thought-system meshing the end-time eschatologies of various religious traditions? Or would it, in the end, turn out to be nothing more than an expression of the cosmic giggle, mocking human pretensions and alchemical dreams? McKenna could never be sure. "The notion of some kind of fantastically complicated visionary revelation that happens to put one at the very center of the action is a symptom of mental illness," he noted, realizing his story had all the trappings of the "messianic ego-inflation" that infected prophets of the past, who passed along their disease in the form of new religious doctrines and dogmas. "My theory may be clinically pathological, but unlike these religious systems, I have enough humor to realize this," he said in his defense. Although tantalized by his timewave, he saw that part of his personal drama involved "the intrinsic comedy of privileged knowledge."

Daniel Pinchbeck is the author of *2012: The Return of Quetzalcoatl* (Tarcher Penguin, 2006) and *Breaking Open the Head* (Broadway Books, 2002). He is also Editorial Director of the alternative web portal 'Reality Sandwich' (www.realitysandwich.com).

This article is a modified excerpt from Daniel Pinchbeck's *2012: The Return of Quetzalcoatl* (Tarcher Penguin, 2006), reprinted with permission.

THE AUTHORS

are in eternity...

Is Great Literature Inspired by the Spirit World?

By *Susan B. Martinez*

o the Irish poet, W.B. Yeats, the sudden flashing of a seabird was an omen. Paragon of the "Irish Renaissance," Yeats – even in his teens – eschewed the scientific materialism of the late Victorian Age. He thought the world "sick with theories," and in his poems would summon the "brotherhood of wisdom and immortal moods." Mystic and butterfly-collector, the lonely poet believed in something more than the five senses; could hear the disembodied Voice (reproving him); conducted occult experiments with his uncle, George Pollaxfen; and attended séances held by Madame Blavatsky. Did William Butler Yeats carry the "psychic gene" of his Hibernian brethren? Or is that all blarney? It was probably through his mother's unwavering belief in Irish tradition, that Yeats accepted the power of the fairies.

In Ireland, the fairy people were called – *the Others*; and it was Yeats's own belief that "minds can flow into one another" to produce a single energy. Minds, not brains. And he called it Divine Mind. But Yeats was not alone, at least among Europe's poets.

Dante had felt "a Deity stronger than I, whose coming shall rule me."[1] Schiller felt his thoughts flowed through him independent of the action of his own mind. Coleridge, that opium-eating supernaturalist, is said to have composed *Kubla Khan* in his sleep. Emily Bronte, it was known among friends, experienced leaving the body and traveling *elsewhere*; she spoke of daring "the final bound" into the Unseen. According to British clairvoyant, Wilma Davidson, many writers have made that 'final bound': "D.H. Lawrence, Virginia Woolf, Ernest Hemingway, Tolstoy, Tennyson, Edgar Allen Poe, and many others, all claimed to have had at least one OBE."[2] (out-of-body-experience).

The Sweet Closing of an Eye...

Some years ago, a St. Louis author named Dorothy Wofford began writing poetry that, amazingly, turned out to be the verses of a 17th century poet named Anne Broadbent. The matter was investigated, cryptomnesia was eliminated (i.e. recalling something unconsciously learned in the past); at the same time it became clear that Dorothy shared some unusual characteristics and tastes with Anne. Dorothy's mediumship and striking similarity to her 17th century counterpart seemed to invoke the law of *rapport*: "Ever molding themselves to mortals of similar tastes and indulgences,"[3] our angel companions abide with us – as George Russell saw it, out of "some affinity of sentiment or soul."[4] Interesting that American's great medium, Arthur Ford, when asked to explain spirit-familiars, simply pointed out that they are "drawn to you because you are doing something that they were doing."[5] The point is well illustrated by a famous American author who, inflamed by the peculiar institution of Slavery, knew that…

> I must write a story to stop the dreadful shame!…the fugitive slave law lashed me into a fury, and I commenced what I meant to be a short story. But it grew, and grew, and grew, and came, and came, and came…I did not plan the book as it turned out. I was only full of wrath, and the story built itself around it…[6]

It was Harriet Beecher Stowe who in the early 1850s began the ever-expanding story of *Uncle Tom's Cabin,* which became the best-selling novel of the age. It was not modesty that caused her to claim "it was written through me, I only holding the pen;"[7] for 'Hattie' Stowe was rather mediumistic herself, occasionally observed by friends to fall into dreamy, trancelike states. She did not shut out the Others in disbelief; her various stories and novels and poems made ample use of ghosts and spirit friends:

> It lies around us like a cloud, / A world we do not see;
> Yet the sweet closing of an eye / May bring us there to be.

Even in her old age, more than forty years after writing *Uncle Tom's Cabin*, Hattie still maintained that the book and its characters "passed before me;" it was simply "blown through her mind as with the rushing of a mighty wind."[8] Every line, she averred, came to her "inner ear by a spirit voice."

It was, of course, the Great Age of Spiritualism, the historic parting of the Veil. In 1860, while in Rome, Stowe organized parties, most notably her Wednesday evening receptions, attended by the Brownings, the Fieldses, and other literary lights. Elizabeth Barrett Browning and Mrs. Stowe became friends and attended séances together. It was Mrs. Browning who, in Italy, would introduce Mrs.

Nathaniel Hawthorne to Spiritualism and "sittings." On one such occasion, the medium (Ada Shepard) began (automatically) writing out a spirit message from Mrs. Hawthorne's deceased mother. "My dearest child," came the words, "I am near you…"

Hattie Stowe sometimes quoted Goethe on the subject of the unseen influence: "It is just as absurd to deny the facts of spiritualism now as it was in the Middle Ages to ascribe them to the Devil." The great German poet had also possessed a touch of second sight, confessing that some of his best poems were written in a condition that bordered on somnambulism. Goethe explained: "Many times has a sheet of blank paper lain on my desk. I am unconscious that I write until I look down and find it filled with poetry."[9]

Disdaining the Darkenened Parlours

Having compiled a list of writers who were sensitive to the spirit world, I noticed that quite a few arose in the 19th century's golden age:

> Louisa May Alcott, Balzac, Emily and Charlotte Bronte, Pearl Buck, Byron, Thomas Carlyle, William Cowper, Lewis Carroll, John Donne, Dostoevsky, Arthur Conan Doyle, Theodore Dreiser, Alexander Dumas, T.S. Eliot, Euripides, Flaubert, Robert Frost, Horace Greeley, Herodotus, Herman Hesse, Homer, Horace, Victor Hugo, Ibsen, Washington Irving, Josephus, Jack London, James Joyce, Kipling, Longfellow, Thomas Mann, Milton, Pascal, Plato, Plutarch, John Ruskin, Rilke, Shakespeare, Socrates, Sophocles, Upton Sinclair, Shelley, Tennyson, Thackery, Thoreau, Tolstoy, Virgil, Whitman, Whittier, Oscar Wilde, Wordsworth, etc.

You may sometimes see Hawthorne's name or Dickens or others on similar lists but there is a reason I have excluded them. Hawthorne, for one, wrote many stories dealing with the supernatural, encountered real-life ghosts, and even lived in a haunted house. But he would ultimately opt for "some very commonplace" explanation of these things; and when his wife received that otherworldly message through the medium Ada Shepard, and breathed to her husband "It is very curious and wonderful," his reply was – "It is unhealthy." As usual, the wives were pro and the husbands, con: After that séance, Elizabeth's husband, the poet Robert Browning, vigorously condemned spiritualism, and Nathaniel Hawthorne joined forces with him, criticizing "the bad judgment common among the spiritual brotherhood."

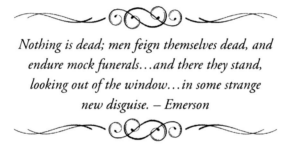

Nothing is dead; men feign themselves dead, and endure mock funerals…and there they stand, looking out of the window…in some strange new disguise. – Emerson

It was the same with Hawthorne's fellow New Englander, Ralph Waldo Emerson, whose writings proclaimed man a deathless being, immortal, transcendent. But he too disdained popular spiritualism with its darkened parlors and spirit-rapping, denouncing it as "rat revelation, the gospel that comes by taps in the wall and humps in the table."[10]

The most fickle and fence-straddling of all Europe's literary elite was Charles Dickens. Despite his numerous psychic experiences, including startling visions of ghosts[11], the great novelist would become a debunker of the mediumistic arts. Like Robert Browning, he would turn his scathing censure on Mrs. Browning's favorite and beloved medium – the renowned D.D. Home. Dickens publicly branded the phenomenal Home a "ruffian" and when Home's stage career flagged (he acted in plays and gave readings to earn the cash he refused to take for his sittings), Dickens sneered "that the public had found out the scoundrel."[12] Dickens, who never did attend a single séance, managed nonetheless to form an opinion of Spiritualism based on its more vulgar aspects: "I have not," he sniffed, "the least belief in the awful unseen being available for evening parties at so much per night." (Both Browning and Dickens, methinks, had reason to be jealous of the terribly attractive, magnetic and immensely popular D.D. Home.) When Dickens failed to disabuse his friend, the popular novelist Lord Bulwer Lytton, of Home's powers, he fretted at Lytton's "delusion."[13]

Yet here is the paradox: Dickens himself was clairvoyant and given to foreknowledge. As early as the 1830s, he had converted to Mesmerism, reversing "all my preconceived opinions," and effectively cured others of tics and so forth by practicing the magnetic arts himself. He also experimented with Ouija boards[14], and by 1862 became a founding member of the London Ghost Club. Most significantly, Charles Dickens developed his ideas *psychically*: many of his plots, he admitted, came from dreams. He once declared to the writer G.H. Lewes that "every word said by his characters was distinctly heard by him."[15]

A LIFE OF THEIR OWN...

William Makepeace Thackery, Dickens' main contender for literary master of the age, also 'received' his *dramatis personae* from Elsewhere, expressing his surprise at his own characters and surmising that "an occult power was moving the pen."[16] The tall and affable Thackery, author of the classic *Vanity Fair*, had sat with both D.D. Home and a Fox Sister, "conversed with the Spirits freely...and was thoroughly convinced" of discarnate powers.[17] Nor did he believe his fictional characters came from his own imagination; it was something on the order of *rapport* – a process once explained by George Russell:

> While we think we are imagining a character, we may – so marvelous
> are the hidden ways – be really interpreting a being actually existing,
> brought into psychic contact with us…To call this imagination…is
> to explain nothing because the explanation is not explained…These
> mental apparitions…have a life of their own.[18]

When the medium J.B. Newbrough asked the spirits, in 1874, how
Shakespeare got his characters, the answer came that the great bard
had been attended by "a vast multitude of spirits…[who] played and
spoke their parts…"[19]

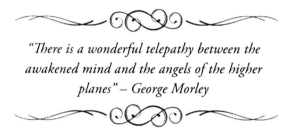

*"There is a wonderful telepathy between the
awakened mind and the angels of the higher
planes" – George Morley*

The poet-artist William Blake was perfectly aware of the Others,
for he had seen, at age nine, a tree filled with angels. Visionary and
self-taught (the child was too temperamental for school), the author
of *Prophetic Books* was certain that he wrote from inspiration, not
of himself.

The inspiration was not there, however, when the poet Longfellow
was asked to write a national song in 1861 at the outbreak of the
Civil War. Longfellow would write: "I am afraid the 'Go to, let us
make a national song' will not succeed. It will be likely to spring
up in some other way."[20] How right he was! Somehow, it had to be
heaven-sent; for the overshadowing that began with the anti-slavery
novel, *Uncle Tom's Cabin* (1852) was to culminate in a torrent of
paranormal incidents that marked the historic struggle for universal
freedom and Mystic Union. Was "Battle Hymn of the Republic"
written first in the heavens of the earth? Are the authors in eternity?

Julia Ward Howe was visiting the front when she heard soldiers singing their favorite tune, "John Brown's Body." Something woke her the next morning before dawn. In a half-dream, words began to scroll through her mind. "Mine eyes have seen the glory…" The verses almost seemed to say that heavenly ranks of spirits were assembling to bring slavery to an end. "Let us die to make men free." The New England poetess later recalled, "…to my astonishment I found that the…lines were arranging themselves in my brain… [I felt] that something of importance had happened to me."[21] The tune put to these verses was that of "John Brown's Body," and the hymn, published the next month, became the fiery gospel of the Union – at "an hundred circling camps…" The *Atlantic Monthly* paid Julia five dollars for her poem.

Mark Twain believed in "mental telegraphy" and in fact coined that term after many years of observing that "mind can act upon mind" through the Invisible. The celebrated storyteller was so keen on thought-transference (between the living) that he reckoned "all my powerful impulses come to me from somebody else…I often feel like a mere *amanuensis* [scribe] when I sit down to write." America's favorite wit was so sold on "this condition of *rapport*," that he toyed with the concept of a *phrenophone* (to connect minds), envisioning

"The authors are in eternity" – William Blake

the day when one could say – "Connect me with the brain of the chief of police at Peking!"[22]

Even writers who do not make much of the Unseen and profess no guiding spirit, like Socrates' *daimon*, can be caught out – in the very words chosen to describe their craft. The delicious Gore Vidal, for example, has recently stated that he starts his (non-historical) novels with "a sentence that has taken possession of me."[23] Many writers, I dare say, are carried on the inspirational tug of that first sentence. But author Isabel Allende, with clairvoyance galloping in her bloodline, is quite conscious of the process and starts her novels by deliberately preparing "my mind and soul to receive the first sentence in a trance…allow[ing] me to peer through and receive the hazy outlines of the story waiting for me." Her Basque lineage, like that of the country Irish, is loaded with the 'psychic gene', and when Isabel began writing fiction, it came with no effort, no thinking. Then, after her grandparents' deaths, she found them reading over her shoulder, and confesses that at the most difficult parts, "ghost came to my aid."

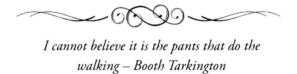

I cannot believe it is the pants that do the walking – Booth Tarkington

Of all the writers we have touched on, Allende (niece of Salavador Allende, the socialist president of Chile, assassinated on Tuesday, September 11, 1973) is the most recent, and in some ways the most enlightened. For she has consciously developed her own natural mediumship and brought it under control. (Danger lurks where psychism goes unrecognized).[24] Isabel Allende confides that her self-induced trance begins "in a secret ceremony" which brings her to "that threshold" dividing this world and the next. In time, and with luck…

...the characters will come alive...and reveal the narrative to me...
[M]y books are not born in my mind, they...are creatures with
their own lives...[T]he subject chooses me, my work consists
simply of providing enough time, solitude, and discipline for the
book to write itself.[25]

Isabel Allende, so closely linked to the People's struggle for justice
and dignity, was not the only modern woman of state to find some
spirit reading over her shoulder. Sometimes late at night, as Eleanor
Roosevelt sat in her study, the Lincoln bedroom, writing her column –
there he was, the Immortal Railsplitter, "peering over her shoulder."[26]
He took some kind of interest, Mrs. R. thought, in her humanitarian
efforts. And that is just how it works: through sympathy and harmony,
through common purpose, nature's *phrenophone* puts us in concert
with kindred spirits, far and near.

Susan B. Martinez, Ph.D., is a spiritualist, freelance writer, activist,
and psychic researcher. Her book, *The Psychic Life of Abraham Lincoln*
was released by New Page Books in October 2007. Susan is currently
the Book Review Editor at the *Journal of Spirituality and Paranormal
Studies*, Inc.

Bigfoot's Bogus Burial

the media
and the wallace myths

By *Loren Coleman*

n December 2002, the media declared that Bigfoot was dead. They did this through the creation of new hoaxes. On December 10th, *Pittsburgh Post-Gazette* columnist Tony Norman wrote: "Sometimes it takes a deathbed confession to put a stake in the heart of long-cherished beliefs. When Ray L. Wallace died of heart failure at 84 last month, he took a sizable piece of American mythology with him." No near death revelation really happened, but that didn't stop such a characterization from taking root in the minds of the media – and hence, the general public.

In fact, Ray Wallace – a long-time Bigfoot 'researcher' considered by many to have instigated hoaxes concerning the famed cryptid – had spun his stories for decades. However, several misstatements of fact were published or broadcast repeatedly in subsequent years following the original reports of his death, manufacturing a 'hoax' mythos that had no basis in fact. The latest example in 2007, for example, published by the *San Francisco Chronicle* upon the death of Bigfooter Archie Buckley, was that Ray Wallace made a "deathbed" confession that his wife was in a gorilla suit for a Bigfoot film. The assumption was that he was talking about the famed "Patterson-Gimlin film" of Bigfoot taken at Bluff Creek on October 20th, 1967. This is a complete fabrication – but the misinformation continues to be published.

As the Patterson-Gimlin footage experiences its 40th anniversary, perhaps the time is right to place on the record the full unfolding of how the newspapers, television, and magazines took the death story of a Bigfoot prankster and extended it to encompass this pivotal piece of evidence. We gain insights into the making of the modern myths now associated with this episode of media mania with a short review of some specific examples of the journalistic untruths presently associated with this story.

Hook, Line, and Sinker

Ray Wallace died November 26th, 2002, the day before Thanksgiving. After sharing an obituary I had written about Wallace with the *Seattle Times*, reporter Bob Young interviewed me via phone and email on December 3rd, 2002, and in the following days. On December 5th, the *Seattle Times* published their article, which has become known as the "Wallace hoax" piece. Bob Young's "Lovable Trickster" article is accompanied by a dramatic Dave Rubert photograph of a Wallace relative displaying fake wooden "Bigfoot" feet, said to have been used to "create" Bigfoot in 1958.

Longtime Canadian Sasquatch researcher John Green's reaction was swift. He said that what the Wallace relative "is holding certainly is not a mold for the 1958 Jerry Crew 16″ 'Bigfoot' cast, of which I have a copy, but it definitely is either a mold for or a copy of a 15″ footprint of the type found by Bob Titmus and Ed Patrick in a Bluff Creek sandbar later the same year, of which I also have copies…As to Ray Wallace having started the whole thing, however, Rene Dahinden and I in 1957 saw a tracing of a British Columbia footprint cast that was a much closer match for the Jerry Crew cast, and that cast had been made in 1941."

This is a significant point. Bigfoot did not pop onto the scene in 1958, although that is the year the *name* came into widespread use. The Native traditions of hundreds of years cannot be ignored, and the old reports and evidence (pre-1958) have been around for decades. Even before the coining of the word *Sasquatch* in the 1920s from a Native Canadian set of names, knowledge of the hairy, upright ape-like giants of the woods was in the record, especially of ethnographers. In cryptozoology, Sasquatch was what we call "ethnoknown" to the natives.

This reminds me of exactly what happened with Christian Spurling's 1991 Loch Ness Monster "revelation," which the media called a "deathbed confession" (even though it was given two years before he died in 1993). Spurling said the 1934 "Surgeon's Photograph" of one of the Loch Ness Monsters was only a toy submarine made with plastic wood (although that material didn't exist in 1934). The British papers declared "Nessie is dead." Debunkers forgot to talk about the second photograph and more. The cracks in the "deathbed confession" slowly began to show, thanks to investigative journalist Richard Smith of Princeton University and others. The 1934 "Surgeon's Photographs" were never that important, except as an icon, anyway.

As to this latest Bigfoot hoax claim, never mind that the original Jerry Crew casts do not match the Wallace fake feet. Never mind that we all knew Wallace was a prankster. Never mind that Wallace wasn't able to put one over on any of us in 44 years. Never mind that no one can actually show how the hoax would have been produced. The media was constructing a new world of Bigfoot myth-making.

THE PATTERSON NONCONNECTION

Bob Young's article set the scene for a flood of badly written items, flowing forth faster than the speed of your cable modem. The original *Seattle Times* article was hastily and harshly rewritten by wire services and electronic outlets, facts were minimized to make sensationalized copy, and the outcome has been a morphing of Ray Wallace's alleged 1958 hoaxes and family films into his being responsible for the 1967 Patterson-Gimlin footage (even though that was never said).

How did the Wallace story spin out of control, to the point of fostering a worldwide belief that Wallace created the whole Bigfoot phenomenon including the Patterson-Gimlin film footage too? The specific evolution of this new media hoax can be seen clearly in how this leapt from one newspaper to the next.

Bob Young's *Seattle Times* article for December 5th, 2002, has this segment: "[Mark] Chorvinsky* believes the Wallace family's admission creates profound doubts about leading evidence of Bigfoot's existence: the so-called Patterson film, the grainy celluloid images of an erect apelike creature striding away from the movie camera of rodeo rider Roger Patterson in 1967. Mr. Wallace said he told Patterson where to go near Bluff Creek, Calif. to spot a Bigfoot, Chorvinsky said."

The article continued: "Ray Wallace dismissed the film as a hoax and said he knew who was in the suit. 'Ray told me that the Patterson film was a hoax, and he knew who was in the suit,' Chorvinsky said. 'Michael Wallace said his father called the Patterson film 'a fake' and said he had nothing to do with it. But he said his mother admitted she had been photographed in a Bigfoot suit'. 'He had several people he used in his movies,' Michael Wallace said."

As is typical of the USA's Associated Press, a rewrite was prepared, and on December 6th, 2002, the AP wire version included this edited paragraph:

> [Ray] Wallace said he told Patterson where to spot a Bigfoot near Bluff Creek, California, Chorvinsky recalled. 'Ray told me that the Patterson film was a hoax, and he knew who was in the suit.' Michael Wallace said his father called the Patterson film 'a fake' but claimed he'd had nothing to do with it. But he said his mother admitted she had been photographed in a Bigfoot suit, and that his father 'had several people he used in his movies'.

Next the story jumped the ocean, and an article, for example, published this misleading paragraph in Edinburgh's *Scotsman* on Saturday, December 7, 2002: "Mr. Wallace later persuaded his wife to dress up in a monkey suit for 'Bigfoot' photographs, and he told Roger Patterson, a rodeo rider, to set up his camera to film the famous footage, shot in 1967, which supposedly showed the creature walking up the hillside."

The above and more were misunderstood or misread, and re-written as the following in the *Evening Telegram* of London later on that same Saturday, in an article headlined, "That's not Bigfoot, that's my wife," written by Oliver Poole, their correspondent 'based in Los Angeles'. Other news outlets such as Singapore's *Strait Times* picked up the story, apparently repeating this mistake.

Poole's article reads, in part: "Mr. Wallace continued with the prank for years, producing photographs of Bigfoot eating elk and frogs. These, it emerged yesterday, were, in fact, members of his family – usually his wife Elna – dressed in a hairy ape suit with giant feet stuck to the bottom. The most famous evidence for Bigfoot's existence, the so-called Patterson film, a grainy, cinefilm image of an erect ape-like creature, was taken by Roger Patterson, a rodeo rider, in 1967. It was another of Mr Wallace's fakes, the family said – he told Mr Patterson where to go to spot the creature and knew who had been inside the suit."

The story then jumped back across the ocean, to land on Sunday, December 8, 2002, in Vancouver's *The Province*, in an article by Stuart Hunter entitled "'Fake' Sasquatch flick won't halt Bigfoot hunt": "Despite a stunning claim last week that the most compelling film footage of the ape-like creature is a fake, Bigfoot hunters say they won't stop pursuing their elusive and smelly quarry. The family of Ray Wallace admitted after his recent death from heart failure in California that while the Bigfoot footprints were huge, the hoax was much, much bigger. *That was no man dressed in a gorilla suit in the infamous Patterson-Gimlin grainy black and white film footage from 1967 – that was Wallace's wife Elna.*" [my emphasis]

Reporter Hunter even then uses an earlier quote from the *Seattle Times* article that was only about the pranks with the fake footprints, not about the Patterson-Gimlin film, and places it as his next paragraph after the above: "'He did it for the joke and then he was afraid to tell anyone because they'd be so mad at him,' admitted Dale Lee Wallace, the hoaxster's nephew." This juxtaposition caused all kinds of problems.

Wallace 'Bigfoot Shoes' (© Dave Rubert)

Therein you have the makings of a media hoax. First it began with Bob Young's mostly factual item (although filled with claims from the Wallaces) about Ray Wallace's death and how the family said he used fake feet, allegedly, in 1958, including opinions and remembered claims of hoaxing. Then it goes to wire service and column creations, and finally to the jump that "the Patterson film is a fake by Ray Wallace with his wife in the suit" – something no one in the Wallace family ever said.

Remember this is the only quote that matters:

> "Michael Wallace said his father called the Patterson film 'a fake' and said he had nothing to do with it." – Bob Young, *Seattle Times*, December 5, 2002.

So what if Ray Wallace said he talked to Patterson and showed him his films? Of course Patterson would have listened to this spinner of tales. Roger Patterson was a Bigfoot hunter in the late 1960s, and as an amateur researcher, he went around and did research. That meant finding those that were there, in Bluff Creek, in 1958, and re-interviewing them. Such behavior makes total sense, and Patterson never hid any of what he was doing. Patterson talked about visiting and interviewing Wallace in his 1966 book. *Strange Magazine's* skeptical editor, the late Mark Chorvinsky – with great fanfare – makes it a cornerstone of some conspiracy theory about Wallace and Patterson. Wallace is, of course, going to say he told Patterson where to go. So what? Others have done the same, to give themselves greater importance in the history of Bigfoot.

January Meanderings

By January 2003, when the media writers decided to compose something about Bigfoot or the Wallace fiasco, they would often carry forth these "newly" created myths into their reports. On January 3rd, 2003, *Inside Edition* did a segment titled "Bigfoot Hoax," in which they framed – uncritically – the Wallace family's stories, and then claimed that Ray Wallace created everything to do with Bigfoot, including linking the Patterson-Gimlin footage to his hoaxes. (My appearance on this program to give a balanced stance on the developing story was cut to a few seconds.)

This same day, in the otherwise rather balanced front page *New York Times* article "Search for Bigfoot Outlives the Man Who Created Him," reporter Timothy Egan turned to discredited Bigfoot Central hobbyist Cliff Crook as his "authority" to proclaim the Patterson-Gimlin footage a "fake." Here, the link between the 1958 alleged Wallace hoax is mashed together with unfounded opinions on the 1967 film.

On January 9th, Scott Herriott's Segment 7 report on CNN's *NewsNight* was broadcast. Herriott's field production presented a good beginning, though highly edited case against the Wallace claim (despite the fact the Wallaces withdrew from Herriott's and John Green's request that they show how the 1958 prints were made). However, it was host Aaron Brown's introduction and final statements (the "outro") that diminished the report. Brown made Herriott appear to be an obsessed eccentric for "still believing" in Bigfoot.

Fox-TV (owned by Rupert Murdoch) was next up, on January 13, with a report on Shepherd Smith's *Fox Reports*. A teaser earlier in the show gives a hint of what was to be expected; it was a frame from the Patterson-Gimlin footage and the words "Trail's End" underneath. Shep Smith gives the introduction by bursting forth, Fox TV-style, by saying "Big Fake. Big Fat Stinking Hoax…" Dan Springer out of Seattle does the reporting, next. He begins with the clipping from the *Seattle Times*, saying that the paper has pronounced the death of Bigfoot when it told of Wallace's passing. Wallace's son is shown talking of Ray, and then old photos of Ray – "who was a logger" in the PNW are shown. The finding of tracks at a location of a crew of his moved the Indian lore of Sasquatch into Bigfoot. John Green (identified as a "Bigfoot Believer") is said to have done "five decades" of looking and is introduced as one of those not convinced by the hoax. A short clip of Green shows him saying the "tracks are real." The reporter says Green gave him some fake feet to walk on the sand to try to debunk the "hoax." The word "tried" is used in the narration.

Reporter Springer then says the "timing" is "bad for believers" as "scientists" were "almost ready" to do some serious research, but now scientists are "ridiculing the famous Patterson" film. (This is not true, as the January 9ᵗʰ broadcast on Discovery of *Sasquatch: Legend Meets Science* demonstrated, by filming scientists analyzing several facets of the Bigfoot questions.) Michael Wallace comes back on to roll his eyes and say he knows who was in the suit. Of course, through editing in this "sound bite," Fox is using the Michael Wallace's quote to make it appear as if he's talking about the Patterson-Gimlin film, when he really was discussing his mother in other films made by his father. The piece ends with comments about the "controversy" of Bigfoot being buried next to Wallace, with a camera pan of Wallace's gravesite.

Time for Kids, on January 17ᵗʰ, 2003, published an article full of errors. Called "Bigfoot? Big Hoax!" by Kathy Hoffman, it appears to have been rushed into publication. Beginning with the supposedly humorous line, "The real story: Dad was the apeman! the article downsized the Wallace claims for children. Using the phrase "recent confession" once again, as if Ray Wallace was hiding his prankish ways when he was alive, the use of the word harkens back to the early "deathbed" confession media mistakes of December 2002.

Then Hoffman writes: "Most scientists agree that Bigfoot is nothing more than a very tall tale. Almost all of the footprints ever found have turned out to be manmade." Of course, "most" scientists have said no such thing, and "almost all" of the footprints are not "manmade." Actually, studies by Dr. Grover Krantz, Dr. Jeff Meldrum, and trackers and forensic experts have shown exactly the opposite to be the case. Only a very small percentage of Sasquatch footprints are human-created fakes. She gets her statistics mixed up again when she says: "Jeff Meldrum of Idaho State University is one of the only scientists who believes Bigfoot could be real." More and more zoologists, anthropologists, and wildlife biologists are open-mindedly examining the evidence everyday, such as famed primatologist and anthropologist Dr. Jane Goodall.

The *New Haven Register* carried an article on January 21st 2003, by Abram Katz, entitled "Self-delusion casts a shadow on Bigfoot stories." After opening with the typical Wallace fake feet claims, and opinions on a "guy in an ape suit," Katz writes: "The question is – and this is a big one – if Sasquatch is an actual animal and has been seen all over the country, why has no zoologist, biologist, or hunter ever seen one?" Of course, this is not a true statement. Many eyewitnesses have been "hunters," of course. The fact that zoologists and biologists who have sighted Bigfoot in the past have not rushed forward has everything to do with the ridicule and academic discrediting that often awaits them. Wildlife biologists appear to be more frequent witnesses than is generally understood.

ALL ABOUT A SKEPTICAL MAGICIAN

Throughout January 2003, we were treated to a hoax about a hoaxer's family, and then in the February 2003 issue of *Fate* magazine, Mark Chorvinsky – a skeptical magician turned magazine writer and editor, and one of the minor players quoted in Young's Wallace article – presented a column claiming that Wallace was marginalized by "Bigfoot enthusiasts." Taking the research field to task for this 'failure', he quickly assured readers that Wallace's role "cannot be overstated." Actually, most of what Chorvinsky writes about in his column is so full of overstatements as to be a superb example of the genre.

First, let us take a look at his thinking and his logic. Everyone knew that Ray Wallace was a hoaxer. What is most important in this article is for Chorvinsky (who died of cancer at the age of 51 in 2005) to establish that he said Wallace was a hoaxer before anyone else did. He sadly fails in this mission. Despite Chorvinsky's claims to the contrary, Wallace was mentioned in the literature from the beginning in 1958 as a prankster and a hoaxer. Even the Sheriff's Department in 1958 was questioning Ray Wallace about whether or not he was behind some of the tracks. When he uses an interview Bigfoot researcher Dennis Pilichis did with Ray Wallace, how does Chorvinsky ignore that the interview came before his own interest in the subject?

"Where did this information appear in their books and articles before I discussed" it in 1993, Chorvinsky asks. Chorvinsky has decided to ignore what is in the literature. In 1989, I wrote a book entitled *Tom Slick and the Search for the Yeti*. Talking of Slick's late 1950s and early 1960s Pacific Northwest Expedition, I wrote: "The expedition's cast of characters also included Ray Wallace and Ivan Marx, both of whom may have gotten into the hunt on the serious side of things, but from all accounts traveled down a dark path of greed and deception..." (I followed this with an entire exposé of Ray Wallace in 1995, in *The Anomalist*.)

Ivan Sanderson, in his 1959-1961 articles, letters, and a book, had noted the links between the road construction work, Ray Wallace, the people he hired, the first prints found, and the sightings. Betty Allen told of the hoax investigations in her 1958 news articles. In the 1970s, Marian T. Place mentions the Wallace brothers and the early days of "strange happenings" around the track sites. In a 1988 book *Brave* that Chorvinsky seemed to be completely unaware of, early Bigfoot hunter Steve M. Matthes entitled his Bigfoot chapter "Big Hoax" because during his involvement with the Slick searchers in 1960, he came upon finds of fake tracks. These tracks clearly appear to match some of the Wallace fake feet. Even *Skeptical Inquirer* was there with pieces of the puzzle before Chorvinsky, declaring in 1982 the firm link between the Rant Mullens foot fakes and Ray Wallace.

In his February 2003 *Fate* column, Chorvinsky tells the reader he was a ten-year correspondent with Wallace, as if this is special. He tells us that Ray Wallace "admitted" to him to be using fake feet. This is no revelation: Wallace said that in letters to almost everyone. Wallace claimed to have seen 2000 UFOs, to know where a Bigfoot guarded a gold mine, and much more. And then there were the films. Lots and lots of films. Ray Wallace made some of the worse Bigfoot films in creation. They were so bad you could almost see the shoes that the people in the store-bought gorilla suits were wearing. They fooled no one, and no one was taken in by them – except perhaps the above-named columnist at *Fate*.

WHOSE IS THE TRUE BELIEVER?

The late Mark Chorvinsky said the Bigfoot "believers" wish to "diminish the importance of such pivotal figures" as Ray Wallace. What is so silly about this is that Ray Wallace was, yes, "diminished," as much as he was tolerated, enjoyed for his funny stories of Bigfoot coming out of UFOs, and yet, nevertheless mentioned in the literature. Wallace was an admitted liar. Why is it that as soon as he is dead that the joke that he is putting on all of us, instead, is to be taken as totally truthful history. Wallace is having a laugh from beyond the grave, and sadly Mark Chorvinsky was the medium channeling this séance.

Take for instance, Chorvinsky's attack on John Green, one of the most moral and sharing researchers in a field filled with sometimes feuding factions. Here's what Chorvinsky said about the man who happened to have been involved in Sasquatch research before the

1958 Bigfoot case even came into the picture: "Green, whose entry into the field was as a journalistic hoaxer...knew that Wallace had no credibility whatsoever [but he] never once stated this in [any of Green's] books and articles. It was only after I [Mark Chorvinsky] began to write about Wallace and his innumerable fake films, photos, and tracks that suddenly Ray Wallace was discussed, and the only way that they could deal with him at this point was to act like he was a minor figure in the scheme of things."

John Green responded: "The reference to my entering the field as a journalistic hoaxer is about as near the truth as Chorvinsky is ever likely to get. I did write a story in an April Fool edition of my paper about a Sasquatch carrying off a tourist. That was two years before I encountered any evidence that the subject is serious. The remark is an attempt to mislead his readers of course, but no doubt he considers that clever. Since there was (and is) no evidence that Ray Wallace (or anyone else) could have faked the Bluff Creek tracks, and ample evidence that Wallace had 'no credibility whatsoever', what reason would there be for me to mention him in a book? If I write another book should I mention that Mark Chorvinsky has written nonsense on this subject and has no credibility whatsoever, or would it not be kinder just to ignore him for the same reason that I never mentioned Wallace, because he is irrelevant? And what possible reason is there for Mark Chorvinsky, knowing that Ray Wallace has no credibility whatsoever, to inflict on his readers false information that he got from Wallace? Specifically, why does he promote the nonsense that Ray Wallace told Roger Patterson where to go to get his movie, knowing that Wallace had also claimed to have taken 10,000 feet of movies of Bigfoot there."

'Patterson-Gimlin Bigfoot'

The Media Forgets

Chorvinsky's February 2003 column thus became the ultimate example of how the media, even within the Fortean genre of *Fate* magazine, became an example of the media getting the Wallace story incredibly mangled in a tangle of personalities and personal views of the Bigfoot mystery – with no regard for the facts.

Newspapers and the electronic media have short-term memory when it comes to hoaxes and the ability of the Sasquatch researchers to monitor their own field. Bigfoot chroniclers have noted fakery in their examinations of the history of Sasquatch evidence for years. Ivan Marx, Ray Pickens, Rant Mullens, and Ray Wallace are the individuals most frequently mentioned in the literature. However, every time a new prankster attempts to gain some publicity for himself, the media reaction is one of surprise and overall acceptance of the new tale as the "whole truth."

For example, in 1982 Rant Mullens said he was responsible for the 1924 Ape Canyon, Oregon reports, and the 1958 carvings of the feet that made the tracks at Bluff Creek, California. News reporters believed Mullens' outrageous allegations, much as the media is swallowing the Wallace family stories today. The Mullens' hoax admissions followed a similar trail as we are seeing with the Wallace fiasco, for it was used by establishment "skeptics" to make what Bigfoot author Mark Hall in his book *Living Fossils* calls "loose and unsupportable statements" that all Bigfoot prints "could easily be fakes" (Daniel Cohen). Or according to Michael Dennett that "Rent Mullens" (his mistaken spelling) talked to one of the "hoaxers" of the Patterson-Gimlin film and told Dennett that the suit was made of bearskins. Hall demonstrates how Dennett's "skeptical" influence spread. A palaeontologist Leonard Krishtalka discusses in his book *Dinosaur Plots and Other Intrigues in Natural History* that the whole Bigfoot mystery is a ruse begun by "Rent Mullins" (adding to the misspelling). Other "skeptics" (like *Skeptical*

Inquirer editor Ben Radford before the Wallace melodrama) have used the Rant Mullens stories to dismiss a good portion of the Bigfoot/Sasquatch evidence.

We are in the midst of seeing this happen all over again through Ray Wallace's 'last laugh'.

Loren Coleman has been involved in fieldwork, bibliographical, and media analysis on Bigfoot since 1960. He has authored over thirty books on cryptozoology, hominology, and media studies. Through his university senior research work, he directed federal government projects producing documentary films, media guides, and conferences. At the University of Southern Maine, as an adjunct associate professor from 1983 through 2004, his every semester course on the impact and analysis of documentaries and broadcast news was one of the most popular on campus. In 2003, Paraview Pocket/Simon and Schuster published *Bigfoot! The True Story of Apes in America*, which devoted further attention to the Ray Wallace fiasco. His 2004 book, *The Copycat Effect*, looks at the influence of media on human behaviors, and his 2006 *The Field Guide to Bigfoot and Other Mystery Primates*, with Patrick Huyghe, updated the question of Bigfoot. He can be found online at www.lorencoleman.com and www.cryptomundo.com.

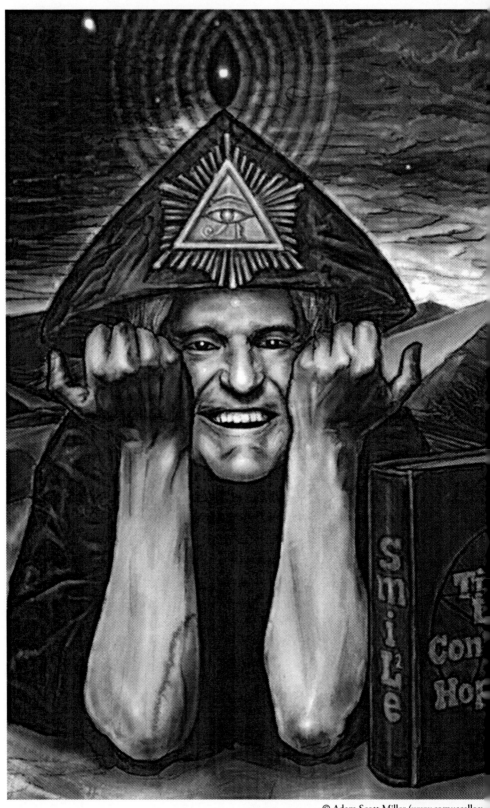

THE HIGH PRIEST AND THE GREAT BEAST

~

THE PARALLEL LIVES OF TIMOTHY LEARY AND ALEISTER CROWLEY

By *John Higgs*

 n 1972, Dr. Timothy Leary picked up a pack of Aleister Crowley-designed tarot cards and asked them the question, "Who am I and what is my destiny?" He then cut the pack and found the Ace of Discs, the card that Crowley believed represented himself. It featured the Greek words To Mega Therion (*To Μεγα Θηριον*), or 'The Great Beast', which was the name Crowley had adopted for himself. This convinced Leary of something that he had recently come to suspect; that he was a 'continuation' of Aleister Crowley and that his role in life was to continue Crowley's 'Great Work', that of bringing about a fundamental shift in human consciousness.

The Timothy Leary of 1972 was a very different man to the Timothy Leary of 1967's 'Summer of Love', when he had been at the height of his fame. Leary was the ex-Harvard professor who preached peace and love, adopted the mantra "tune in, turn on and drop out," and led the exploding psychedelic movement. In the five years that followed he had been repeatedly arrested, imprisoned, had escaped from jail, been smuggled out of America by terrorists, was kidnapped by revolutionaries in North Africa, escaped again, fled to Switzerland, been jailed by the Swiss and was currently living a nomadic life moving between different Swiss Cantons under the protection of an exiled French arms dealer. Nixon had called him "the most dangerous man in America" and had sent John Mitchell, his Attorney General, to Switzerland to try and obtain his extradition. Leary's life was playing out on such a grand, dangerous scale that it was tempting to believe that he had been somehow selected by the hand of history, and that great deeds were expected of him.

GALACTIC SPACESHIPS IN ALGERIA

Leary's identification with Crowley began in earnest after he took an acid trip in the Sahara desert with an English beatnik artist and writer named Brian Barritt. Barritt was, in Leary's words, "a fucking genius." "Brian is an English Untouchable," Leary wrote in 1971. "His shadow falling across the path of the middle class is enough to contaminate twenty lives. He is highly toxic. Brian is ancient but not old. He has put as many drugs as possible into his body for thirty six years and is obscenely healthy, diabolically wealthy, and looks about twenty. He intends to maintain this state for an indefinite period. He is not going to die; they will have to kill him."

Leary and Barritt first tripped together over the night of Easter Saturday and Sunday, 1971. The pair drove from the Algerian coast to a place called Bou Saada, on the edge of the Sahara. 'Bou

Saada' means 'City of Happiness' and it was rumoured to be a very magical place. Leary had to collect some belongings from the Hotel Caid, where he and his wife Rosemary had previously stayed. These included the foreword that he had written for one of Barritt's books, and some of his wife's clothes. It was the clothes that they were primarily interested in, for there were tabs of Orange Sunshine acid sewn into the hems, and some high quality Afghan hashish in the heels of the shoes.

They ate the acid, and some hash, and drove out into the endless dunes until they found a dried up riverbed. Here they sat on the ever shifting, pepper-fine sand and watched the sun set while they waited for the LSD to hit. A full moon rose. Night fell on the desert.

"The sky was on fire," is how Barritt later described the trip that followed. "Massive galactic spaceships blinked into being, golden vessels with the faces of Egyptian Gods on their prows, gliding between life and death....Beauteous cities glide by composed of materials not yet invented, towers twisted skywards. Through a window a woman with the face of an angel and the body of a spider was chatting me up with her eyes..." Leary, meanwhile, seemed to be performing some form of ceremony. He was pacing up and down reciting the alchemical phrase *solve et coagula*.

Even by Leary and Barritt's standards, it was a memorable night. But the trip included a few synchronicities that seemed to indicate that there was more to it than just a string of imaginative hallucinations. At the start of the trip Barritt became aware of a hooded man in the middle of a dust devil or a whirlwind of sand. He had a scroll or manuscript that seemed to be important, and which was linked to the Elizabethan magician and alchemist Dr. John Dee.

Dr. Dee was one of the leading scholars of his day, and a man who played a leading role in the development of the science of navigation. He was also the court astrologer to Queen Elizabeth I, and he used her horoscope to choose the day of her coronation in 1558. He possessed what was believed to be the largest library in Britain, until the local townsfolk, believing him to be an evil sorcerer, burnt it down. He was also a spy for the Crown, and was sent on intelligence missions in various other European countries. It seems fitting, therefore, that he used to sign documents with the code '007'.

Dee was also an alchemist and deeply involved in occult studies, even though these practices were extremely politically dangerous in the religious turmoil of the times. He became involved with the thief and grave-robber Edward Kelly, believing that Kelly had the ability to hear spirits and demons. Over many months Dee transcribed the information that was channelled 'through' Kelly, and the result was a body of magical work, including the language of the angels, that is known as Enochian Magic.

A year after their trip at Bou Saada, Leary and Brian discovered that, in 1909, Aleister Crowley and the poet Victor Neuberg conducted a magical ceremony at that exact same riverbed in the dunes outside Bou Saada where they had taken LSD. Crowley and Neuberg summoned demons by invoking nineteen 'calls' that had originated with Doctor John Dee and Edward Kelly. Enochian magic was integral to Crowley's magical system, and it was Dee and Kelly's angelic script that Crowley was invoking at Bou Saada.

The work took a few weeks as they invoked one 'key' of the manuscript a day, bidding a string of angels and demons to appear inside a magical triangle marked in the sand. Mescaline was used, as was sexual magic, with Neuberg at one point buggering Crowley at an altar in a makeshift stone circle and dedicating the act to the god Pan. When the day came to invoke Choronzon, the demon of chaos and

Barritt in 2004 (courtesy J. Higgs)

the abyss, Crowley did not remain outside the magic triangle. Instead he deliberately sat inside it.

The pair would have made quite a sight as they performed their strange works amongst the shifting Saharan dunes. Crowley was dressed in a long black hooded robe with a revolver around his waist. Neuberg, with two tufts of dyed red hair twisted into horns, sat watching in a magic circle created for his own protection, and made notes. Crowley instructed Neuberg that, whatever happened, he must resist any attempt from the demon to be released. The invocation was completed, three pigeons were sacrificed and, according to Neuberg and Crowley's accounts, Choronzon appeared. The demon possessed Crowley and began to taunt Neuberg, pleading to be released. They later claimed that Crowley/Choronzon began to change shape, appearing to Neuberg in a string of forms including an old lover and a snake with a human head. It begged the poet for a drink of water and promised that it would sit at his feet and obey him if it was freed. With Neuberg distracted by the dazzling images materialising before his eyes, the demon gradually dribbled the fine sand on the magic circle, slowly erasing it. Then the entity that possessed Crowley's body rushed at Neuberg and, according to *The Confessions of Aleister Crowley*, "flung him to the earth and tried to tear out his throat with froth-covered fangs." Fortunately, Neuberg had been armed with a consecrated magical dagger and managed to fend the beast off. Choronzon was banished, leaving Crowley lying naked in the sand. With the ceremony over, the magic circle and triangle were erased and a fire was lit to purify the place.

Leary and Barritt were astounded when they discovered this, a year after their desert trip. That they had been at exactly the same riverbed was coincidence enough, but the cowled figure inside a dust devil that Barritt had 'seen' matched Crowley's description of his possessed self. Crowley, who had been wearing a black hooded robe, described the demon possessing him as being a coagulation of forms that "swirl senselessly into haphazard heaps like dust devils."

The fact that he had been using a manuscript of the work of Dr. John Dee, which had also appeared to Barritt, pushed the incident way beyond coincidence.

It's About Time...

There were many similarities between Timothy Leary and Aleister Crowley, and this had not gone unnoticed at the time. Andy Warhol, for example, had commented on it. They had both come from repressive middle class backgrounds, and both rejected those values to found liberated and hedonistic religious sects. They both put great value on sex and drugs, and there are strong parallels between Leary's Millbrook commune and Crowley's Abbey of Thelema on Sicily. Crowley was dubbed the 'wickedest man in the world' during his lifetime, while Leary was called "the most dangerous man in the America" by President Nixon. Crowley's commandment 'Do What Thou Wilt Shall Be The Whole Of The Law' has similar libertine values to the commandments of the League of Spiritual Development, a "personal religion" of Leary's invention, although Leary's were softened to disallow controlling others. Both wrote re-interpretations of the *Tao Te Ching*. This is an indicator of the similar size of their egos, as the *Tao Te Ching* is arguably one of the most complete pieces of text ever written, and there are few who believe that they can improve on it. As Robert Anton Wilson demonstrated in *Cosmic Trigger*, there are many parallels between the 'Starseed Transmissions', the information received during Leary's experiments with channelling whilst in Folsom Prison, and Crowley's *The Book of The Law*. There are also parallels between the decline of each man's life during their later years, and on the people, such as John Lennon, whom they have both influenced. They both had wives named Rosemary.

Leary started to think of himself as a 'continuation' of Crowley, as opposed to a 'reincarnation' as it is normally understood. There were strong parallels between Dee and Kelly, Crowley and Neuberg, and Leary and Barritt, and Leary saw himself as part of a line of sorcerers that reoccurred throughout history. This was something that Crowley appeared to be aware of, although he believed that he was a reincarnation of Kelly, rather than Dee. (From what we know of Crowley, it is not surprising that he would wish to associate himself with the one considered to be the most evil!)

Leary believed that he was playing out a 'script' for a regular transformative current that repeated itself throughout time. These 'scripts' existed in a similar manner to a song. A song only exists in time, not space, but it still exists enough for patterns, harmony and meaning to be detectable. Indeed, 'time' was the key here, or rather the change in the qualities of time that could be detected under LSD. There were moments during a trip, Leary believed, that his awareness outgrew the normal, unstopping, linear flow of time. After all, just as a two-dimensional drawing can only be properly observed from three-dimensions, so time, the fourth dimension, should only really make sense from a fifth dimension or higher. The expanded awareness of LSD seemed, on occasions, to give just such a higher perspective. From this point otherwise invisible patterns and currents in history became apparent.

Leary's belief that his awareness had gone beyond the linear flow of time is actually not as absurd as it might seem at first glance. There is a growing consensus amongst scientists that, while time itself is real, the perceived onward march of time is an illusion. As Einstein once famously wrote to a friend, "The past, present and future are only illusions, even if stubborn ones." Writing in *The Scientific American* (Vol. 15 No. 3 2005, p. 82) Paul Davies concludes that, "The passage of time is probably an illusion. Consciousness may involve thermodynamic or quantum processes that lend the impression of living moment to moment."

He then goes on to note that, "It is possible to imagine drugs that could suspend the subject's impression that time is passing."

During this period Leary was writing a book at about his jail break called *It's About Time*, and he would later end his autobiography with the exact same words. The book was later renamed in a direct homage to Crowley; it was published under the name *Confessions of a Hope Fiend*, a title chosen to consciously reference Crowley's *Diary of a Drug Fiend* and *Confessions of Aleister Crowley*.

Shortly afterwards Leary was kidnapped at gunpoint in Afghanistan, brought back to America and placed in solitary confinement in Folsom prison. After making a deal with the FBI that destroyed his reputation amongst many of his hippy followers, he became an evangelist of personal computers and the Internet. He died of cancer on May 31st, 1996.

According to William Burroughs, "Tim changed the world. It may be another century before he is accorded his rightful stature. Let his detractors shake their heads, a hundred years from now." It is certainly true that a re-assessment of Leary's ideas and his impact on our culture is long overdue. There are those who believe that Leary was successful and did bring about a fundamental and lasting shift in human consciousness for millions of people. There are others who believe he should take the blame for the problems and disillusionment that ended the Sixties dream. But one thing is clear: there is no figure from the second half of the twentieth century who has a better claim on the continuation of Crowley's 'Great Work' than Dr. Timothy Leary.

John Higgs is a BAFTA-nominated writer and producer from Brighton, England. His book *I Have America Surrounded* chronicles Timothy Leary's life of "flat-out epic grandeur." More information about the book can be found at www.ihaveamericasurrounded.com.

The Multilingual MEDIUM

Conversations with the Spirit of Confucius?

by *Michael E. Tymn*

ike many mediums, George Valiantine apparently began losing some of his powers after a dozen or so years of producing awesome phenomena. As a result, he was accused of being a charlatan and his reputation was thereafter tainted. It is, however, difficult to read the accounts of Valiantine's mediumship by many credible and intelligent men and believe that he was anything but a true medium before his powers began leaving him, or before low-level spirits began controlling him.

It was reported that at least 14 languages, including Portuguese, Italian, Basque, Welsh, Japanese, Spanish, Russian, Hindustani, and Chinese were spoken by spirits through his mediumship. In a 1931 book, *Psychic Adventures in New York*, Neville Whymant, Ph.D. – a professor of linguistics at Oxford and London Universities – told of his sittings with Valiantine during an extended visit to the United States in 1926. Whymant had lived in the Far East for several years and had mastered a variety of Oriental languages, and had come to the United States to study the languages of the American Indian. According to an article in the April 6th, 1927 edition of the *New York Herald-Tribune*, he spoke more than 30 languages. Cursory searches show that Whymant was indeed a world-renowned explorer, author, philologist, and linguist.

A Surprising Séance

While in New York City, Whymant was invited to the Park Avenue home of Judge and Mrs. William Cannon. Some months after that dinner party, on October 15th, 1926, Whymant and his wife received another invitation to visit the Cannon home. Mrs. Cannon explained that she needed someone with knowledge of Oriental languages to do a little interpreting for some people interested in discussing psychical research.

"It is important to state here," Whymant wrote, "that we did not know until we arrived at the Cannon apartment that we were being invited to a spiritualist séance." Mrs. Cannon later explained to Whymant that she was afraid he would have declined the invitation had she told him what it was all about. She told him that a voice had been breaking through in previous sittings in what appeared to be Chinese. Whymant added that he had no idea that the Cannons had any interest in spiritualism or psychical research, and he had no real interest in the subject.

Other guests arrived for the Cannon's "spiritualist study circle." Upon entering the dining room, Whymant observed chairs set around a center space. One of the chairs was occupied by Valiantine, whom he described as a stout, genial figure. It was explained to

Whymant that Valiantine was a direct-voice medium, and that his vocal cords did not produce the voices or sounds he would hear during the séance. Rather, an aluminum trumpet, which was placed in the center of the circle of chairs, would be used by the spirits in amplifying their otherwise weak or whispered voices. The medium, Whymant was told, simply provided the ectoplasm from which the spirits molded vocal cords and larynxes.

It was all very new to Whymant and his wife. "It was obvious we knew nothing of recent developments in the psychic arts," he continued the story. "We were even unable to understand the jargon of the new cult." Valiantine appeared to Whymant as "the simpler kind of American citizen." He clearly did not belong to the upper-class of people who had gathered for the séance.

The Whymants and an American physician were the only newcomers. They were invited to examine the room before the doors were closed. "There was no appearance or suspicion of trickery, but I mention these things to show that I was alert from the beginning, and I was prepared to apply all the tests possible to whatever phenomena might appear," Whymant went on. It was explained to him that light could injure the medium and thus the lights would have to be turned off. Moreover, no one could leave his or her seat as it might break the "circle of power" and reduce the possibility of good results. Whymant noted that the trumpet had phosphorous paint on it, so that its movement in the darkness could be followed.

As soon as the lights were turned off, the group recited the Lord's Prayer and then sacred music was played on a gramophone in order to "bring the vibrations into harmony with those of the spirit world."

"Suddenly into the sound of the singing came the sound of a strong voice raised in greeting," Whymant recorded. "It seemed to rise up from the floor and was so strong that for some moments I felt convinced that I could actually feel the vibrations of the floor." The voice, Whymant was informed, was that of Dr. Barnett, the spirit leader of the circle, who opened and closed it at will. Shortly thereafter, another voice "totally different in timbre and quality" was heard. This voice, the newcomers were informed, was that of Blackfoot, an American Indian of the tribe of that name, who was the keeper of the "spirit door." Some whispered messages to regular members of the circle from deceased relatives or friends then followed.

Whymant was then startled by a very strong voice singing 'Christo di Angelo' at "full lung force." The voice seemed to soar up to the ceiling and hover there. "Speaking at first in pure and clear Italian, the voice soon dropped into a Sicilian dialect of which I knew nothing," Whymant further noted. The voice then provided a Sicilian ballad, after which more personal messages, some of a very intimate nature, followed. Whymant wrote that he felt almost like an eavesdropper in listening to the messages.

The group then heard the "sound of an old wheezy flute not too skillfully played." It reminded Whymant of sounds he had heard in the streets of China. All the while, Whymant kept an eye on Valiantine, who sat directly across from him a few feet in the dark room, which still had enough light to see movement.

CHINESE SO DEAD

When the flute-like sound faded, Whymant heard a "voice" directed at him through the trumpet say in an ancient Chinese dialect: "Greeting, O son of learning and reader of strange books! This unworthy servant bows humbly before such excellence."

Whymant responded in more modern Chinese: "Peace be upon thee, O illustrious one. This uncultured menial ventures to ask thy name and illustrious style."

The 'voice' replied: "My mean name is K'ung, men call me Fu-tsu, and my lowly style is *Kiu*." Whymant recognized this as the name by which Confucius was canonized. Not certain that he heard right,

Whymant asked for the voice to repeat the name. "This time without any hesitation at all came the name K'ung-fu-tzu," Whymant wrote. "Now I thought, was my opportunity. Chinese I had long regarded as my own special research area, and he would be a wise man, medium or other, who would attempt to trick me on such soil. If this tremulous voice were that of the old ethicist who had personally edited the Chinese classics, then I had an abundance of questions to ask him."

Neville Whymant

At that point, the voice was difficult to understand, and Whymant had to ask for repetition. "Then it burst upon me that I was listening to Chinese of a purity and delicacy not now spoken in any part of China." Whymant came to realize that the language was that of the *Chinese Classics*, edited by Confucius 2500 years earlier. It was Chinese so dead colloquially as Sanskrit or Latin, Whymant explained. "If this was a hoax, it was a particularly clever one, far beyond the scope of any of the sinologues now living," he continued.

Apparently the communicating spirit recognized that Whymant was having a difficult time understanding the ancient dialect and changed to a more modern dialect. Whymant wondered how he could test the voice and remembered that there are several poems in Confucius' *Shih King* which have baffled both Chinese and Western scholars.

Whymant addressed the voice: "This stupid one would know the correct reading of the verse in *Shih King*. It has been hidden from understanding for long centuries, and men look upon it with eyes that are blind. The passage begins thus: *Ts'ai ts'ai chüan êrh...*"

Whymant had recalled that line as the first line of the third ode of the first book of Chou nan, although he did not recall the remaining fourteen lines. "The 'voice' took up the poem and recited it to the end," Whymant wrote.

The voice put a new construction on the verses so that it made sense to Whymant. It was, the voice explained, a psychic poem. The mystery was solved. But Whymant had another test. He asked the voice if he could ask for further wisdom.

"Ask not of an empty barrel much fish, O wise one! Many things which are now dark shall be light to thee, but the time is not yet...," the voice answered.

Whymant addressed the voice: "...In Lun Yü, Hsia Pien, there is a passage that is wrongly written. Should it not read thus:...?" Before Whymant could finish the sentence, the voice carried the passage to the end and explained that the copyists were in error, as the character written as *sê* should have been *i*, and the character written as *yen* is an error for *fou*.

"Again, all the winds had been taken out of my sails!" Whymant wrote, pointing out that the telepathic theory – i.e. that the medium was reading his mind – would not hold up since he was unaware of the nature of the errors.

There were several additional exchanges between Whymant and Confucius before the power began to fade. Confucius closed with: "I go, my son, but I shall return...Wouldst thou hear the melody of eternity? Keep then thy ears alert..."

Whymant also recorded that prior to the dialogue with Confucius, his wife's father communicated in his characteristic drawl, reminiscent of the West County of England. Whymant attended 11 additional sittings, dialoguing with the voice claiming to be Confucius in a number of them. At one sitting another voice broke in, speaking a strange French dialect. Whymant recognized it as Labourdin Basque. Although he was more accustomed to speaking Spanish Basque, he managed to carry on a conversation with this new 'personality'.

"Altogether fourteen foreign languages were used in the course of the twelve sittings I attended," Whymant concluded his short book. "They included Chinese, Hindi, Persian, Basque, Sanskrit, Arabic, Portuguese, Italian, Yiddish (spoken with great fluency when a Yiddish- and Hebrew-speaking Jew was a member of the circle), German and modern Greek." Whymant also recorded that at one sitting, Valiantine was carrying on a conversation in American English with the person next to him while foreign languages were coming through the trumpet. "I am assured, too, that it is impossible for anyone to 'throw his voice,' this being merely an illusion of the ventriloquist," he wrote.

Not being a spiritualist or psychical researcher, Whymant did not initially plan to write the book. However, tiring of telling the story so many times, he agreed to put it in writing, asking that with the publication of the book that others not ask him to tell the story again.

Michael E. Tymn graduated from San Jose State College in 1958 with a degree in journalism. He has been a freelance writer since his college days, having contributed more than 1,400 articles to some 35 publications over the past 50 years. His primary interest now is in the metaphysical arena – he is the editor of *The Searchlight*, a quarterly magazine published by the Academy of Spirituality and Paranormal Studies, Inc. His book *The Articulate Dead* is being published by Galde Press.

HELLFIRE AND DAMNATION

Sir Francis Dashwood and the Ancient Mysteries

By *Philip Coppens*

 eople have often come together to advance learning as a community, rather than continue on an individual basis. From medieval monasteries to modern 'workshops' or 'off-sites', such endeavours are there for the greater rather than individual good. In esoteric circles, the Florentine Academy, organised by the 15th century Florentine merchant Cosimo de Medici, was such an initiative. Under the directorship of Marsilio Ficino, the Academy became the driving force behind the Renaissance, the breeding ground of Michelangelo and Botticelli – and was so exclusive that even Leonardo da Vinci was never admitted.

A century later, in France, there was the *Abbaye de Thélème*, a model that would later be made famous by the self-proclaimed

Beast of magic, Aleister Crowley. The original Abbey of Thelema was the brainchild of François Rabelais, an author who did much to standardise French grammar, while also working for the famous printer Sébastian Gryphe. Gryphe was the man who published the French version of the *Hypnerotomachia Poliphili*, one of the most enigmatic occult books in history (and which formed the backbone of the recent bestselling novel *The Rule of Four*). Gryphe was also involved in the so-called "Angelic Society," a group of artists that met in a private garden in Lyon to exchange ideas, and which may have contributed to the creation of the other "secret societies" that began to sprout up in Western European esoteric circles from the 17th century onwards.

In the 15th century, the Florentine Academy wanted a redefinition of Christianity; in the 16th century, so did Rabelais, who in his bestseller *Gargantua* wrote his famous motto "Do what you will" (*Fais ce que vouldra*), which he had borrowed from St Augustine of Hippo. As a Franciscan friar and later a Benedictine monk, Rabelais was intimately acquainted with the religious life of his day, and like so many others, became disenchanted with it. Rabelais' Abbey of Thelema was the thought experiment that was meant to serve as the template for a grand reform. He depicted this ideal abbey as a splendid Renaissance castle: there were no external walls and no clocks. It was co-educational, admitting girls from 10 to 15 years and boys from 12 to 18. They could even marry, amass riches and live in freedom. Rabelais thus made Thelema the very antithesis of the monastic life that prevailed in his day.

Key to the concept of Rabelais' Abbey of Thelema was that a person's life was governed not by laws, statutes or rules, but according to free will. They got up when they wanted to, drank, ate, worked, and slept when they had the desire to do so. No one awakened them or forced them to drink or to eat or do anything else – in their rule, there was only one regulation: *Do what you want*. Total freedom.

Total freedom is often interpreted as a licence to drink, have sex and do nothing productively whatsoever. It is the life of the *bon vivant*, who goes through life doing precious little. It is this concept that seems to have inspired Aleister Crowley in the creation of his Abbey of Thelema on Sicily, which largely seems to have been chosen as a location for Crowley to have various imaginative forms of sex with a multitude of women, as well as performing his magical experiments – often, both at the same time.

THE HELLFIRE CLUB

When it comes to the 18th century English "Hellfire Club," the question is indeed whether we are confronted with a serious endeavour, as outlined by Rabelais, or whether his ideology was simply used to provide a licence for sexual extravaganza. The Hellfire Club. It is a spectacular name, one which suggests that anyone who was a member may have liked some of those 'luxuries' of life which would warrant a future imprisonment in the eternal flames of hell. Indeed, if we are to believe the rumours, the members did just that.

Today, the Hellfire club is mostly remembered through the name of the "Hellfire Caves" in West Wycombe, but the club began its meetings in London in the 1740s, in the George and Vulture Inn in the City, though some meetings were also held in Sir Francis Dashwood's house in Hanover Square, as well as members' houses elsewhere. It seems the club needed a home of its own and Dashwood leased Medmenham Abbey in 1751 and had it fitted for the benefit of the members of his club – all belonging to the highest ranks of English society. From then on, the former Cistercian abbey would be home to the Hellfire Club, where they would meet, apparently all dressed in a white hat, white jacket and white trousers, whilst the Prior – Dashwood; who else? – wore a red hat and a red bonnet.

The Hellfire Caves were excavated between 1748 and 1754 on Dashwood's orders, but it remains unclear whether the club ever actually used the caves for their meetings, or whether it was simply a personal project. Though it is often said that they were created to keep the local people at work during perilous economic times, the truth of the matter is that Dashwood used a labour force coming from Cornwall to build his subterranean world – hardly local. Still, the present-day Sir Francis Dashwood, in the guidebook to the caves, sees no mystery: "I believe that Sir Francis was just having a bit of fun. It was a time when follies and artificial caves were fashionable – Horace Walpole had built a cave in his London house, Strawberry Hill, and had purloined some stalactites from the natural caves at Wookey Hill in Somerset, and there were many other examples such as those at Stourhead and Stowe – but Sir Francis' artificial cave is the largest and most curious of all."

The caves are one long tunnel, along which various niches and halls have been inserted. Towards the end is an artificial river, ending in the so-called "Inner Temple," which sits 300 feet underneath St Lawrence's Church located at the top of the hill. The entrance to the caves is

Entrance to the Hellfire Caves (courtesy P. Coppens)

through a Gothic façade. If they were ever meant to be the venue for meetings of a secret society, it is clear that very few secrets were hidden inside: the caves were open to visitors from the day they were built, though it seems that no-one besides the locals knew of them and thus they can only have attracted a small number of visitors.

After two centuries of neglect, the caves were officially reopened in 1951, but they remained a dangerous site – if only because the local vicar stated that evil influences emanated from the cave. An impressive 10,000 visitors nevertheless still passed through them that summer. Specifically the Great Hall was in a perilous condition (its ceiling collapsing), as a result of which a corridor bypassing the Great Hall was dug in the 1950s. In the following decades, the Great Hall was made safe, and today visitors can once again pass through it. It remains a very popular tourist attraction and keeps the memory of the Club alive.

Secrets of the Temple

Inside the caves are two Roman numerals. The first is "XXII" ('22'), located on the left hand side of the wall some distance inside the caves. Some believe that they are a measurement in poles of the distance from the entrance. But why would anyone need to know such information? Furthermore, why 22, and not 20, or any other number? No wonder then that two poems have it that the location of the number XXII marks the location of a secret passage, which is said to run from the caves to the church above. The other number is XXXIV ('34'), which is carved before the entrance of the tunnel which leads to the main chapter room. Again, no logical reason for its presence has been offered; no story is attached to this number.

The end of the cave complex is the so-called "Inner Temple," where it is believed that meetings of the Hellfire Club were occasionally held. Some have labelled the room as the "vulva" of the Great Mother goddess. Just before is an artificial river, which from at least 1863 was labelled the "River Styx," referring to the river that flows through the Greek Underworld and which the souls of the deceased had to cross in order to reach the Afterlife. In 1796, a Mrs Philip Lybbe Powys stated that the pool of water had to be crossed on stepping stones, whereas previously there had been a boat. Today, a bridge has been built over the 'river'.

Whether or not they were incorporated into the rituals of Dashwood's Hellfire Club, most agree that the design was inspired by the Eleusian mysteries of ancient Greece. Modern visitors will feel that the statues in the niches of the Great Hall, some of which are of Mithraic design, underline this possibility. However, these statues are fairly modern additions, for the benefit of the modern visitors. What was in the niches originally is not known. If based on the Eleusian mysteries, then the question is whether this inspiration was purely on an architectural level, or whether Dashwood wanted to make the venue into an initiatory site central to the inner workings of the Hellfire Club.

Which brings us back to the question of what the club was up to. The name "Hellfire Club" is open to various interpretations. We know that the group were also known as the Knights of St Francis of Wycombe, and that the famous painter Hogarth painted Dashwood as a Franciscan friar. But Dashwood's first name was Francis, so this cannot be seen as a major clue to solving any potential mystery. However, a clue does come from Dashwood's biography: In 1738, he visited Italy and developed an antipathy towards the Roman Catholic Church. But rather than become an atheist, he seems to have embraced another religion. In paintings, he is depicted in the presence of a statue of Venus. From Rabelais, he copied the motto "Do as you will" and had it inscribed over the archway of the entrance of Medmenham Abbey, thus making it his very own "Abbey of Thelema" – the first realisation of Rabelais' aspiration.

Dashwood made another journey to Italy in 1752, this time without his wife. Most commentators label the voyage "mysterious" as its purpose remains unknown. Some assume he went to Venice, as it was still the centre of esoteric studies. Dashwood's library discloses books about magic that were bought in Venice, but the date of purchase is unclear. Venice was the town where the *Hypnerotomachia Poliphili* had been written and published; from here, the book made a journey across the Alps, to be published in a French translation by Gryphe, Rabelais' employer. Did Dashwood make a pilgrimage?

Others have proposed that he visited Naples, which he had visited on his first voyage, to view the initial excavations of the Herculaneum (Pompeii). His return visit, some argue, was to visit the art in the "House of Mysteries": a Roman brothel. Even if he did come to Naples, perhaps Dashwood did not make a sexual pilgrimage, but wanted to learn the location of a site that is very similar to the Hellfire Caves, but which was largely lost during Dashwood's time. Just outside of Naples is the Oracle of Cumae, the site of one of the greatest oracles in the world, the Sibyll, originally installed by the Greeks, later operated by the Romans.

In any case, Dashwood certainly created an ancient Egyptian-Graeco-Roman theme for the club. The visitor to Medmenham was welcomed by a statue of Harpocrates, the Egyptian god of silence, as well as of his female equivalent, the goddess Angerona. They seemed to be there to remind the members that they were required to be silent about what went on inside – the need for secrecy being the cornerstone of any secret society.

PLAYING WITH PENITENCE

As was customary of the time, specific care was not only given to the house, but also to its gardens. At the entrance of Medmenham

Abbey, there was a statue of Venus, stooping to pull a thorn out of her foot. There is also an inscription from Virgil, Naples' famous poet:

Hic locus est, partes ubi se via findit in ambas;
Hac iter Elyzium nobis ; at laeva malorum
Exercet poenas, et ad impia Tartara mittit.

"Here is the place where the way divided into two; this on the right is our route to Heaven, but the left-hand path exacts punishment from the wicked, and sends them to pitiless Hell."

The quote is not any random quote, but underlines the vital choice the soul of the deceased faces in the Afterlife. Within a Christian context, souls either went to Heaven or the Hell. But there was a third option: Purgatory. Purgatory was where the soul's sins were "washed" away by fire. It was similar to the fires of hell, except that the purgatorial fire was not one of condemnation, but of cleansing, required to gain admittance to Heaven.

Medieval times saw several penitent movements. Today, these penitential movements are most visible in the Catalan regions of Spain and France, where on Good Friday they walk in procession through the streets. Their dress looks identical to that of the Ku Klux Klan, who borrowed their habit from these penitent movements. Like the KKK, they carry crosses, but in a peaceful manner. Today, the movement is folklore, whereas in origin, the procession was a bloody affair: participants wore the *cagoule* (a pointed headdress), while their torso was naked. Walking through the streets, they flagellated themselves, blood landing along the route. During this procession, they identified themselves with Jesus, whose blood also rolled through the streets of Jerusalem on his Calvary.

The penitent movement, largely a group of lay monks that lived together in an imitation of a religious community, saw themselves as preparing for death while alive, seeing the flagellations as the equivalent of the purgatorial flames; they literally believed they were buying their access to heaven while still alive.

The question needs to be asked whether these Franciscan priors of Medmenham Abbey were such penitents. The answer comes in the form of a statue of Priapus. In myth, Priapus was the son of Pan and Venus, and was born with a constant erection. The phallus of the statue was tipped with a flame, underlining the "fire" aspect of the club. There was another inscription underneath:

PENI TENTO
non
PENITENTI

"A tense penis, not penitence"

Needless to say, this is suggestive that the club was not in fact a Christian penitent movement…but a sex club.

BACCHANALIA OR BUST

That sex was on the order's agenda should not be in doubt. Next to the chapel in Medmenham were some cells which, according to Horace Walpole, were fitted with cots and the "brothers take their women there." According to John Wilkes, "they had sometimes a mock celebration of the more ridiculous rites of the foreign religious orders, of the Church of Rome, of the Franciscans in particular…" Yet, Wilkes stated he was never admitted to the chapter-room where these rites occurred, so his opinion is just that; it is not evidence. At the same time, it is known that women were allowed to partake in the joys of the flesh too.

Still, to dismiss the club as "just" a sex club would not do it justice. Though sex was important, the members placed sex within a religious framework. In 1977, Jesse Lasky Jr and Pat Silver argued that Dashwood was restoring pagan worship, suggesting that the Hellfire Friars drank in honour of Bacchus, or Dionysos. Dashwood biographer Lt.-Col. Towers confirms this: "My interpretation of the caves remains as stated, that they were used as a Dionysian oracular temple, based upon Dashwood's reading of the relevant chapters of Rabelais."

The dining room in Dashwood's house also had depictions of Bacchus. The east wing, built in 1754, around the time the caves were completed, is based on a Greek temple; the west wing is a reconstruction of the temple of Bacchus, as seen by Dashwood at Smyrna. The food during meetings of the Club was consumed in the Bacchian tradition and the subsequent sexual exploits were deemed to be nothing but a parallel to the famous drinking, eating and sexual activities that were known to be held in honour of the deity in ancient times. It seems that the members even considered masturbation a sacred act, as long as it was pledged to the goddess – just as Bacchus drank in honour of the Goddess.

Many have also observed that Dashwood was influenced by *The Golden Ass* by Apuleius, in which the central theme is an initiation into the Mysteries of Isis – the Egyptian Venus – which also involves sexual rites.

RECLAIMING THE MYSTERIES

Medmenham or the caves – with only the number 22 and 34 as "decoration" – are not the only constructions that incorporate aspects of Dashwood's religious framework. The church of St Lawrence, built above the cave system, has a ceiling that is a copy of that of the ruined Temple of the Sun at Palmyra. The church itself has a golden ball on top. Both elements reveal that Dashwood was also influenced by the ancient sun cults.

Furthermore, Dashwood's library reveals that he was interested in the Kaballah. Thus, the number 22, found inside the cave, can be linked with the number of paths between the various spheres of the Tree of Life. As for the local poem that talks about a secret passage that is rumoured to be present near the number 22:

> Take twenty steps and rest awhile
> Then take a pick and find the style
> Where once I did my love beguile
> T'was twenty-two in Dashwood's time
> Perhaps to hid this cell divine
> Where lay my love in peace sublime.

The presence of a secret "divine cell" in which a loved one is resting in a sublime peace is very reminiscent of the tomb of Venus, as she is portrayed in the Rosicrucian literature, which revolves around the discovery of this secret chamber by Christian Rosenkreutz, the mythical founder of the movement. As this literature had circulated across Europe at the beginning of the 17th century, Dashwood would have no doubt been familiar with it.

It underlines that the Hellfire Club was not a group of aristocrats purely out to have a good time; there was a larger vision, that vision apparently being a return to a type of pagan religion, with hints of Rabelais' Abbey of Thelema, apparently focusing on the goddess Venus (or her equivalent, Isis).

In ancient times, heads of states came to Cumae and other oracles to hear the priestess prophesise the fate of kings and nations, showing there was a political dimension to the divination game. The Platonic Academy was, apart from being an artistic centre, also a breeding ground of social and political reform; the Renaissance was not solely an artistic movement, it also changed society. Dashwood and several – if not most – of the members of his Hellfire Club, were key politicians. Those who have studied Dashwood believe they can sum up his political vision in the following statements:

- Britain should be ruled by a wise elite.
- This elite should represent true aristocracy.
- This elite should practice a religion based on the truths of Nature.
- Women should be admitted, as equal partners.

When we note that there were supposed to always be nine members present at meetings of the Club (the Florentine Academy too had nine members), we should wonder – in light of his interest in sex, including masturbation, and the sun cult – whether Dashwood had perhaps been exposed to a system of political thought, known as synarchy, that would be codified by Saint-Yves d'Alveydre in the latter half of the 19th century, and which would equally incorporate ancient symbolism, much of which is prominent in the Hellfire Club.

Saint-Yves d'Alveydre saw synarchy as a system of government, whereby key positions in government were controlled by individuals who in secret were part of one pact or organisation; the public should however be unaware of this. Two centuries before synarchy was officially invented, the Hellfire Club already conformed to this model. Indeed, the Hellfire club had at one point the most prominent members of British society amongst its members. Suster notes that the Friars, by 1762, dominated the government of Great Britain. When their existence was made public that same year, it was revealed that the Prime Minister, The Marquis of Bute, along with The Chancellor of the Exchequer, Sir Francis Dashwood and another Cabinet member, were all members.

The public outing of the Hellfire Friars resulted in most members deciding to no longer attend meetings, initiating the decline of the club. In 1766, the chapter room and other rooms in the abbey were apparently stripped naked. Eventually, in 1777, the lease on the abbey was not renewed – the last meeting of the club is believed to have been held in 1774. Still, no harm or ridicule befell Dashwood after the existence of his Club was exposed; he would become friends with Benjamin Franklin, the future mastermind of the American Revolution. With popular theories that the United States of America was a Masonic project, we can only wonder how much Dashwood and the Hellfire Club inspired Franklin to pursue the American Dream.

The caves thus entered centuries of neglect, before becoming the only surviving legacy of the Club. Though the destroyed Medmenham Abbey had been the centre of the Club, the caves do seem to have played a role. Dashwood's daughter, Rachel Fanny Antonina, got a reputation as being a "magnificent witch" after her father's death, studying the occult books her father had left her. She once said about the caves: "The clue to all my troubles can be found in the heart of the hill," never explaining fully what she meant, but obviously referring to the caves, if not the Inner Temple and what went on in there. It is clear that the Club practiced sexual activity, but most likely there was also a magical dimension to it. This may have been why the caves were later believed to be "evil."

The caves are unlikely to ever reveal their final secret, if only because the Club went to great lengths to make sure no-one would ever know. Gerald Suster writes: "It is said that the steward, Paul Whitehead, spent the three days before his death painstakingly burning all papers. If he did, one wonders why. If he didn't, one wonders why it was said." Whitehead died in 1774 – the year when the final meeting of the club is believed to have occurred – and left his heart to Sir Francis, together with 50 pounds for a marble urn, so that it would be placed in Dashwood's mausoleum at West Wycombe.

In *Pantagruel*, Rabelais relates the story of Gargantua the giant, who gives him an estate along the Loire, where John, a Friar, realises his dream in founding the Abbey of Thelema. Did Dashwood see himself as Friar John? Medmenham, an estate along the river

Thames, definitely became the site of his Abbey. Rabelais gives the Abbey's exact dimensions, which are taken from the Kaballah. It has six sides, which echoes the design of the mausoleum that Dashwood created. Let us note that the river Thames itself was named after Isis, the Egyptian Venus. Venus was the goddess of love; sexual rituals in honour of her would indeed be expected, just as drinking sessions would be the norm for worshippers of Bacchus.

Whether the Hellfire Club was purely an exclusive club of powerful aristocrats, whose sole purpose was creating a pagan environment in which the members were relieved of their daily bonds – allowing them to "do what they wanted," including acting out their sexual fantasies – or whether there was a magical dimension to it, is a very hard question to answer; and one, for which no definitive answer can be given. But it is known that Dashwood was legitimately interested in magic and the Kabbalah; Dashwood had a series of ethics and visions that were innovative for his time, and in line with Rabelais' thinking two centuries previously. It is clear that if the Hellfire Club was just meant to be sex club, at least it had a setting that was full of meaning. But like a soul that goes into death and is faced with two roads, so the true nature of the Hellfire Club is either that of a secret initiatory society or of a sex club. Like Purgatory, no doubt, the club was a mixture of both, and something in between.

Philip Coppens is an author and investigative journalist on topics ranging from the world of politics to ancient history and mystery. He is the editor-in-chief of the Dutch magazine *Frontier* and is a frequent contributor to *Nexus Magazine*. Since 1995, he has lectured extensively across the world. He is the author of *The Stone Puzzle of Rosslyn Chapel*, *The Canopus Revelation*, *Land of the Gods* and the recently released *The New Pyramid Age*. His website is www.philipcoppens.com.

VISIONS OF THE BLIND

By *Paul Devereux*

It had been many years since I had last seen Don, one of my favourite college lecturers, so I was delighted to bump into him at a conference. Back in the old college days he had been something of a Sean Connery look-a-like and was much admired by the girl students, so it was a shock to see him now carrying a white stick and being accompanied by a (rather attractive) female helper. He informed me that he had recently become registered as blind, yet it was apparent that he could still see to a limited extent. He explained that he had some usable peripheral eyesight but that his central area of vision was seriously affected; it transpired that he was suffering from "macular degeneration." I had never heard of the condition, so we found a place to sit and talk and he set about repairing my ignorance – and in the process he introduced me to a weird area of human experience that I had no idea existed.

The Dying of the Light

I learned that macular degeneration is a disease that damages the central portion of the retina known as the 'macula'. This area deals with what is called 'fine acuity vision' used in 'straight ahead' visual tasks such as reading, writing, driving, watching television, sewing, and similar activities. The disease produces what is in effect the opposite of tunnel vision. It can occur in two different forms, known as 'wet' and 'dry', and though there is as yet no cure for either there are some preventative procedures available in cases where the condition has not progressed too far. Macular degeneration in one eye usually indicates that the other will soon become similarly afflicted. Incidence of the disease becomes more prevalent with age, though it can occur earlier in life, and its first symptoms are easily missed – they are literally overlooked. (Having hypochondriacal tendencies, I made a mental note while Don was talking to have a check-up with my eye doctor within the week.)

With Don the disease had reached a fairly advanced stage, and he explained to me how he could no longer read or write as before, or even type. This was because both letters and numbers would vanish suddenly from his sight and then reappear, disrupting any attempt at protracted reading or writing. This still occurred even when he used large print or magnifying glasses, though he had found that leaning down towards a page while wearing a jeweller's loop enabled him to read and write adequately for short and simple tasks such as completing cheques.

I praised Don for the calm, measured way in which he was dealing with his disability – a particularly distressing one for someone like him who so valued books. He smiled and shrugged, saying it was a matter of getting on with an unavoidable situation. "But it is the visions that take some getting used to," he muttered, his voice suddenly taking on a darker tone.

BLINDSIDED BY VISIONS

"Visions? What do you mean, Don?" I asked, totally nonplussed. He outlined several forms of hallucination that were plaguing him. The first one to manifest was what Don described as looking like "a ball of string or basketwork, a globular shape with an aperture on one side." He would see this image as if projected onto walls or other surfaces. He could sometimes make out a small face inside the aperture, and on the occasions this became particularly evident the basket-like effect would adjust around it like a bizarre head-dress. A similar effect was the occurrence of a "pool of pale grey light" which would often appear a few yards in front of him when he was walking along. Faces would also appear within this strange pool of light.

Don explained to me that these visual effects were developing into more complex imagery. When seated at breakfast and looking out of his window into the garden, he had on several occasions seen a kind of illumination within which not just one but a number of figures appeared, walking in a column. They were seemingly all male, some wearing hats, others caps. They would silently advance towards the window then turn to the right near the garden shed, but one figure would often break away from the others at this point and come right up to the window as if peering in at Don before it too moved out of sight to one side.

I learned that an even more startling version of this type of vision had occurred shortly before our meeting. When Don was visiting the graveyard where his wife is buried he sat for a while on a bench. He suddenly saw one end of the church on the far side of the cemetery become illuminated. Then there appeared "great crowds of figures" of both sexes and in all manner of dresses moving in a stately way towards the church – this time they were not advancing towards him. They entered the large area of illumination and vanished.

A further visual effect – which Don considered to be "rather spectacular" – was the disappearance of people in front of him, especially presenters on stage in lecture situations. First the person's head would vanish and then the torso, yet Don would be able to see the background behind where the now invisible figure was standing with perfect, uninterrupted clarity.

I asked Don if he was in a normal state consciousness when he had all these odd visions and he confirmed that he was. Moreover, he had been talking to another sufferer of macular degeneration who quietly admitted that he, too, was seeing curious visions. I promised my old tutor that I would research the subject to see what, if anything, could be found out about these bizarre visual effects.

Enter Charles Bonnet

I read a paper on macular degeneration but it failed to mention anything about visions or hallucinations, so I asked a neuroscientist friend about the matter. He replied at once, saying that the effect in visually impaired people was known to medical specialists as the "Charles Bonnet Syndrome." He directed me to some references on it.

Charles Bonnet was an eighteenth-century Swiss philosopher who was the first person to describe the presence of visual hallucinations in psychologically normal people when he noticed his grandfather, who was blinded by cataracts, claiming to see birds and buildings that were not there. It was thought to be a fairly rare condition until as recently as the 1980s when research indicated that its incidence was in fact moderately widespread in elderly and visually handicapped people. One factor that had held up the full appreciation of the situation was that people experiencing the visions were often unwilling to mention them to anyone, especially their doctors, in case they were judged to be going insane.

The research reveals that the hallucinations can last from a few seconds to several hours and can be of many things, both familiar and unfamiliar to the person viewing them. Hallucinatory content can include inanimate objects, people, animals, plants and bunches of flowers, trees, and complete scenes. Some people see strange things such as monsters, shining angels, or transparent figures floating in a ghostly manner through rooms and hallways. A small percentage of reported cases involve visions of recently deceased people who had been known to the patient. Although most of the content of the hallucinations are life-size, there are also reports of visions of miniature people – for example, one person saw two tiny policemen putting a midget villain into a diminutive prison van! The hallucinated objects can float in the air, but more typically they merge with the physical surroundings – so a visionary person might be seen sitting in a physically real armchair. In a few instances a person's whole surroundings can become visually altered, and rooms or even streets can seem to change their shape making it difficult for the person to get around; one extreme case of this in the literature involved a man who when approaching the top of a flight of stairs had the vision of being on top of a mountain, rendering his descent of the staircase somewhat difficult. Another case study recorded in the literature reminded me of Don's experiences: a retired lawyer saw people dressed in soldier-like uniforms putting on street parties outside his house. They were always very busy, he said.

PICTURE THIS

The Charles Bonnet Syndrome is merely an observation, not an explanation, so what exactly causes these hallucinations? On that subject the medical literature becomes less helpful, and it is clear, even admitted, that no one really knows. I could buy the idea that patches of light in the central visual region could be related to pathological conditions in the macula, and could cause people and writing to apparently disappear intermittently, but faces at the window, and people dressed in various costumes walking toward churches or driving vehicles or holding street parties seem more of a push. This was especially the case for me in that I was also aware that people claiming to encounter spirits, whether psychic mediums or ordinary individuals in spontaneous cases, tend to report seeing them in their peripheral vision rather than directly, 'head on'. I could not help but wonder with these macular degeneration visions whether we were dealing with hallucinations or spirits or some subtle level of perception between them both.

Although the actual mechanics are currently unknown, the basic official theory explaining the visions associated with visual impairment like macular degeneration is that the brain, on receiving incomplete visual data through the eyes, 'fills in' the missing elements as best it can – a kind of 'best fit' process. In fact, there is evidence that it is only the input of a constant visual stream through our eyes that prevents the brain making up its own imagery in any case. This has been demonstrated in sensory deprivation experiments, in which subjects who are placed in total blackout conditions for long periods experience hallucinatory imagery to lighten their darkness. All of us experience this in another form and to a lesser degree when we dream.

If this explanation is true, then a whole host of other implications are raised. If animated figures in costumes, shades of the dead, processions leading to physically real churches, whole landscapes and entire, complex scenes can be rendered in intricate detail by the brain struggling to 'fill in' gaps in sensory data, what then is 'reality'? Could what we take to be concrete materiality be a kind of hallucination sustained by cultural conditioning, and are paranormal phenomena simply glitches in that illusion? Are the different, spirit-based worldviews held by tribal societies simply other forms of hallucination no less 'real' than our own? Is the Hindu doctrine of apparent reality being but the "Veil of Maya," of illusion, correct?

Whatever the answers are to such questions, one thing is certain – we do not see with our eyes alone.

Paul Devereux is an experienced and respected author and researcher primarily dealing with archaeological themes and ancient lifeways, unusual geophysical phenomena, and consciousness studies. His work spans the range from academic to popular. While making his subject matter attractive and accessible to a wide audience, his material is factually based. He has written or co-written 25 books since 1979, been involved in a number of television productions, and has also written a range of peer-reviewed academic papers. For more information, visit his official website (www.pauldevereux.co.uk).

T.T.O.U.F.O.

TENTATIVE SECRET
FORWARD TO MAJCOM

TOP SECRET/MJ-12

INCREDIBLE AS IT MAY SEEM...

A Look Inside 'The Flying Saucer'

By *Blair MacKenzie Blake*

The timing was incredible – and, perhaps, not coincidental. I was sitting in the lounge of the 'Roswell Inn', sipping happy-hour draughts while watching CNN's continued coverage of two historic events occurring simultaneously, although quite literally worlds apart. One was the festivities marking the golden anniversary of the alleged crash/retrieval of a flying disc on a ranch near Roswell, New Mexico in 1947, with the other being the designed 'crash'-landing of NASA's *Pathfinder* on the surface of Mars.

As one pro-UFO investigator speculated about the various theories concerning the Roswell incident on the fuzzy television monitor, sitting at the bar across from me, a tall, lanky fellow in a corny western getup

– complete with faux pearl snaps on his shirt and a turquoise bolo tie – muttered that the most believable explanation was that recently put forth by the young daughter of the rancher whose property was now accepted by one camp of researchers to encompass the actual impact site. According to Kristin Corn, as recounted in an article in *Time* magazine ("Roswell or Bust," June 23rd, 1997), "the crash was caused by alien teenagers who slipped away from the mothership and went for a joyride." Although I didn't exactly agree that this was the most likely answer for the complex series of events that happened in these parts a half-century ago, I had to admit to the guy in the new Stetson hat that it was as good as many of the other fanciful notions being bandied about during the six-day gala. This was certainly a kinder way of saying what the writer for *Time* obviously thought of the current Roswell mania when, in the first paragraph of the article, he commented on the "rich manure-like odor" that his olfactories detected while deplaning onto the tarmac at the local airport. That he arrived with an agenda was also apparent (without reading between the lines) in that he neglected to mention that 'Kristin's' theory actually came from a short animation film made by a Harvard graduate. But getting back to the poor television reception: earlier, when CNN mentioned the Martian meteorite found in Antarctica – which many scientists believed yielded fossilized evidence of past primitive life on the Red Planet – the Roswellian scoffed at the academic debate over the unique properties of organic molecules on "a goddarned rock," when 50 years ago the military recovered several dead alien bodies just up the road. "There may have been a survivor," I reminded him as I downed my Budweiser…

Meanwhile, outside on Main Street, "UFO Encounter '97" was in full swing. While running the gantlet through a tee-shirted crowd of the UFO faithful and participants in the alien costume contest, I noticed a doe-eyed grey alien manikin attached to a camouflage parachute dangling from some power lines. This, I assumed, was the Chamber of Commerce's way of mocking the Air Force's latest attempt to spoil the party. While local merchants were busy putting the final touches on colorful and often humorous crashed flying saucer displays in their store fronts, the government had offered a more prosaic explanation for the Roswell "folklore" concerning the alleged observation of alien bodies in the desert.

After an "exhaustive search for the records" the GAO concluded that what these witnesses had chanced upon during their ventures onto the range, were anthropomorphic dummies used in high-altitude parachute tests. When the UFO enthusiasts countered that such tests weren't conducted until almost a decade after the "Roswell Incident," the Air Force shot itself in the foot, as spokesman Col. John Haynes chalked the time disparity up to faulty memories – or, more technically, to a mental syndrome known as "time compression"…an idea that was quickly ridiculed even by arch-skeptics of the crashed saucer scenarios.

Stars Blowing in the Wind?

What became known as "the dummy solution" was the fourth such explanation offered by the military, hoping to rid itself of the crashed saucer gadflies once and for all. Back in 1994, the GAO published a lengthy "case closed" report stating the scattered debris found at the Corona site was the less-than-fantastic wreckage of a Top Secret program code-named "Project MOGUL," which used a balloon array equipped with acoustic sensors to eavesdrop on any Soviet nuclear detonations. To ufologists, they had simply re-invented the weather balloon cover story that the world placidly accepted hours after the original July 8, 1947 press release, where the "intelligence office of the 509th Bombardment group at Roswell Army Air Field" announced that they had captured a flying saucer on a ranch in the Roswell region. As to this downed weather gadget (a tinfoil radar target was said to be attached to the neoprene balloon), I had to agree with those who cried foul. It boggles the mind how Major Jesse Marcel, the Intelligence Officer of the world's only atomic strike force, could possibly mistake materials of such a mundane nature for something far more exotic, especially when average American citizens all across the country easily identified such instruments that landed on their property, and were more than happy to return them for the small cash reward as the label (written in plain English) instructed them to do.

But even more mind-boggling is what Marcel's son (now a doctor) related to the authors of the first book about the subject, entitled *The Roswell Incident* (1980): After his father brought a portion of the strange metal debris home and spread it out on the kitchen floor, commenting some thirty years later the younger Marcel doubted if all the smaller fragments were picked up, with his mother saying that some of it was probably swept out the back door. He then added that: "About that time we poured a concrete slab around the back door for a patio. I don't recall if this was before or after the incident, but if it was shortly after, what better way to preserve some of these fragments that were swept away?" In this day when miles of the Corona debris field has been dug up and sifted through by dozens, nay hundreds, of researchers looking for extraterrestrial artifacts missed during the military's initial clean up, why is it that one never hears anything about any attempts to excavate this small patio? Incredible as it may seem, could it be for the reason mentioned in the book's next paragraph: "Although this would not be the first time in the chronicles of archaeology that potentially and incalculably valuable shards or records had been unconsciously *destroyed* [my emphasis], researchers would no doubt meet with some difficulties explaining to the present owners of the Marcel house the imperative need for breaking up the patio, piece by piece, in order to locate writings from space." After reading this passage again, I made a mental note that one of the book's authors, William Moore, had later publicly admitted to being part of a government disinformation campaign with regards to UFOs.

Returning now to the what the military passed off as the third explanation for the whole Roswell affair (after admitting that the original *rawinsonde* weather balloon was a fabrication), as dissenters of the MOGUL balloon-train solution will tell you, the project may have been classified at the time, but the components used weren't. In other words, it was a common weather balloon (with a listening device), the only difference being that there were more of them. That is, a weather balloon is a weather balloon is a weather balloon! It was the firsthand accounts of the inexplicable characteristics of the debris that littered a near mile-long stretch of the Foster ranch that made Roswell a household word, something the "balloon buffoons" seem to miss – although they are quick to point out that the scotch-like tape from a toy manufacturer, that was used in the construction of the MOGUL research project, was curiously decorated with flowerlike patterns similar to what the "harassed rancher" who handled the materials had described. Of course, proponents of the crashed alien spaceship scenario retorted that these descriptions of flowers and such (as opposed to unintelligible extraterrestrial markings) came only after the operator of the sheep ranch, Mack Brazel, had been detained and possibly threatened into submission by military authorities. Words like 'rubber', 'paper', 'scotch tape', 'sticks' and 'tinfoil' may have been a way of pouring cold water on the media frenzy back on that day in July, but, as we shall later see, the descriptions might be consistent with a much darker aspect of the now famous incident.

Roswell Newspaper Headline

Taking the 'r' Out of 'Crash'

As I made my way towards the International UFO Museum and Research Center (IUFOMRC) for the scheduled symposium (having missed the "quilt presentation"), in the circus atmosphere it was evident that what really happened back in 1947 wasn't quite as important as promoting tourism. For all the time and effort put into maintaining the curtain of secrecy, everywhere I looked there were peddlers of souvenirs commemorating the amazing event: Flying saucer trinkets, bumper-stickers, plastic I-beam replicas, coffee mugs, jewelry and alien head glow-pops. Seeing the aging witnesses (phony or otherwise) of the recovery of that-which-wasn't-ours wearing spaceship pendants, and even the stick-in-the-mud researchers enjoying themselves, I couldn't help but wonder as a sidewalk theorist if any surviving higher-ups, who participated in military intel or strong-arm tactics to cover the trail, were watching from the shadows, perhaps seated in 'The Alien Caffeine Espresso Bar', mumbling "If you talk, we'll kill you and your whole family." Although I got the significance (and necessity) of the 'Flying Saucer Pancake Eating Contest', the one thing I absolutely couldn't understand was why none of the boosters of the "Encounter" ever thought about stringing multicolored lights on the large silver water tower in the middle of town, Surely this mothership-looking structure would have been as impressive as the crash-site dioramas in the museum. Oh well, at least there was a night-time golf tourney...

The big buzz at the museum centered on a metallic sample purported to be crash debris. Described as looking like a "shiny charcoal briquette," a university chemist had analyzed the fragment and, due to its unique isotopic ratios, concluded that it was of extraterrestrial origin. A year earlier, a mysterious piece of metal that was also believed to be "proof" of the Roswell crash had been brought to the museum. Unfortunately, Pinkerton guards weren't needed, as this turned out to be nothing more than the scrap from a Utah jeweler's shop, with the material's strange appearance being produced by using a Japanese technique of layering metals of "terrestrial isotopic abundance."

Whether or not this latest fragment was a genuine artifact of the Roswell incident, or just another cruel prank to discredit the whole thing (strangely enough, to my knowledge, after the impromptu press release, the metallic sample has never been seen again), it definitely wasn't a piece of the much sought after "memory foil" that is considered by most researchers to be the UFO equivalent of The Holy Grail (although the body of a dead alien wouldn't exactly be chopped liver...or would it!?) Strips of this foil material have been described by first-hand witnesses as having certain liquid metal properties, with the most unique characteristic being that the feather light material instantly retained its original shape after being crumpled into a ball. I could see how such an extraordinary material could have practical applications right here on earth, but it is definitely an auto body shop's worst nightmare. This is the stuff that everybody can't help but look for while checking out the debris field and various alleged impact sites (although they'd probably settle for a rusty GI-issued P-38 can opener after a few hours in the desert heat), believing that such a find would constitute irrefutable proof of the extraterrestrial nature of the event. However, all these years later, it might not be the smoking gun that everyone thinks it is. At the time of my writing this piece, I have been informed that there already exists a "liquid metal" technology, that advertises a revolutionary alloy with an "amorphous atomic structure." In that this material is proclaimed to have a "superior strength/weight ratio" as well as *"superior elastic limit - i.e. the ability to retain its original shape (memory) after undergoing very high loads and stress"* [my emphasis], the best present day researchers might be able to claim is that this new technology was duplicated (reverse-engineered) from the debris recovered at Roswell back in 1947. So, unless the chain of custody is universally accepted (a virtual impossibility) it looks like they're going to need a dead (or, better yet, living) alien body after all. Although at the time I considered the chances of such momentous evidence being produced as highly unlikely (particularly the living occupant of an alien spacecraft), it was after a 'chance' encounter at the place that I was going next, one of the widely-acclaimed impact sites, that I came to view all the military activity and subsequent 'cover-up' of the Roswell incident in an entirely new light.

Leaving those celebrating the fiftieth bash on Main Street, my brother and I drove to the "Corn impact site," located some 30 miles north of Roswell, just off U.S. 285. With a ticket purchased through TicketMaster (seat #1, I'm very proud to say), priced at $90.00 for "UFO Crash Site Camping," I parked our rental van on a vast expanse of semi-desert scrub under a vibrant twilight sky. Although we (like a lot of other people) were expecting a UFO Woodstock, much to our surprise, it appeared that we were the only ones spending the night on this private land.

Off in the distance we did see one other tent amid the yuccas, but a cursory look through a pair of binoculars revealed that no one was home. Perhaps they were back in town, still swinging at glow-in-the-dark golf balls.

As stars began to come out in scattered patches, flashes of heat lightning bounced around on the horizon in all directions. Having earlier signed a waiver relinquishing the ranch owner from all responsibility – namely, from the possible danger of cactus, scorpions and rattlesnakes – we wandered somewhat off the beaten track, glancing down at the ground, looking for anything shiny. Soon, with tiny spiked burrs clinging to our khaki socks, we reached what we'd come all this way to see.

Above an arroyo stood a 40-foot rocky cliff where the distressed Roswell craft was said to have skidded to its final resting place. Now a shrine of sorts to the victims of the wreck, visitors had placed bouquets of colorful flowers and tiny American flags to mark the spot and to pay their respects. Consecrated hours ago by Laguna Pueblo dancers, I have to admit that it was an eerie sight, although perhaps not quite as scary as the "alien beef jerky" being sold back at the Convention Center. Down a dusty path, just past two newly erected sandstone obelisks, a large boulder was inscribed with the words:

WE DON'T KNOW WHO THEY WERE. WE DON'T KNOW WHY THEY CAME. WE ONLY KNOW THEY CHANGED OUR VIEW OF THE UNIVERSE...

Back at our campsite, as lightning illuminated the flapjack-flat terrain better than any Fourth of July fireworks could, at precisely 11:59 PM I looked up at the stormy night sky, hoping against all odds to hear a strange, deafening clap of thunder. This never happened, but as sure as the day had been hot enough to melt snakes, at that exact moment I noticed the headlights of a vehicle that had turned off Highway 285 (a couple of miles away) and was kicking up clouds of dust while heading towards us. Who were these staunch believers, I wondered? The $15 escorted bus tours to the crash site had ended at sundown. Perhaps it was those whose tent the strong gusts of wind had earlier blown over, sending it tumbling across the ranchland until it disappeared from sight. Or maybe it was more damned reporters? Earlier, several writers from the major Southwest newspapers had made the bumpy trip in the rain, hoping to interview anyone who paid $90 to spend the night with the coyotes. Was it the New Mexico Highway Patrol? Already one officer had showed up right where we were sitting, blinding us with his spotlight before he got out of the car, uttering in an excited tone, "So this is where it crashed!" Shielding my eyes from the glare of the headlights as the vehicle stopped a few yards in front of us, after a couple of seconds I heard a loud voice call out my name. Seeing the decrepit black pickup with its equally battered black camper shell, I was somewhat surprised to see that 'G' had returned.

Close Encounters of the Fifth Kind

While camping in a slightly different area on the Corn ranch the previous night (July 3rd), a man in his late 60s or early 70s had showed up in the middle of the night, asking us if we minded some company.

This fellow – who I'll simply call by his first initial, 'G' – told us that he was a ghost town buff traveling cross-country looking for the spirit of the old West. While in the area, he had heard about the Roswell incident, and decided to see what all the hoopla was about. It didn't take long, however, to determine that he was quite knowledgeable about the subject of UFOs in general and the whole Roswell affair (was he what Stanton Friedman termed an apologist ufologist?) Although there was something a bit strange about the stranger (besides the fact that he was following phantom trails to abandoned saloons, banks, and sheriff's jails), there was nothing to suggest that he was some oily ex-government spook, a kook, or, even worse, one of those sinister "Men in Black" that haunt us ufoers out on the windswept plains. In fact, he was wearing a flannel shirt and faded jeans. As he chain-smoked and drank Millers, all the while complaining about how he couldn't find any imported beer in Roswell (hopefully he wasn't looking for it in those general stores maintained by the state's preservationists!), we spent the night talking about some of the more interesting facets of the Roswell incident. When morning came, unable to tolerate the heat and arriving tour coaches, as my brother and I were about to head into town, we saw that he was passed out in the back of his camper. Littering the dusty ground all around us were hundreds and hundreds of tiny pieces of what was once his Styrofoam cooler. Weird! How'd this happen, we wondered? When I told him that we were going to spend the day hanging out in Roswell, and wished him well on his adventures, he stirred and with a puzzled expression uttered, "Who are you?" Which is why I was now so surprised to see him again. I thought he'd be half way to Calico by now. Instead, he sprightly climbed out of the grime-caked camper proudly displaying a brand new plastic ice-chest. And, incredible as it may seem, he'd found some imported beer in Roswell. He also produced from a paper bag a bottle of whiskey, telling us that he was, as the Roswell tavern joke goes, "ready for a Close Encounter of the Fifth Kind."

Close Encounters, the film, was one of the subjects brought up when talking about some of the stranger coincidences associated with the Roswell incident. Written and directed by Steven Spielberg (born in 1947), in the movie the contact with aliens occurs on Devil's Tower, Wyoming – which just happens to be on the same longitude as the Roswell crash site. And wasn't a mysterious personage whose last name was Spielberg the owner of the controversial "Alien Autopsy" footage, linked with what has now become generically referred to as the Roswell crash? As a NASA probe with a wheeled robot rover explored the surface of Mars on this Independence Day, which marked the 50th anniversary of the day when something believed to be of alien manufacture fell out of the dark skies, another coincidence came to mind: In the 1953 version of the film *War of the Worlds*, the location of the crash of one of the Martian cylinders is reported, on two occasions, to be near Corona. Although the Corona referred to in the film is in California, southeast of Corona, New Mexico is where the foreman of the Foster sheep ranch, Mack Brazel, initiated the Roswell incident after finding debris purported to be of extraterrestrial origin. To some Roswell die-hards, the mentioning of Corona was a veiled reference to highly classified information about a crashed alien spaceship that was inserted into the movie by its producer, George Pal. Pal, they claim, was friends with ex-Nazi rocket scientists Willy Ley and Werner von Braun, two men who likely had inside information about certain particulars of the Roswell event, and who possibly served as consultants for the film.

Rare Lightning and Dark Fireworks

Lightning strikes and the occasional peal of thunder over the Corn ranch sprawl led to speculations about Mack Brazel's silver pastures and what might have been responsible for the odd explosion that he heard during a severe electrical storm. Watching from his dinky shack, the rancher thought it was strange that the lightning kept wanting to strike the same place time and again, "almost as if there was something attracting it to those spots." (Again, 'coincidentally', in Spielberg's recent film version of *War of the Worlds*, the buried alien ships come to life after lightning continually strikes the same spot.) Although this might seem little more than a footnote to the event, it nevertheless shouldn't be overlooked by researchers and could offer an important clue as to what really happened on that night, as well as the true nature of the object that caused an ever-growing military presence, not to mention alien Christmas stockings 50 years later.

What this object was, of course, is the real question, and subject of countless debates. An alien-controlled interstellar spacecraft or unmanned planetary probe are the solutions favored by most UFO advocates, but if you, like many skeptics, discount these as possibilities (or the weather balloons and parachute dummies offered by the military as an explanation), you're still left with plenty. Some theorize that what crashed was us – time travelers from our future whose journey met with disaster during a freak electrical storm, that or an advanced aerospace platform with biologically-manufactured humanoid pilots caught in a *Twilight Zone*-like time warp. Other less exotic explanations that have not been ruled out include: a jet-powered flying wing (YB-49); secret prototype vertical-take-off-and-landing Nazi saucers or other tailless lifting-body aeroforms developed near the end of the war and brought over here during Operation Paperclip; Japanese second-generation Fugo balloons or combinations of advanced balloon arrays with flying wing-type gliders or other aeronautical curiosities; variants of V2 rockets launched from the White Sands complex; an atomic bomb accidentally dropped by the elite 509th; or something else nuclear related which resulted in dead bodies that appeared to be very deformed and slightly Asian looking – a story hotter than a firecracker lit at both ends and a politically deadly secret to two American presidents at the time. Then there are those who claim that absolutely nothing happened in the vicinity of Roswell. Incredible as it may seem, it wasn't two different groups of aliens shooting it out in a high-tech dog-fight over the enchanted New Mexico desert, with one of the pilots having blood as black as tar in its veins.

For me, the problem with the Roswell incident (and most other UFO stories) is that nothing seems very 'alien.' Of course, it's always possible that we were given a gift of sorts – that is, the crash was staged by some unknown civilization and the advanced technology left at the scene for us to discover didn't necessarily represent the pinnacle of their scientific achievement, but was deemed to be enough of a 'boost' for us at this particular stage of human development. If this scenario was in fact true, one hopes that, unlike what certain insiders have claimed, after all these years we've managed to figure out how to open the thing.

One insider who maintained that we did, indeed, breach the downed alien vehicle was the late Lieutenant Colonel Philip J. Corso, a former Pentagon official and the co-author of *The Day After Roswell*. According to Corso, as a staff officer to the Army's Foreign Technology Division back in the 1960s, he was responsible for seeding bits of alien technology taken from the "Roswell File" to the giants of American industry, so that they might duplicate it for military purposes. The back-engineering project of the Roswell debris led to the development of integrated circuit chips, night vision, lasers, transistors, fiber optics, and super-tenacity materials, all which sounded pretty good until the colonel kept talking. Evidently, he had also once pried open a wooden crate to find a dead alien body suspended in blue liquid inside a glass container. Even more impressive, perhaps, in an interview on NBC's *Dateline*, he shocked the interviewer (who was somewhat accepting of the whole laundry list of *really* foreign technology) by claiming on one occasion to have seen a time machine.

In discussing Corso's book with 'G', I mentioned that while I was having lunch on the outskirts of Roswell that afternoon, I noticed long-time UFO researcher Linda Moulton Howe sitting next to me. When I went over to talk to her about Encounter '97, during our conversation, when I brought up Corso's 'time machine' episode, she dismissed it by smiling and saying that the man was now in his 80s. (Curiously enough, when I first mentioned Linda's name, 'G' responded by saying: "She's not so hot." Although the former Miss Idaho looked just fine to me, I didn't understand what her physical appearance had to do with ufological polemics. But, as I was soon to learn, this was a cryptic remark that had nothing to do with the Roswell investigator's looks, but instead, involved a coded reference to the racy narrative of a possible MI5 disclosure, disguised as a spy thriller.) Whatever the case about the time machine, here was a high-ranking retired military officer who had connections to the intelligence community, writing and speaking about being a conduit of alien technology that – for my 2 cents – didn't seem particularly alien or advanced. More realistically, the items purported to be harvested via an extraterrestrial source could be seen as the logical next R&D step in the evolution of our own technological advancement. But if he knew that the stuff wasn't otherworldly, why subject himself (and his family) to intense scrutiny and possible (actually, inevitable) ridicule? Why, in his twilight years, would a member of "America's Greatest Generation" tarnish his reputation with the 'batty' notion of an alien explanation for the Roswell incident? When I put this question to 'G', after a dramatic pause (or was it a drag from his cigarette), he asked if I had ever read a book called *The Flying Saucer*?

Stranger Things Haven't Happened

Taking Roy Neary's line from *Close Encounters*, I stared at 'G' and asked, "Who are you people?" Being an avid collector of vintage flying saucer books, and particularly fond of the really obscure ones, I knew that *The Flying Saucer* was a work of 'fiction' published in 1948 by a prolific British author named Bernard Newman (1879–1968). I also knew that it was possibly the first book to deal with the subject of flying saucers, and that its enigmatic author was almost certainly an intelligence agent whose career remains to this very day shrouded in secrecy and deceit.

As a satire of international politics, inspired in part by H.G. Wells's *War of the Worlds*, the plot involves a "League of Scientists" who stage a series of flying saucer crashes, in the hope that the world's leaders will unite against a common foe (i.e. the deliberately created extraterrestrial threat), thus bringing about world disarmament. Newman's novel contains many elements that will be familiar to Roswell aficionados, and the story often mirrors the labyrinthine intrigue of today's UFO psy-ops and military disinformation tactics.

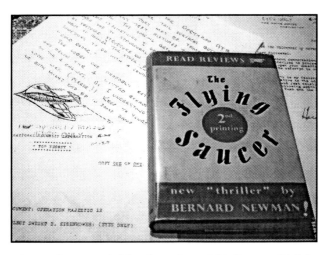

Bernard Newman's 'The Flying Saucer' (© Duncan Blake)

Included in the narrative is the contrived crash of a flying saucer in the wastes of New Mexico, complete with a considerable quantity of strange lightweight, though extraordinarily hard metallic debris, hieroglyphic-like markings, a glass-like substance attached to the craft with "properties hitherto unknown that confused radar," no signs of propellers or jets and, my personal favorite, "no sign of a parachute." At one point in the story, when confronted with the problem of those who might deny the possibility of the perceived ET threat, at great financial cost the elite group (shades of the MJ-12 committee?) manufacture a mangled alien victim of the wreck whose yellowish skin (treated with infrared light) came from a dead Asian person, with the internal organs composed of exotic animal parts, all of which brings to mind the dissection of the humanoid seen in the conveniently out of focus Ray Santilli video. And speaking of that latex-based lifeform (?) – regarding the alien invaders in *The Flying Saucer*, through the decipherment of certain astronomical data found in the saucer, the most brilliant scientists deduced that whoever they were, they must have six-fingers!

If the Roswell incident involved a similar charade designed to convince people that such a crash really occurred, then, as 'G' reminded me (or did I remind him?), the "perpetrators of this magnificent, unscrupulous deceit" (to quote the back flap of the dust-jacket of Bernard's book) already had a template from which to work. This was the Aurora, Texas spaceship crash that allegedly occurred in 1897 (coincidently the year that Bernard Newman was born, and 50 years before the Roswell incident). As the story goes, a mysterious airship piloted by a not-so-infallible Martian collided with a windmill, causing a terrific explosion and scattering debris over a wide area. Witnesses to the event spoke of unusual metal fragments, paper records written in unknown hieroglyphics, and a terribly disfigured dead alien pilot who was later buried in the local cemetery. Today, most ufologists consider the incident to be a non-event hoax, but even if it was just a whopper of a Texas tale – one cylindrical gas-bag spouting off about another cylindrical gas-bag – stories of this wondrous machine falling out of the heavens might still have served the purposes of a later conspiracy, not to suppress the truth about a crashed alien craft on a isolated ranch, but to promote it as part of someone's elaborate scheme.

In *The Flying Saucer*, the first task of those responsible for the scheme is to prepare the mind of the people well in advance – "to make it receptive to ideas about other planets." This was achieved, among other things, by stimulating articles in the popular press.

The person whose job it was to do this, Newman himself, knew that in the case of the Orson Welles' Halloween radio broadcast of *The War of the Worlds* – incredible as it may seem – thousands of Americans believed that it was a real news transmission. But even more importantly, the author was aware that at the same time the authorities were inundated with calls of alarm from people who actually saw the Martians.

In discussing mass hallucinations – where hundreds of witnesses spread the tale that was 'introduced' to them, to hundreds of other people – Newman draws our attention to pilot Kenneth Arnold's sighting of nine bright objects moving at a great rate of speed on June 24th, 1947. In describing these craft, "the man who started it all," as Arnold is often called, used an analogy of a saucer, saying that the objects skipped through the air like a saucer skipping across the surface of a body of water. And, so, even though the objects he saw were described as roughly boomerang or crescent shaped, because of his analogy the word "flying saucer" was coined, and with the press flap, days later the newly-labeled flying *saucers* were being seen in other parts of the country. In a news clipping from an Indiana paper at the time of the 1947 saucer scare, one local resident is even confined to a mental ward after the police found her hacking holes in the sidewalk with a hatchet in order to drive away the saucers. In Newman's book, once the public was made ripe for it, the 'invasion' – "masterminded by a handful of the best brains in the world" – could begin.

As 'G' and I talked about how so many of the key players in the early days of saucerdom were either military-types or had connections with the intelligence community (the same as it is today), we also had some chuckles at those who might have been the unwitting dupes of psy-op machinations. Didn't the 1950s contactee and saucer-ride boy Truman Bethurum find it a bit odd that he later saw the beautiful female saucer captain, Aura Rhanes from the planet Clarion, drinking orange juice in a restaurant where she pretended not to recognize him? (Was it also an inside joke that the Clarions told the road construction worker that the correct name for a flying saucer is a "scow" – some of us being aware that scows are used to haul garbage!) And how hard would it be to fool a Missouri farmer who told the world about a craft of unimaginable technological sophistication, whose occupants expressed their concerns about the labels on cans of 'pork beans' (shouldn't it be 'beans & pork' they suggested, seeing how the greater percentage of the contents were beans?). And then there was the short order cook of a hamburger stand at Mount Palomar. All this was making me wish I had bought some of that alien popcorn back at the Encounter '97 marketplace. At least I still had some leftover KFC (and, yes, they also jumped on the Roswell bandwagon, although I don't think Colonel Sanders ever claimed to have seen a time machine.)

If the Roswell incident was deliberately contrived, and making sure that people were receptive to the idea of flying saucers was the first component of the plan, then the second thing needed would be absolute secrecy. About this time, 'G' pulled out that bottle. Even though I was glad to see that he was drinking whiskey, and not Vodka, he wanted to talk about the beautiful Russian spy in Newman's thriller, a fortune-teller named Madame Hermina. It was this woman who one FBI sergeant working for the "world peace-makers" described as being "a good looker, a sizzler." In another relevant sentence, he says: "I've had a glance at this dame. Gee, she's something. Dolled up to the nines – and the tens. Her clothes set some guy back a few grand. And even without her clothes she'd be worth looking at." According to 'G', this last line – although the kind of British humor one expects from a gag-laden 1940s thriller that takes more than one jab at the FBI agent's naivety of certain things – is the first clue that certain references to the Russian beauty contain hidden meanings that Newman wished to convey to other players – meaning those well placed in the intelligence community.

'G' also said that repeated references to this magnificent woman's clothing should be scrupulously examined, and that the author practically gives the game away when he writes that there was "something fishy about this dame, must be to have a name like that." When I later dissected certain passages in the book that 'G' thought I'd find interesting (with regards to this revelation about the fortune teller's name, Madame Hermina), I thought it might have something to do with the Hermes missile project that other researchers have attempted to portray as a likely explanation for the Roswell crash and subsequent cover up. According to the available records, on May 29, 1947, a modified V-2, called a Hermes B-1 vehicle, crashed into a cemetery near Juarez, Mexico. However, in checking this out, I crossed the Hermes project off the list of suspects, as I did the other errant V-2s and A-9s, even though I understood how the remains of certain components such as Duraluminum, the use of foreign alphabets and/or geometric symbols on captured Nazi rocket parts, and even the possibility of shaved Rhesus monkey passengers could explain how these investigators reached their conclusions. If Newman and others at MI5 wanted to settle the score with the Yanks for pulling a fast one on the British with regards to the whole Operation Paperclip thing, then it might have been something else that was recovered from the Peenemunde site that he wanted to divulge, or at least let the CIA know that he knew. As many veteran researches have shown, the V-2 theory just doesn't stand up as a Roswell candidate when carefully scrutinized.

Shocked into Unity by Freaks in Silver

As for Madame Hermina's fashion parade, it turned out that this had to do with her espionage activities and the old spy cliché of using chemicals such as invisible ink which were cleverly concealed in certain of her silky garments, along with the mordant (reagent) required to make visible any secret communications. In this case, the mordant brings out a jumble of letters that form part of a simple code. Once decoded, the plain text spells out "CONTACT ZETETICS." In *The Flying Saucer*, the zetetics or "Flat Earth Society" are meant to represent all those religious fundamentalists who might not readily accept the idea of Martians posing a common threat to humankind, simply because they deny the existence of any extraterrestrials. To the League of Scientists responsible for the deception, when confronted with the problem of unbelievers who threaten to thwart the entire plan, they decide to play one of their trump cards and "send them a man from Mars." What occurs is pure theater – a constructed alien being that would make Phineas T. Barnum proud, who is killed in a crashed saucer. This, of course, brings to mind the Santilli "Alien Autopsy" and other videos, etc, especially if they are fakes. However, it is important to keep in mind that the zetetic suspicions and arguments mentioned in the book apply to any skeptics of such an ET presence, with the "Flat Earth Society" just happening to be the first open avowal of the scheme. As the plan proceeds, the elite group pulling the strings behind the scenes, those whose science is said to be "a generation ahead of others," continues to produce more tangible evidence of the invasion. At one point in the story, they even arrange for a 'living' Martian to be observed by credible individuals moments before it's eliminated.

If we are to seriously entertain the idea that the Roswell incident as a psychological warfare tool was the blueprint for Newman's novel – that is, that Roswell was an ultra-secret military operation created, if for no other reason then to send all the Russian intelligence agents in the area on a wild goose chase – then, shape memory aside, is it not conceivable that unusual prototype aeroforms (American, German, Japanese or otherwise) and other materials on the cutting edge of science – those not yet available in the private sector, were used to fool the various witnesses to the event? Seen in this light, the puzzlingly mundane nature of some of the debris described by those who saw it first-hand makes a lot more sense (and while we're talking about a product of the intelligence community, it could also be that certain "poison pills" or self-destruct tactics were built in to the elaborate plan.) Of course, if prized witnesses like Brazel, Marcel and a few others were knowingly in on the scheme from the very beginning, then the architects of the deception merely had to rely on their imagination (limited, I would suggest!) when designing the alien technology, and offer minimal evidence of it to the public. Detractors of the Roswell affair as a crashed extraterrestrial spaceship might not have as many problems with this scenario, and the same would go for those who have used character assassination to discredit people like Major Jesse Marcel Sr. This might also explain many of the inconsistencies in the stories that have occurred over the last fifty years, especially if the great hoax was only designed to have a limited effect. And if it wasn't, and the back-room types are still hard at work exploiting the 'crash', it might explain the parting shots by Marcel, Brazel and others that what they saw was not of this earth.

The more I thought about the distinguished group of scientists with their plan for world disarmament (shades of Reagan and Colonel Corso) as outlined in the 'fictional' *The Flying Saucer*, the more intrigued I became with certain connections in the sequence of events of the Roswell incident. Perhaps this is the leak that ufologists are looking for, with a former British secret agent and author of the spy/thriller genre as the shadowy informant. With this "hall of mirrors" mentality in mind, I recalled that when I had first met 'G' out on one of the widely-accepted impact sites, he had originally told me that he was a ghost town buff, and was on his way to see Elizabethtown, an abandoned gold-mining settlement in New Mexico. Whether or not it was just a coincidence, I was nevertheless a bit amused to later find out that the place was founded by a guy named William Moore. As I have already mentioned, a different William Moore was the co-author of *The Roswell Incident*, as well as the most likely source (if not the creator – possibly with the express permission of certain government spooks) of the apparently fraudulent "Eyes Only" MJ-12 documents. Interestingly enough, the "who'da ever thunk it" member of this 'above' top-secret saucer-study panel, if we are to believe that the documents are authentic (meaning genuine, even as the bait of a contrived military program to promote the Roswell incident) – Harvard astronomer and UFO debunker Dr. Donald Menzel – was known to have a fascination with "mythical" Martians, which doodled and painted for others. Strange!

Certain admissions in recent years of Moore's involvement with the Air Force Office of Special Investigations (AFOSI) – including the dissemination of disinformation to the UFO community – have made the researcher a rather controversial figure, although he must still be considered one of the major players in the Roswell episode. With his intimate knowledge of the UFO phenomenon, I wondered if 'G' had been playing some kind of mind game with me by mentioning the rich history of Elizabethtown? In short, was he offering me fool's

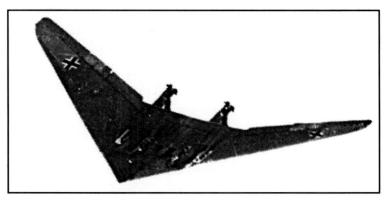

Horten Brothers 'Flying Wing'

gold with his hints that Newman's book contained specific revelations about Roswell, or was it worthy of further investigation? Ten years later, I'm still not sure. Perhaps I don't yet have the correct mordant needed to render the 'invisible' ink of the book's cryptic passages visible as if by 'Majik'.

Made in Japan?

After all the traffic at the "Roswell Encounter '97" marketplace had died down a bit, "a shockingly plausible new theory on the Roswell incident" was laid out by researcher Nick Redfern (*Body Snatchers in the Desert*, 2005). Actually, Nick's theory isn't that new, having first been suggested in one form by seasoned ufologist/ Fortean phenomenon expert John Keel, and later expanded upon by Jim Wilson (boo, hiss) in the July 1997 issue of *Popular Mechanics*, but he does add many disturbing, darker elements to the story.

If I understand it correctly, according to Nick's insiders, the culprit for the Roswell crash(es) was an experimental hybrid aircraft that combined a German Horten brothers-inspired lifting body design attached to something similar to an advanced high-altitude Japanese Fugo balloon array, that was piloted by a crew of "human guinea-pig" Japanese pilots "who had been specifically trained for the task," but which crashed in the Roswell region after being struck by lightning during one of the worse electrical storms in the area in recent memory (damn, where's a weather observation balloon when you need one!) Although described as being futuristic, at a time of jet-engine propulsion systems and fledgling rocket technology, to me this contraption sounds a bit like the old phantom airships with their ponderous frames and mechanical contrivances. Maybe the Martian spaceship from 1897 was transported back to Roswell through Colonel Corso's time machine? That might explain those repeated strikes of lightning in the same area that Mack Brazel saw. All kidding aside, this sounds like another diversion "surreptitiously" leaked to a Roswell investigator. At any rate, members of America's "Greatest Generation" will not be happy to hear that – according to one of Nick Redfern's whistleblowers – in the post-war 1940s, in our most secret government installations and advanced military complexes, "a lot of this was people not really knowing what the hell they were doing and just coming up with dipshit ideas and hoping for the best." Insensitive as it may seem, considering the post-war sentiments of the time, and the looming threat of the Cold War, these same Americans might not be as upset to learn that we were conducting radiation-shielding experiments with deformed, handicapped, and disfigured Japanese POWs inside captured hybrid Nazi flying machines and Japanese kamikaze balloon technology.

That these prototype craft had ejection capsules might be a slight problem (where are these nifty escape pods today?), but I still don't think anyone would mistake an even "horrible-looking" oriental crew member for an extraterrestrial, what with the stereotypical images of said people on propaganda posters that appeared everywhere just a few years earlier.

In describing some of these biological experiments, and early research into nuclear-shielding issues that was part of the darker truth about the Roswell incident, in one passage in *Body Snatchers* we are told that "on board each flight was a pilot who had undergone intense high-altitude training and who was protected from *any* [my emphasis] hazards by a modified pressure suit." Okay, so what was the problem? Why did we need those terribly unfortunate Japanese UNIT 731 victims? Weren't there enough modified pressure suits to go around? If Nick Redfern's insiders are correct, and stranger things *haven't* happened, I truly believe "the horrible truth at the heart of the Roswell story" would most certainly be covered up, not so much by the American government, but by all the Roswell boosters and merchants. Those who have for decades glorified and profited on the crashed alien saucer would go to great lengths to keep the world from knowing the truth about "human guinea-pigs" recovered from the desert. Besides the ethical considerations, it would also put a new spin on all those UFO suckers (lollipops) being sold on Main Street during the gala. Not only that, the U-Haul Company would definitely have to re-think the colorful graphics promoting the State of New Mexico and "What really happened in Roswell" on their moving trucks and vans.

Perhaps not surprisingly, one of Nick Redfern's sources speaks of "a covert group operating on the fringes of British intelligence that had been involved in the Roswell controversy as far back as 1948. Exactly who these shadowy people were, the source claimed not to know, but he did add that they were not to be fucked around with." Well, what have we here? Does this sound familiar to anyone? Might this covert group be responsible for the insider information concerning a crashed alien saucer plot, orchestrated by an elite team that appeared in the pages of an obscure spy novel published in 1948? As he gave his fascinating account of certain players in the British government UFO controversy, Redfern described his informant as speaking with what he perceived to be a "deliberately exaggerated conspiratorial tone" and "faked nervousness." This "Mr. Levine," even without martinis and boilermakers, sounds like he, indeed, might be familiar with *The Flying Saucer*. (Note: In a chapter in his book entitled "The Crashed UFOs That Never Were," Redfern does mention Bernard Newman's novel, and its possible connection to the Roswell incident – only, if I'm correct in my interpretation, he seems to feel that such stories of crashed alien saucers were devised to hide dark government secrets, as opposed to misleading the Russians into believing that we possess such alien hardware, or for putting munitions manufacturers out of business.) I personally don't doubt that such cruel human radiation and high-altitude experiments as revealed in *Body Snatchers* were sponsored by the government and performed on American soil back in the 1940s (and much later), I just don't think that Redfern's theory contains all of the pieces of the Roswell puzzle.

Puzzle of the Pieces

In attempting to put the puzzle together, the first thing to keep in mind is that the military itself said that they had captured a flying saucer in the Roswell region before their statement was quickly retracted. This is the foundation stone of the event, and we should ask ourselves whether or not it was a series of blunders by the base Public Information Officer and others involved, a preemptive strike by the military brass to divert attention away from something else until the necessary security measures could be put into place, or a clever ploy as part of a psy-op campaign to trick the Russians, keeping in mind the spy hysteria of the time? Most people agree that something strange definitely occurred at Roswell. With this book of third-rate fiction that we have been examining, the question is: Was the author translating fact into fiction (as he'd done in the past with the atomic bomb), or fiction into fact, as he, himself, tells us that he is doing with this hoaxed threat to global security?

I was to see the evidence of such cloak-and-dagger exploits for myself after reading certain letters and documents given to me by a member of an alphabet-soup government agency (yep, everyone has a mysterious source, so why should it be any different with me?). One of the most interesting things in this cache of 'sensitive' material was a sketch that is a dead ringer for the latest "biomorphic" Roswell craft (as forensically reproduced by William M. McDonald) in a letter dated from the mid 1980s, and said to be the flying prototype for an advanced aerospace weapons platform. The letter mentions "something to do with a condition termed cold radar." In the last sentence, its author, the late George Andrews – a well-known aviation expert – warns the recipient of the letter to please keep this information to himself or they both might end up in some "damp pokey." Reading this, I wondered if the crude drawings showed a reverse-engineered version of the downed alien craft that Newman described in 1948 when he wrote, "the glass-like substance attached to the craft had some properties, hitherto unknown, that confused radar reception?" According to McDonald, Andrews "personally confirmed the design connection" between the "Roswell interplanetary aerospace skiff" and our latest spy-planes, UAVs , space shuttles and aerial weapons platforms. So, was Newman's inclusion of this 'little' detail just imaginative, and prophetic writing, or was he, in effect, spilling the beans as to the real crash/retrieval of something technologically advanced near Roswell?

Personally, I hope that it was an alien vehicle, even if just a dumbed-down gift to give us a push in the right direction. In that case, we could look at the unfolding Roswell incident as part of an ongoing conditioning tool to acclimatize us to the reality of the alien presence. But even if the whole thing turned out to be a charade, in sticking to the fabricated story, Brazel, Marcel and the others involved would still be doing their patriotic duty. And if we dismiss the rumors of all the UFO darksiders – the MJ-12 "aviary" of William Moore and others, with their strawberry ice cream-eating EBEs, there is still another scenario that should be considered. This involves Admiral Byrd's missions to Antarctica (you know, that place where the Marian meteorite was discovered). Suppose…just suppose…that they found something else there, and the military experimented with it, or a plane crashed while transporting it…

Incredible as it may seem, what they discovered was something so earthshaking that a cover story was created, about a flying saucer not so different from our own technology that crashed (hence, it was not infallible), killing the humanoid occupants who turned out to be not so different from us (hence, not invincible). With the current mindset of our planet – excluding a few zetetics – most people don't seem to have a problem knowing that, as Mack Brazel, Major Jesse Marcel and a CIC officer spent the night in a tiny rancher's shack with nothing to eat but crackers and some pork & beans, outside in the desert was the body of a dead alien (maybe even an alien teenager who went for a joyride in the "Sports Model") who traveled light years, possibly to warn us about the erroneous and misleading label on that can. In fact, millions of people even celebrate the very notion.

In an ironic twist (provided Corso wasn't pulling our leg), the truth of the matter might be found in the telegram held in the hand of Brigadier General Roger Ramey, the commanding officer of the Eighth Air Force in 1947. At the time, the General was posing for a photographer with the debris of a downed weather balloon – the one that was initially mistaken for a crashed flying saucer. Using high resolution scans, the "Ramey memo" has been analyzed, with some researchers seeing the words "VICTIMS OF THE WRECK" among other suggestive phrases (skeptics claim these are just "faces in the clouds"). Some day when the technology permits it, the actual words might be more discernable and, because of the indisputable provenance of the telegram, the Roswell case might finally be solved. But then again, why would a General be holding a classified document (with the text facing the camera) in front of a civilian photographer in the first place? Something maybe Bernard Newman could answer.

Blair Mackenzie Blake has been studying, practicing, and writing about the western esoteric tradition for over twenty years. More recently, he has been focusing his attention on the neurochemical basis of successful magickal workings (and paranormal activity in general). Incorporating a magical vocabulary and nightside symbolism, his first book, *IJYNX*, a collection of occult prose-poems, attempts to convey the ritually-machined ecstatic states that allow one access to hyper-dimensions of consciousness and encounters with transmundane entities. BMB is also the writer for www.toolband.com and www.dannycarey.org.

TEMPLAR REVELATIONS

After 700 Years, the Truth Deserves to be Told

By *Lynn Picknett and Clive Prince*

Cliché though it might be, as anyone in this field knows, the Knights Templar are often cited as major players in the Western Mystery Tradition as guardians and transmitters of esoteric – but usually irritatingly elusive - secrets. But is this reputation really justified? While historians routinely wave away claims that the Templars kept occult secrets, or had a covert agenda beyond their official purpose, there is undeniable evidence that there was more to them than meets the eye. But on the other hand, even a little dedicated delving reveals that a great deal of nonsense is written about the Knights, and claims that are based on very slender or sometimes no evidence at all have been repeated so often that they have become 'fact' in the alternative history world. The 700th anniversary year of the suppression of the Templars is the perfect time to revisit some of these claims, and the results can be somewhat surprising…

A MURKY BEGINNING

Most people in our field are well-versed in the story of the Templars' origins: how, after the First Crusade seized Jerusalem and the Holy Land from the Muslims, a French knight named Hugues de Payens and eight companions pledged the King of Jerusalem that they would create a band of knights to protect the pilgrimage routes. The King approved their mission, and gave them quarters in the Al-Aqsa Mosque on the Temple Mount, then being used as the royal palace. And the story goes on that for nine years these nine knights carried out their task without adding to their number. Then, in 1128, under the sponsorship of leading churchman Bernard of Clairvaux, Hugues and his knights received a papal blessing and recognition for their new chivalric order, which then erupted into a massive organization throughout Europe.

This well-worn story comes from a chronicle of William of Tyre, written around 1180 – that is, about 60 years after the event. There are no *contemporary* accounts of the founding of the Templars – even in the writings of chroniclers who *should* have recorded it. In fact, there are no records of Hugues and his companions before the Council of Troyes – although there are documents, for example recording grants of property, that confirm the existence of the Order, the first one dating from 1121. So, beside William of Tyre, and beyond the fact that Hugues de Payens was their founder and first Grand Master, there is actually no solid information at all about the creation of the Order. (Perhaps it was no coincidence that William of

Tyre was distinctly anti-Templar. He certainly got a lot wrong, such as declaring that no new recruits entered the order for nine years, whereas documents exist that unequivocally record the admission of new knights during that period.)

Nearly every account – conventional or alternative – gives the year the Order was founded as 1118, but this is certainly wrong. It was given official approval at the Council of Troyes in January 1128, at which Hugues de Payens was recognized as the first Grand Master. This gave the Templars their official Rule, which begins:

> ...we, in all joy and all brotherhood, at the request of Master Hugues de Payens, by whom the aforementioned knighthood was founded by the grace of the Holy Spirit, assembled at Troyes from divers provinces beyond the mountains on the feast of my lord Hilary [13 January], in the year of the incarnation of Jesus Christ 1128, *in the ninth year after the founding of the aforesaid knighthood.*[1]

1128 minus 9 is 1119. Presumably the Templars and Hugues de Payens knew when they were formed! And 1119 makes sense because 300 pilgrims were massacred at Easter of that year, *en route* to the River Jordan – an event that sent shockwaves through Christendom and would have inspired the idea of keeping the roads safe for pilgrims.

Dating becomes a little more complicated because in 12th-century France the New Year began on 25 March, so any dates from 1 January to 24 March at the time would be a year later according to our calendar. For example, the Templar Rule is dated January 1128, but this would be January 1129 in our reckoning. So the Templars could even have been founded in early 1120. But what is certain is that this could not have happened in 1118...

Does just one year matter? Not really, except that over the centuries there have been many attempts to find a numerological significance in 1118, and also because there are groups around today who claim not only to be the direct descendants of the medieval Templars but who base their authority on their alleged possession of the authentic archives of the original Order. But basically, if any such groups declare that the Templars were founded in 1118, then they have no claim to authority. (And if anyone specifically announces that the Templars were founded on 12th June 1118, be very careful, because they are from the Solar Temple...)

DIGGING UNDER THE TEMPLE MOUNT

Another, much more significant 'fact' is often repeated in most alternative books about the Templars (including our *Templar Revelation*!). This is the claim that Hugues de Payens and his companions, during those 'lost' nine years, spent their time digging under the Temple Mount, where they had been granted quarters by King Baldwin. This implies that they were searching for something, which in turn implies that they knew that something specific and to them, highly desirable, was hidden there. This fuels the theory that the original nine Templars were on some kind of secret mission, using their vow to protect pilgrims as a cover story, and that the whole thing was the result of a conspiracy by people in the know in Europe. The theories go further and suggest that Hugues and his fellow knights found whatever it was they went looking for, and it was this that gave the Order the power and influence it needed to expand.

There *is* definite historical evidence that the Templars were founded as the result of a conspiracy in which the two key players were Bernard of Clairvaux, the head of the powerful Cistercian monastic order and the most powerful churchman of his day, and the Count of Champagne. But we need to tread cautiously. The conspiracy may have aimed at nothing more than the creation of the Templars as a military order. The idea of a standing army under the control of the Church – a dream of Bernard's – would encounter opposition from secular and religious interests, and would need to be carefully managed by puppet-masters working from the shadows. So there may be a mundane explanation for the evidence of conspiracy.

However, actively seeking something important in Jerusalem is harder to explain on these grounds. Graham Hancock in *The Sign and the Seal* suggests that they were looking for the Ark of the Covenant; Christopher Knight and Robert Lomas in *The Hiram Key* argue that the Templars' secret quest was crowned by a discovery of something similar to the Dead Sea Scrolls, hidden in the first century which and later secreted under Rosslyn Chapel. But where does this idea come from?

It is entirely derived from the discovery, in the early years of the 20th century, of alleged 'Templar artefacts' beneath the Temple Mount during excavations carried out by the British Army's Royal Engineers, led by Lieutenant Charles Wilson. These objects apparently showed that the Templars themselves had dug there, prompting the speculation that it was Hugues de Payens and his early companions who had done the digging.

The objects are described as 'Templar', implying that they must bear recognizably associated symbols or images. But until the Council of Troyes in 1128, which marked the expansion of the Order, there were no Templar symbols or insignia. Before that they fought in standard military kit.[2] It was the Council that established the Templars' uniform – a white mantle and cloak. And the familiar red cross *pattée* was added even later.

If these objects found under the Temple Mount bear recognisable Templar symbols, then they must date from after 1128 – in which case Hugues de Payens and his men certainly had no hand in putting them there. But is it even certain that these objects belonged to the Templars? And indeed, what exactly are they? Few writers describe them, but as it happens, they are in the possession of Edinburgh-based Robert Brydon, with whom we have had the privilege of collaborating on several books. Bob relates how Lieutenant Wilson had sent them to his father, as they shared an interest in the Crusades generally and the Templars in particular, and were involved with modern revival orders.

Bob has never claimed that they are Templar artefacts, and indeed it seems pretty obvious that they are objects belonging to *medieval Crusaders* – bits of chain mail and similar stuff. There is nothing specifically Templar about them at all. Because of his own interests, Wilson simply assumed them to belong to the Knights. In fact, all these objects really prove is that at some time during the occupation of Jerusalem by the Crusaders – which lasted from 1099 to 1187 – somebody, for some reason, did some digging under the Temple Mount. As a story it is considerably less impressive than the usual tale about secret or magical Templar artefacts.

A Dangerous Secret

Although so far we might seem dyed-in-the-wool debunkers, clearly as authors of *Templar Revelation* we agree whole-heartedly that there really was a secret side to the Templars.

Esoteric and alternative theories about the Knights take one of two paths. The first is that they were motivated by secrets from the beginning, that they were actually founded to carry out clandestine agendas – so that certain initiates could operate in the Middle East. The second is that at some time during their presence in the Holy Land, the Templar top brass discovered something – an artefact or information, which significantly changed the beliefs and motivation of the Order. (Strangely, there are virtually no records about the structure and running of the Order between 1150 and 1250, almost as if the Templars deliberately weeded their own records for this period.)

There is no doubt that the Knights were obsessively secret. But then, they had good reasons to be. They were engaged in what we today would call military intelligence, as well as international diplomacy, besides acting as the major banking organisation of medieval Europe – all of which required secrecy and tight security. If there was no mystery about the Templars, then they had failed at their job.

But there are signs of something unorthodox, even heretical, hidden at the heart of the Order. There is very little doubt that there was a major connection between the Templars and the Holy Grail stories that flourished while they were at the height of their power, and which are indisputably heretical, and specifically Gnostic.

There are some intriguing clues. As a huge, diverse, international organisation the Templars used many different seals for identification and the authorization of documents, and French researchers have highlighted one particular seal, now in the French National Archives. This bears the words *Secretum Templi*, prompting the speculation that it was used by a secret, inner order within the Templars. This is unlikely, seeing as it appeared quite openly on various documents. More probably it was the Templar equivalent of a 'Top Secret' stamp, being found on the most important documents, for example on records of transactions between the Templars and the King of France.[3]

However, the significant point is which image they used on this important seal – an entity called Abraxas, a mystical semi-deity venerated by Gnostics in the 1st century. Surely this is a very strange symbol to find being employed by an organization that supposedly existed purely and simply to protect the Church and uphold conventional Christianity. In fact, about 10% of surviving Templar seals bear Gnostic images, including several of Abraxas, and all of these, for some reason, date from 1210 to 1290 (i.e. the later phase of the Order). And some authorities on symbolism equate Abraxas with John the Baptist...

An Unexpected Judas

As many will know, in *Templar Revelation* we concluded that if the Templars had adopted any form of Gnosticism, it was the Johannite heresy – a heterodox religion that venerates John the Baptist above Jesus and even considers that Christ betrayed him. (Indeed, it could be said without a whisper of exaggeration that Jesus is the Judas of the Johannites).

We reached this conclusion for the following reasons. According to esoteric traditions that can be traced back for about 250 years, soon after the founding of their Order the Templar leaders in the Middle East encountered a sect known as the Johannites of the East, or the Church of John of the East, and that an inner circle adopted their doctrines and beliefs. And even the 19th century Pope Pius IX stated that the Templars had been "Johannite from the very beginning."

Satisfyingly, there was a sect that fits this description – devotees of the Gnostic religion known as the Mandaeans, who still exist in southern Iraq. They are the followers of a religion of which John the Baptist was a luminary (but which he did not actually create). Given the fact that the Mandaeans were more widespread in the Middle East at the time of the Crusades – not to mention the Templars' otherwise inexplicable preoccupation with John the Baptist – it is at least a reasonable speculation that in this case those modern esoteric traditions of an encounter are based on some solid facts.

This may not be conclusive, but the information fits very neatly. However, there are two gaps that need to be filled. The first is evidence that the Templars really did encounter a sect that retained information from the first century (we can prove that such sects existed in the Middle East at the time of the Crusades, as they do today, but that they had any dealings with the Templars has to remain speculative, even if it is reasonable to make such an assumption). And then, if that was the case, how did knowledge of that encounter find its way into the esoteric traditions of the second half of the eighteenth century at the latest? The second gap can be filled by assuming the survival of the Templars and their influence on European esotericism – and there is some evidence for their survival. But what about the first?

There *is* evidence of such contact – and we have been kicking ourselves for missing it when writing *Templar Revelation*. In fact, it comes from the eminent New Testament scholar Hugh Schonfield, who in the 1980s became interested in the mystery of the name Baphomet – the idol that the Templars were accused of worshipping – to which he decided to apply a coding system known as the Atbash Cipher. This is a system of letter substitution, used specifically to conceal names in the Middle East in the late centuries BCE and the early centuries CE, particularly by some of the groups associated with the origins of Christianity, for example by the writers of some of the Dead Sea Scrolls. Schonfield was surprised to find that the Atbash Cipher decodes 'Baphomet' perfectly – turning it into 'Sophia', the Greek word for wisdom.[4]

As the Atbash Cipher is an extremely simple letter substitution, it would hardly be so amazing if the Templars had invented it independently – except for the fact that the 'Baphomet' decoding only works when the *Hebrew* alphabet is used. This suggests that rather than it originating in medieval France, the Templars learned it from some group in the Holy Land. And, as Hebrew had long ceased to be the language of the masses there, that group must have survived since the early centuries CE.

If Schonfield is correct – and he seems to be, as the decoding *works* – then this is proof that the Templars did make contact with some group or sect that descended from the early days of the Christian era. As the Atbash Cipher was not specific to any one group, it is impossible to pinpoint which one, but it does at least show that some contact of this kind was made.

Capud 58m

One of the most famous discoveries in the Paris Temple at the time of the Templars' suppression, which is always ripe for heated debate among alternative circles, was that of a silver-gilded head of a woman. This was a reliquary containing fragments of a female skull bearing the inscription *Capud 58* followed by what was either the letter 'M' or, more likely, the astrological sign for Virgo.

There has been a great deal of excited speculation – for example in *The Holy Blood and the Holy Grail* – about the significance of this head, what it might reveal about the Templars, and whose skull it might be. (Could it be connected with Mary Magdalene?) Disappointingly, the object no longer exists – it disappeared during the suppression – but it is mentioned in the records of Templar trials, when they were accused of worshipping it.

In fact, it is possible to identify whose head it was, or was supposed to be. In the trial records it is specifically identified as belonging to "one of the 11,000 virgins," identifying it precisely as a relic of St Ursula (or one of her companions).[5] In legend, Ursula led a group of maidens who, on a pilgrimage to Rome, were attacked by the Huns and chose martyrdom to dishonour. The group was originally 110-strong, but a copyist accidentally turned it into 11,000 – and by the Middle Ages this had become hard fact.

Because of the legend, Ursula became celebrated as patron saint of virgins – explaining the Virgo symbol on the reliquary. She was also associated with pilgrimage, making her attractive to the Templars, who began as the protectors of pilgrims. And, coincidentally, the design and colours of her banner – white with a red cross – were the same as the Templars'. Obviously all of this made St Ursula the perfect Templar saint, explaining why they owned her relic and why they 'worshipped' it, presumably by praying to it on her feast day.

If this is correct, it shows that during the Templars' trial, once again the Inquisition were twisting quite conventional and innocent religious practices and making them out to be heretical, even diabolical, rites.

FRIDAY 13TH – AND AFTER…

Another myth (or perhaps wrong-headed impression), when corrected, actually works in favour of 'alternative' theories that the Templars survived the suppression of 1312. Although on a day that would live in infamy – Friday, 13th October 1307 – the Templars in France were arrested on the orders of the King Philip the Fair, as a whole the Order would only be abolished after another four and a half years. The Council of Vienne met from October 1311 to May 1312, partly to consider the fate of the Templars, and Pope Clement V decided to dissolve the Order, forbidding the wearing of its colours or insignia, on pain of excommunication – a powerful deterrent to those who believed in everlasting Hell.

Although most accounts tend to give the impression that the Order was wiped out – with virtually the whole membership being rounded up, tortured and executed – the truth is rather different. At the time of the suppression, the total membership of the Order is estimated to have been about 15,000, of which only about 10% were knights – as the organization required a huge back-up staff. Out of a total of 15,000, only 1500 were knights and about 5000 sergeants, the other fighting rank (a Templar invention). The round-up began in France, where there were – at the most generous estimate – 5000 members of the Order, giving a total of a maximum of 500 knights.

Outside France, however, not much happened. In England no action was taken against the Order for two years, and Edward II refused to allow torture. Under a kind of plea-bargaining between the king and the Pope, all members of the Order were allowed to go free if they publicly rejected the crimes with which they were charged (without an admission of personal guilt), and asked for the Church's forgiveness. (The Templar Master of England refused even this and died in the Tower of London.)

In Scotland, no action was taken until October 1309 – and then only two Templars could be found (both of whom were English). Interestingly, their leading accusers were two members of the St Clair family, but in any case the two Templars were absolved of their sins and dispatched to a Cistercian monastery.

Outside France, very few Templars made confessions, few were condemned, and none were executed. The vast majority were, essentially, set free – being commanded to undertake a light penance and allowed to join other religious or knightly orders (as they were still bound by their original oath).

Of the 15,000 members, records survive of the trials of just over 1000. Of these, only about 150 died, some 120 being executed and around 35 dying under torture – nearly all of these in France. *All the rest went free*, sometimes joining other monastic or chivalric orders – in some countries the Order simply changed its name and carried on as if nothing had happened – sometimes being allowed to live on former Templar lands with a pension. In other words, only 1% of the members of the Order died during the suppression. Of the remaining 99%, nearly all of them were freed. After the Order was abolished, about 14,000 ex-Templars were left, of which over 1000 were knights, still in Europe.

A Secret Survival?

As this is a huge and very controversial subject, it is enough now to make just one major point. Historians dismiss the idea of a secret

Templar survival, mainly because it is unlikely that any group could survive successfully for so long outside of the mainstream. But the historical record fails to bear this out. Many groups have survived longer – the Knights Hospitaller, for example, were founded a few years before the Templars and still exist as the Knights of Malta, with an unbroken history. In fact, it is hard to think of *any* movement or organisation that has ever been totally suppressed, especially when it sees itself as the victim of an injustice. And given the number of Templars left free, it is even harder to imagine that they *didn't* want to perpetuate the Order in secret.

In any case, the Order as such was not condemned. Pope Clement declared that the evidence failed to justify such a draconian step, but that the scandal attached to individual knights was so great that it was untenable for the Order to continue. Essentially, the Templars as an organisation were found innocent, but too tainted to retain credibility.

Then, dramatically, in 2002 the Vatican announced that it had found a long-lost document that shows that Clement V actually believed the Order to be innocent, and which blamed the suppression of the Order on the political machinations of Philip the Fair. This is somewhat curious because it was hardly a huge revelation – as we have seen, the terms of Clement's decree of 1312 make it clear that he had not found the Order guilty. So why the Vatican made such a splash about it in 2002 is a mystery – except that, in 1995, the largest modern Templar Order began negotiations with the then Pope with the aim of re-establishing papal recognition. The Pope's position was that he was willing to do so in principle, provided that the modern Order made no claim on the property and money confiscated in 1312. Coincidence?

So far we have either debunked some of the most cherished alternative ideas about the Templars, or hopefully presented a new perspective on some of the more familiar ideas. So at this point we ought to add a new mystery. One intriguing event that occurred during the dissolution of the Order of the Temple remains unexplained – and, curiously, has failed to attract much attention.

Two weeks into the Council of Vienne, just as Clement and his prelates were in St Maurice's Cathedral beginning their deliberations on the Order, seven Templar knights, armed and wearing full regalia, entered without warning. Their leader declared that they had come to defend their Order and warned that 2000 knights were hidden in the hills around nearby Lyons, ready to come to their assistance if need be. At this point two more knights entered.[6]

It was a tense stand-off. Who were these nine knights, the assembly wondered, where had they sprung from – and was their claim that thousands of armed Templars were ready to come to their aid simply a bluff?

Clement decided that it was a bluff, and called it. He ordered his guards to arrest the nine knights and imprison them. This was done, and no Templar army came to their aid.

This strange interruption to the proceedings certainly happened – it appears in the official records of the Council. The nine are referred to later in the records, in December, when the Pope asked his prelates to come to a decision on whether the Order should be allowed to make a defence. Among the options he gave them if they decided that the Templars should be given this right, was that the nine imprisoned knights should be the ones to speak on the Order's behalf. (The Council decided that there should not be a defence at all.) But there is no record of what happened to them.

Who were these men, who appeared a full four years after the roundup of the Templars of France, at a time when all members throughout Europe were supposedly in custody? Where did they come from, and where had they been in the intervening years? And how did they manage to get into the cathedral, and into the presence of the Pope without being challenged?

The fact that Clement ordered no inquiry into what was essentially a very significant breach of security, and seemed to show no curiosity about these rogue Templars and how they came to be free, suggests he knew their identity. But if so, why were their names not recorded in the proceedings of the Council of Vienne?

So what with old, new – and not to mention unfeasible – mysteries, in the 700 years since their suppression, the Knights continue to surprise and mystify. What would we do without them?

Lynn Picknett and Clive Prince first met in 1989, and have since collaborated on researching and writing a number of books which investigate various mysteries, from the esoteric history of secret societies to the real origins of Christianity. Their book *The Templar Revelation* was one of the key sources used by Dan Brown in his research for *The Da Vinci Code*. In their latest book *The Sion Revelation*, Picknett and Prince return once again to the controversy surrounding the secret society The Priory of Sion.

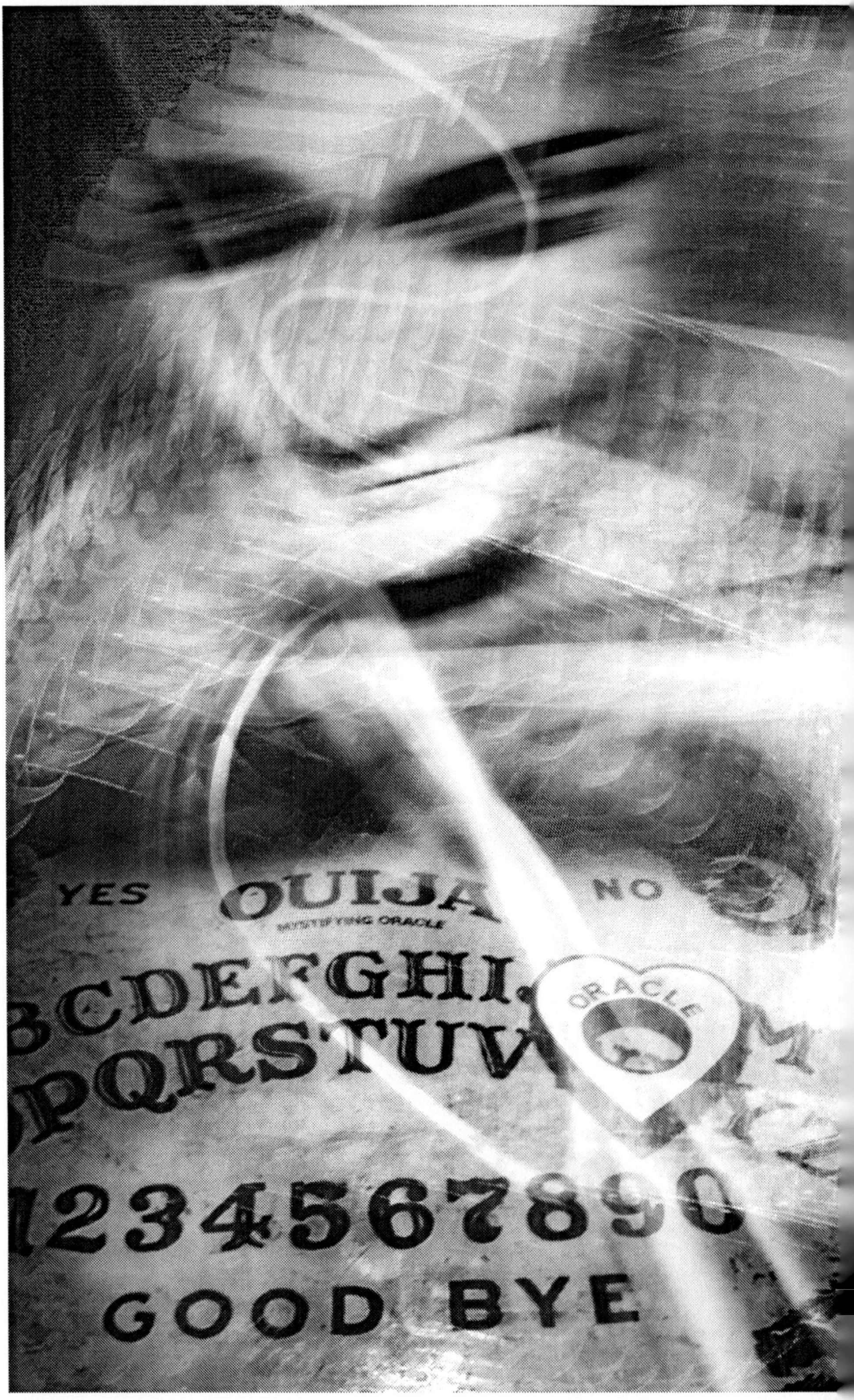
YES
OUIJA
NO
ORACLE
GOOD BYE

How this American Anomaly Became
More than Just Fun and Games

By *Mitch Horowitz*

uija. For some the rectangular board evokes memories of late-night sleepover parties, shrieks of laughter, and toy shelves brimming with Magic Eight Balls, Frisbees, and Barbie dolls. For others, Ouija boards – known more generally as talking boards or spirit boards – have darker associations. Stories abound of fearsome entities making threats, dire predictions, and even physical assaults on innocent users after a night of Ouija experimentation. And the fantastic claims don't stop there: Pulitzer Prize-winning poet James Merrill vowed until his death in 1995 that his most celebrated work was written with the use of a homemade Ouija board.

For my part, I first discovered the mysterious workings of Ouija nearly twenty years ago during a typically freezing-cold winter on eastern Long Island. While heaters clanked and hummed within the institutional-white walls of my college dormitory, friends allayed boredom with a Parker Brothers Ouija board. As is often the case with Ouija, one young woman became the ringleader of board readings. She reprised the role of spirit medium that had typically fallen to women in past eras, when the respectable clergy was a male-only affair. Under the gaze of her dark eyes – which others said gave them chills – the late-night Ouija sessions came into vogue.

Most of my evenings were given over to editing the college newspaper, but I often arrived home at the dorm to frightening stories: The board, one night, kept spelling out the name "Seth," which my friends associated with evil. (Probably connecting it with the malevolent Egyptian god Set, who is seen as a Satan prototype.) When asked, "Who's Seth?" the board directed its attention to a member of the group, and repeatedly replied: "Ask Carlos." A visibly shaken Carlos began breathing heavily and refused to answer.

Consumed as I was with exposing scandals within the campus food service, I never took the opportunity to sit-in on these séances – a move I came to regard with a mixture of relief and regret. The idea that a mass-produced game board and its plastic pointer could display some occult faculty, or could tap into a user's subconscious, got under my skin. And I wasn't alone: In its heyday, Ouija outsold Monopoly.

Ouija boards have sharply declined in popularity since the 1960s and 70s, when you could find one in nearly every toy-cluttered basement. But they remain among the most peculiar consumer items in American history. Indeed, controversy endures to this day over their origin. To get a better sense of what Ouija boards are – and where they came from – requires going back to an era in which even an American president dabbled in talking to the dead.

Spiritualism Triumphant

Today, it is difficult to imagine the popularity enjoyed by the movement called Spiritualism in the nineteenth century, when table rapping, séances, mediumistic trances, and other forms of contacting the "other side" were practiced by an estimated ten percent of the population. It began in 1848 when the teenaged sisters Kate and Margaret Fox introduced "spirit rapping" to a lonely hamlet in upstate New York called Hydesville. While every age and culture had known hauntings, Spiritualism appeared to foster actual communication with the beyond. Within a few years, people from every walk of life took seriously the contention that one could talk to the dead.

For many, Spiritualism seemed to extend the hope of reaching loved ones, and perhaps easing the pain of losing a child to one of the diseases of the day. The allure of immortality or of feeling oneself lifted beyond workaday realities attracted others. For others still, spirit counsels became a way to cope with anxiety about the future, providing otherworldly advice in matters of health, love, or money.

According to newspaper accounts of the era, President Abraham Lincoln hosted a séance in the White House – though more as a good-humored parlor game than as a serious spiritual inquiry. Yet at least one vividly rendered Spiritualist memoir places a trance medium in the private quarters of the White House, advising the President and Mrs. Lincoln just after the outbreak of the Civil War.

Making Contact

In this atmosphere of ghostly knocks and earnest pleas to hidden forces, nineteenth-century occultists began looking for easier ways to communicate with the beyond. And in the best American fashion, they took a do-it-yourself approach to the matter. Their homespun efforts at contacting the spirit world led toward something we call Ouija – but not until they worked through several other methods.

One involved a form of table rapping in which questioners solicited spirit knocks when letters of the alphabet were called out, thus spelling a word. This was, however, a tedious and time-consuming exercise. A faster means was by "automatic writing," in which spirit beings could communicate through the pen of a channeler; but some complained that this produced many pages of unclear or meandering prose.

One invention directly prefigured the heart-shaped pointer that moves around the Ouija board. The *planchette* – French for "little plank" – was a three-legged writing tool with a hole at the top for the insertion of a pencil. The *planchette* was designed for one person or more to rest their fingers on it and allow it to "glide" across a page, writing out a spirit message. The device originated in Europe in the early 1850s; by 1860 commercially manufactured *planchettes* were advertised in America.

Two other items from the 1850s are direct forebears to Ouija: "dial plates" and alphabet paste boards. In 1853 a Connecticut Spiritualist invented the "Spiritual Telegraph Dial," a roulette-like wheel with letters and numerals around its circumference. Dial plates came in various forms, sometimes of a complex variety. Some were rigged

1920 Patent Diagram for Ouija Board

to tables to respond to "spirit tilts," while others were presumably guided – like a *planchette* – by the hands of questioners.

Alphabet boards further simplified matters. In use as early as 1852, these talking-board precursors allowed seekers to point to a letter as a means of prompting a "spirit rap," thereby quickly spelling a word. It was, perhaps, the easiest method yet. And it was only a matter of time until inventors and entrepreneurs began to see the possibilities.

Baltimore Oracles

More than 150 years after the dawn of the Spiritualist era, contention endures over who created Ouija. The conventional history of American toy manufacturing credits a Baltimore businessman named William Fuld. Fuld, we are told, "invented" Ouija around 1890. So it is repeated online and in books of trivia, reference works, and "ask me" columns in newspapers. For many decades, the manufacturer itself – first Fuld's company and later the toy giant Parker Brothers – insinuated as much by running the term "William Fuld Talking Board Set" across the top of every board.

The conventional history is wrong. The patent for a "Ouija or Egyptian luck-board" was filed on May 28th, 1890 by Baltimore resident and patent attorney Elijah H. Bond, who assigned the rights to two city businessmen, Charles W. Kennard and William H.A. Maupin. The patent was granted on February 10th, 1891, and so was born the Ouija-brand talking board.

The first patent reveals a familiarly oblong board, with the alphabet running in double rows across the top, and numbers in a single row along the bottom. The sun and moon, marked respectively by the words "yes" and "no," adorn the upper left and right corners, while the words "Good bye" appear at the bottom center. Later on, instructions and the illustrations accompanying them, prescribed an expressly social - even flirtatious - experience: Two parties, preferably a man and woman, were to balance the board between them on their knees, placing their fingers lightly upon the *planchette*. ("It draws the two people using it into close companionship and weaves about them a feeling of mysterious isolation," the box read.) In an age of buttoned-up morals, it was a tempting dalliance.

True Origins

The Kennard Novelty Company of Baltimore employed a teenaged varnisher who helped run shop operations, and this was William Fuld. By 1892, however, Charles W. Kennard's partners removed him from the company amid financial disputes and a new patent – this time for an improved pointer, or *planchette* – was filed by a 19-year-old Fuld. In years to come, it was Fuld who would take over the company and affix his name to every board.

Based on an account in a 1920 magazine article, inventor's credit sometimes goes to an E.C. Reichie, alternately identified as a Maryland cabinetmaker or coffin maker. This theory was popularized by a defunct Baltimore business monthly called *Warfield's*, which ran a richly detailed – and at points, one suspects, richly imagined – history of Ouija boards in 1990. The article opens with a misspelled E.C. "Reiche" as the board's inventor, and calls him a coffin maker with an interest in the afterlife – a name and a claim that have been repeated and circulated ever since.

Yet this figure appears virtually nowhere else in Ouija history, including on the first patent. His name came up during a period of patent litigation about thirty years after Ouija's inception. A 1920 account in New York's *World Magazine* – widely disseminated that year in the popular weekly *The Literary Digest* – reports that one of Ouija's early investors told a judge that E.C. Reichie had invented the board. But no reference to an E.C. Reichie – be he a cabinetmaker or coffin maker – appears in the court transcript, according to Ouija historian and talking-board manufacturer Robert Murch.

Ultimately, Reichie's role, or whether there was a Reichie, may be moot, at least in terms of the board's invention. Talking boards of a homemade variety were already a popular craze among Spiritualists by the mid-1880s. At his online Museum of Talking Boards, Ouija collector and chronicler Eugene Orlando posts an 1886 article from the *New-York Daily Tribune* (as reprinted that year in a Spiritualist monthly, *The Carrier Dove*) describing the breathless excitement around the new-fangled alphabet board and its message indicator. "I know of whole communities that are wild over the 'talking board,'" says a man in the article. This was a full four years before the first Ouija patent was filed. Obviously Bond, Kennard, and their associates were capitalizing on an invention – not conceiving of one.

And what of the name Ouija? Alternately pronounced wee-JA and wee-GEE, its origin may never be known. Kennard at one time claimed it was Egyptian for "good luck" (it's not). Fuld later said it was simply a marriage of the French and German words for "yes." One early investor claimed the board spelled out its own name. As with other aspects of Ouija history, the board seems determined to withhold a few secrets of its own.

ANCIENT OUIJA?

Another oft-repeated, but misleading, claim is that Ouija, or talking boards, have ancient roots. In a typical example, Frank Gaynor's 1953 *Dictionary of Mysticism* states that ancient boards of different shapes and sizes "were used in the sixth century before Christ." In a wide range of books and articles, everyone from Pythagoras to the Mongols to the Ancient Egyptians is said to have possessed Ouija-like devices. But the claims rarely withstand scrutiny.

Chronicler-curator Orlando points
out that the primary reference to Ouija
existing in the pre-modern world appears
in a passage from Lewis Spence's 1920
Encyclopedia of Occultism – which is
repeated in Nandor Fodor's popular 1934
Encyclopedia of Psychic Science. The Fodor
passage reads, in part: "As an invention
it is very old. It was in use in the days of
Pythagoras, about 540 B.C. According to a French historical
account of the philosopher's life, his sect held frequent séances or
circles at which 'a mystic table, moving on wheels, moved towards
signs, which the philosopher and his pupil Philolaus, interpreted to
the audience...'" It is, Orlando points out, "the one recurring quote
found in almost every academic article on the Ouija board." But
the story presents two problems: The "French historical account" is
never identified; and the Pythagorean scribe Philolaus lived not in
Pythagoras's time, but in the following century.

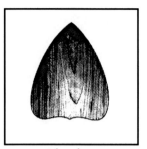

Planchette

It is also worth keeping in mind that we know precious little
today about Pythagoras and his school. No writings of Pythagoras
survive, and the historical record depends upon later works
– some of which were written centuries after his death. Hence,
commentators on occult topics are sometimes tempted to project
backwards onto Pythagoras all sorts of arcane practices, Ouija and
modern numerology among them.

Still other writers – when they are not repeating claims like the one
above – tend to misread ancient historical accounts and mistake other
divinatory tools, such as pendulum dishes, for Ouija boards. Oracles
were rich and varied from culture to culture – from Germanic runes
to Greek Delphic rites – but the prevailing literature on oracular
traditions supports no suggestion that talking boards, as we know
them, were in use before the Spiritualist era.

Ouija Boom

After William Fuld took the reins of Ouija manufacturing in America, business was brisk – if not always happy. Fuld formed a quickly shattered business alliance with his brother Isaac, which landed the two in court battles for nearly twenty years. Isaac was eventually found to have violated an injunction against creating a competing board, called the Oriole, after being forced from the family business in 1901. The two brothers would never speak again. Ouija, and anything that looked directly like it, was firmly in the hands of William Fuld.

By 1920, the board was so well known that artist Norman Rockwell painted a send-up of a couple using one – the woman dreamy and credulous, the man fixing her with a cloying grin – for a cover of *The Saturday Evening Post*. For Fuld, though, everything was strictly business. "Believe in the Ouija board?" he once told a reporter. "I should say not. I'm no spiritualist. I'm a Presbyterian – been one ever since I was so high." In 1920, the *Baltimore Sun* reported that Fuld, by his own "conservative estimate," had pocketed an astounding $1 million from sales.

Whatever satisfaction Fuld's success may have brought him was soon lost: On February 26, 1927, he fell to his death from the roof of his Baltimore factory. The 54-year-old manufacturer was supervising the replacement of a flagpole when an iron support bar he held gave way, and he fell three stories backward.

Fuld's children took over his business – and generally prospered. While sales dipped and rose – and competing boards came and went – only the Ouija brand endured. And by the 1940s, Ouija was experiencing a new surge in popularity.

Historically, séances and other Spiritualist methods proliferate during times of war. Spiritualism had seen its last great explosion of interest in the period around World War I, when parents yearned to contact children lost to the battlefield carnage. In World War

II, many anxious families turned to Ouija. In a 1944 article, "The Ouija Comes Back," *The New York Times* reported that one New York City department store alone sold 50,000 Ouija boards in a five-month period.

American toy manufacturers were taking notice. Some attempted knock-off products. But Parker Brothers developed bigger plans. In a move that would place a carryover from the age of Spiritualism into playrooms all across America, the toy giant bought the rights for an undisclosed sum in 1966. The Fuld family was out of the picture, and Ouija was about to achieve its biggest success ever.

The following year, Parker Brothers is reported to have sold more than two million Ouija boards – topping sales of its most popular game, Monopoly. The occult boom that began in the late 1960s, as astrologers adorned the cover of *Time* magazine and witchcraft became a fast-growing "new" religion, fueled the board's sales for the following decades. A Parker spokesperson says the company has sold over ten million boards since 1967.

The sixties and seventies also saw the rise of Ouija as a product of the youth culture. Ouija circles sprang up in college dormitories, and the board emerged as a fad among adolescents, for whom its ritual of secret messages and intimate communications became a form of rebellion. One youthful experimenter recalls an enticing atmosphere of danger and intrigue – "like shoplifting or taking drugs" – that allowed her and a girlfriend to bond together over Ouija sessions in which they contacted the spirit of "Candelyn," a nineteenth-century girl who had perished in a fire. Sociologists suggested that Ouija sessions were a way for young people to project, and work through, their own fears. But many Ouija users claimed that the verisimilitude of the communications were reason enough to return to the board.

OUIJA TODAY

While officials at Parker Brothers (now a division of Hasbro) would not get into the ebb and flow of sales, there's little question that Ouija has declined precipitously in recent years. In 1999, the company brought an era to an end when it discontinued the vintage Fuld design and switched to a smaller, glow-in-the-dark version of the board. In consumer manufacturing, the redesign of a classic product often signals an effort to reverse falling sales. Listed at $19.95, Ouija costs about 60% more than standards like Monopoly and Scrabble, which further suggests that it has become something of a specialty item.

In a far remove from the days when Ouija led Parker Brothers' lineup, the product now seems more like a corporate stepchild. The "Ouija Game" ("ages 8 to Adult") merits barely a mention on Hasbro's website. The company posts no official history for Ouija, as it does for its other storied products. And the claims from the original 1960s-era box – "Weird and mysterious. Surpasses, in its unique results, mind reading, clairvoyance and second sight" – have since been significantly toned down. Given the negative attention the board sometimes attracts – both from frightened users and religionists who smell a whiff of Satan's doings – Ouija, its sales likely on the wane, may be a product that Hasbro would just as soon forget.

And yet…Ouija receives more customer reviews – alternately written in tones of outrage, fear, delight, or ridicule – than any other "toy" for sale on Amazon.com (280 at last count). What other "game" so polarizes opinion among those who dismiss it as a childhood plaything and those who condemn or extol it as a portal to the other side? As it did decades ago in *The Exorcist*, Ouija figures into the recent fright films *What Lies Beneath* and *White Noise*. And it sustains an urban mythology that continues to make it a household name in the early twenty-first century. There would seem little doubt that Ouija – as it has arisen time and again – awaits a revival in the future. But what makes this game board and its molded plastic pointer so resilient in our culture, and, some might add, in our nightmares?

"An Occult Splendor"

Among the first things one notices when looking into Ouija is its vast – and sometimes authentically frightening – history of stories. Claims abound from users who experienced the presence of malevolent entities during Ouija sessions, sometimes even being physically harassed by unseen forces. A typical storyline involves communication that is at first reassuring and even useful – a lost object may be recovered – but eventually gives way to threatening or terrorizing messages. Hugh Lynn Cayce, son of the eminent American psychic Edgar Cayce, cautioned that his researches found Ouija boards among the most "dangerous doorways to the unconscious."

For their part, Ouija enthusiasts note that teachings such as the inspirational "Seth material," channeled by Jane Roberts, first came through a Ouija board. Other channeled writings, such as an early twentieth-century series of historical novels and poems by an entity called "Patience Worth" and a posthumous "novel" by Mark Twain (pulled from the shelves after a legal outcry from the writer's estate), have reputedly come through the board. Such works, however, have rarely attracted enduring readerships. Poets Sylvia Plath and Ted Hughes wrote haunting and dark passages about their experiences with Ouija; but none attain the level of their best work.

So, can anything of lasting value be attributed to the board – this mysterious object that has, in one form or another, been with us for nearly 120 years? The answer is yes, and it has stared us in the face for so long that we have nearly forgotten it is there.

In 1976, the American poet James Merrill published – and won the Pulitzer Prize for – an epic poem that recounted his experience, with his partner David Jackson, of using a Ouija board from 1955 to 1974. His work *The Book of Ephraim* was later combined with two other Ouija-inspired long poems and published in 1982 as *The Changing Light at Sandover*. "Many readers," wrote critic Judith Moffett in her penetrating study entitled *James Merrill*, "may well feel they have been waiting for this trilogy all their lives."

First using a manufactured board and then a homemade one – with a teacup in place of a *planchette* – Merrill and Jackson encounter a world of spirit "patrons" who recount to them a sprawling and profoundly involving creation myth. It is poetry steeped in the epic tradition, in which myriad characters – from W.H. Auden, to lost friends and family members, to the Greek muse/interlocutor called Ephraim – walk on and off stage. The voices of Merrill, Jackson, and those that emerge from the teacup and board, alternately offer theories of reincarnation, worldly advice, and painfully poignant reflections on the passing of life and ever-hovering presence of death.

The Changing Light at Sandover gives life to a new mythology of world creation, destruction, resurrection, and the vast, unknowable mechanizations of God Biology ('GOD B', in the words of the Ouija board) and those mysterious figures who enact his will: Bat-winged creatures who, in their cosmological laboratory, reconstruct departed souls for new life on earth. And yet we are never far from the human, grounding voice of Merrill, joking about the selection of new wallpaper in his Stonington, Connecticut home; or from the moving council of voices from the board, urging: *In life, stand for something.*

"It is common knowledge – and glaringly obvious in the poems, though not taken seriously by his critics – that these three works, and their final compilation, were based on conversations…through a Ouija board," wrote John Chambers in his outstanding analysis of Merrill in the Summer 1997 issue of *The Anomalist*.

Critic Harold Bloom, in a departure from others who sidestep the question of the work's source, calls the first of the *Sandover* poems "an occult splendor." Indeed, it is not difficult to argue that, in literary terms, *The Changing Light at Sandover* is a masterpiece – perhaps *the* masterpiece – of occult experimentation. In some respects, it is like an unintended response to Mary Shelley's *Frankenstein*, in which not one man acting alone, but two acting and thinking together, successfully pierce the veil of life's inner and cosmic mysteries – and live not only to tell, but to teach.

One wonders, then, why the work is so little known and read within a spiritual subculture that embraces other channeled works, such as the Ouija-received "Seth material," the automatic writing of *A Course In Miracles*, or the currently popular Abraham-Hicks channeled readings. *The Changing Light at Sandover* ought to be evidence that *something* – be it inner or outer – is available through this kind of communication, however rare. It is up to the reader to find out what.

Voices Within?

Of course, the Merrill case begs the question of whether the Ouija board channels something from beyond or merely reflects the ideas found in one's subconscious. After all, who but a poetic genius like James Merrill could have recorded channeled passages of such literary grace and epic dimension? Plainly put, this wasn't Joe Schmoe at the board.

In a 1970 book on psychical phenomena, *ESP, Seers & Psychics*, researcher-skeptic Milbourne Christopher announces – a tad too triumphantly, perhaps – that if you effectively blindfold a board's user and rearrange the order of letters, communication ceases. A believable enough claim – but what does it really tell us? In 1915, a specialist in abnormal psychology proposed the same test to the channeled entity called Patience Worth, who, through a St. Louis housewife named Pearl Curran, had produced a remarkable range of novels, plays, and poems – some of them hugely ambitious in scale and written in a Middle English dialect that Curran (who didn't finish high school) would have had no means of knowing.

As reported in Irving Litvag's 1972 study, *Singer in the Shadows*, Patience Worth responded to the request that Curran be blindfolded in her typically inimitable fashion: "I be aset athin the throb o' her. Aye, and doth thee to take then the lute awhither that she see not, think ye then she may to set up musics for the hear o' thee?" In other words, how can you remove the instrument and expect music?

Some authorities in psychical research support the contention that Ouija is a tool of our subconscious. For years J.B. Rhine, the veritable dean of psychical research in America, worked with his wife, Louisa, a trained biologist and well-regarded researcher in her own right, to bring scientific rigor to the study of psychical phenomena. Responding to the occult fads of the day, Louisa wrote an item on Ouija boards and automatic writing adapted in the winter 1970 newsletter of the American Society for Psychical Research. Whatever messages come through the board, she maintained, are a product of the user's subconscious – not any metaphysical force: "In several ways the very nature of automatic writing and the Ouija board makes them particularly open to misunderstanding. For one thing, because [such communications] are unconscious, the person does not get the feeling of his own involvement. Instead, it seems to him that some personality outside of himself is responsible. In addition, and possibly because of this, the material is usually cast in a form as if originating from another intelligence."

For his part, the poet Merrill took a subtler view of the matter. "If it's still *yourself* that you're drawing upon," he said, "then that self is much stranger and freer and more far-seeking than the one you thought you knew." And at another point: "If the spirits aren't external, how astonishing the mediums become!"

To Ouija – Or Not to Ouija?

As I was preparing for this article, I began to revisit notes I had made months earlier. These presented me with several questions. Among them:

Should I be practicing with the Ouija board myself, testing its occult powers in person? Just at this time, I received an email, impeccably and even mysteriously timed, warning me off Ouija boards. The sender, whom I didn't know, told in sensitive and vivid tones of her family's harrowing experiences with a board.

As my exchange with the sender continued, however, my relatively few lines of response elicited back pages and pages of material, each progressively more pedantic and judgmental in tone, reading – or projecting – multiple levels into what little I had written in reply (most of which was in appreciation). And so I wondered: In terms of the influences to which we open ourselves, how do we sort out the fine from the coarse, allowing in communications that are useful and generative, rather than those that become simply depleting?

Ouija is intriguing, interesting, even oddly magnetic – a survey of users in the 2001 *International Journal of Parapsychology* found that one half "felt a compulsion to use it." But, in a culture filled with possibilities, and in a modern life of limited time and energy, is Ouija really the place to search? Clearly, for a James Merrill, it was. But there exists a deeper intuition than what comes through a board, or any outer object – one that answers that kind of question for every clear-thinking person. For me, the answer was no.

It was time to pack up my antique Ouija board in its box and return to what I found most lasting on the journey: The work of Merrill, who passed through the uses of this instrument and, with it, created a body of art that perhaps justifies the tumultuous, serpentine history from which Ouija has come.

Mitch Horowitz is the editor-in-chief of Tarcher/Penguin in New York and a frequent writer and speaker on metaphysical themes. He is currently writing a book, *Occult America: The Secret History of How Mysticism Conquered America*, for Bantam. You can visit his website at: www.mitchhorowitz.com.

This article was originally published in the Fall 2006 issue of *Esopus* magazine (www.esopusmag.com), a biannual of arts and culture.

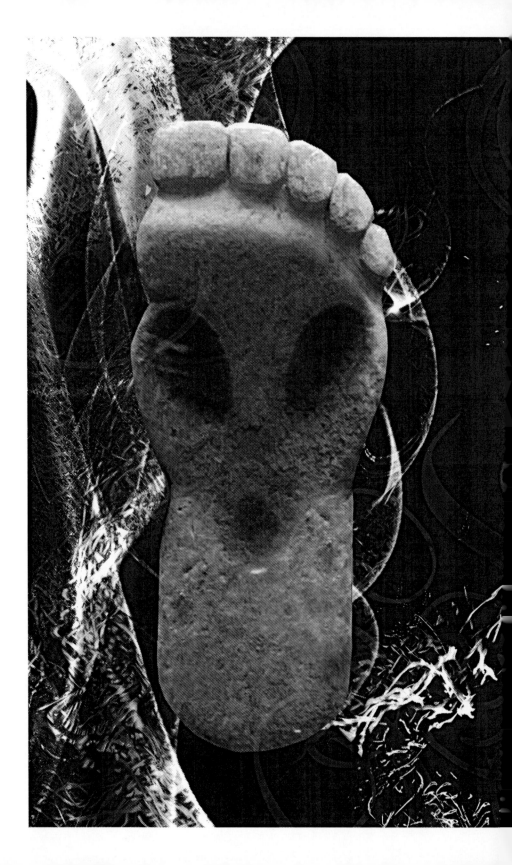

THE UNBELIEVABLE

STRANGENESS

OF BIGFOOT

Tales of the Legendary Monster
...and his *Spaceship?*

By *The Emperor*

here has been an ongoing problem with the Extraterrestrial Hypothesis (ETH), and other "nuts and bolts" explanations for UFOs, and it is a problem that has been increasingly noticed in the studies of other anomalous phenomena. Jacques Vallee has studied UFOs for decades and concludes that "ufologists have consistently ignored or minimized reports of seemingly absurd behaviors that contradict the ETH, by selectively extracting data that best fits their agenda or version of the theory."[1]

He describes the problem in UFO studies and the related debate as "like saying the moon is either made of green cheese or it does not exist. In such polarized debates we are given no room for a third, a fourth, or a fifth hypothesis."[2] He lays the blame at the door of the media who need a simple black and white story. However, other reasons might include a search for respectability among researchers, the need for skeptics to have a simple strawman to demolish (often with the evidence that things are much weirder than they seem), and even filtering by witnesses who might leave out the odder aspects for fear of not being believed.

Although this situation exists in a number of areas of anomaly research, what we'll be looking at here are the issues in cryptozoology and, amongst all the strange beasties, it seems to be Bigfoot that really demonstrates the problems. In his book *Alien Impact* Michael Craft sums up the situation well:

> Despite frequent Bigfoot-UFO sightings over the years, most UFO researchers ignore hairy monsters as too absurd or irrelevant to follow up. The same is true of the (far fewer) Bigfoot hunters, who also ignore possible connections with lights in the sky or paranormal phenomena. If you were trying to get scientific or public acceptance for the possible existence of a large North American primate, then would you investigate UFOs?[3]

Obviously, this is not a universally held division and there are some researchers out there exploring the no-mans-land between Fortean disciplines (we will meet them in the course of this article). However, the issue is still prominent and the data poorly disseminated. What I'll be doing is taking a survey of the landscape and looking at ways of moving the discussion forward.

Also, as we'll see, the issue goes well beyond the linkage of Bigfoot and flying saucers. I'm not going to be claiming that the reason we have never captured a Bigfoot is because they slip off to their base on the far side of the Moon every night (no matter how fine a mental image that is) – that is just the shallow end of a pool which gets much deeper and odder. The problem is that this oddity is being explained away (a different thing from simply explaining something), ignored and generally sidelined. This isn't to say this is anything new and other researchers have mentioned this issue.

Patrick Harpur's classic work *Daimonic Reality* deals with a lot of these concerns:

> It is our culture which is divided over whether these animals are spirits and ghosts or whether – absurd as it must seem to a tribal society – they are actual, literal animals. We even have a quasi-science – cryptozoology – whose adherents go out hunting for black cats or Bigfoot. They are to mystery animals what extraterrestrialists are to UFOs. However, they are not to be despised – everyone who has an encounter with one of these beasts, no less than with a UFO, cannot doubt its reality. The only question is what sort of reality are we talking about?[4]

The authors of the recent book on the investigation of the 'Skinwalker Ranch' express similar, if broader, concerns:

> The apparent paranormal aspects of many Bigfoot accounts make many cryptozoologists uncomfortable. In fact, most Bigfoot researchers choose to downplay some of the more exotic aspects of their research. After all, they believe that Bigfoot, Yeti and their assorted cousins are flesh-and-blood beings that just haven't been found yet. Whenever witnesses discuss Bigfoot in connection with such topics as UFO sighting or psychic phenomena, cryptozoologists get understandably antsy. After all, mixing in a plethora of other weird topics could not only strengthen the hand of Sasquatch skeptics but also give scientists and journalists another reason to sidestep any serious examination of the Bigfoot mystery.[5]

So now let us avoid the sidestepping, and meet the mystery head on....

CAN BIGFOOT FLY A SAUCER?

John Keel, well known for staking out the crossroads of paranormal phenomena, highlights the odd conjunction of UFOs and Bigfoot: "It is a curious fact that flying saucers have been repeatedly seen in ABSM-infested areas."[6] The main questions are: why might this be, and are there closer links between UFOs and Bigfoot?

While short hirsute humanoids are of interest to cryptozoologists[7], they are best known for their links with UFOs, in particular with cases from South America.[8] What we are interested in is whether their larger cousins are also up to no good in flying saucers? It turns out that, while we can't put them behind whatever passes for a steering wheel, there is plenty of evidence to suggest a link of some kind.

Curt Sutherly, for example, has described the 1975-1976 "flap" in America (a suitable term as it also featured man-sized birds) when "encounters with hairy man-beasts and UFOs were numerous at the time, as were reports of cattle mutilation."[9] Importantly for this study, he details a series of sightings at a trailer park in Elizabethtown, Pennsylvania, stretching from early in 1975 through to mid 1976, seemingly with a break in reports between August and February. Repeated banging on the sides of the trailers was annoying the residents, so in an attempt to catch the culprits the owners installed floodlights. This seems to have had the unfortunate effect of bringing the residents face-to-face with...something. The first resident encountered a large man-ape creature outside her home, although the monster left no tracks. Numerous sightings and attacks followed. When the encounters restarted in 1976, the witnesses saw a bright light between the park and the woods, followed by growling and sightings of a shambling figure. Interestingly, not only did the police get involved but in August 1976 the National Guard arrived and staked out the area, although they refused to explain what they were doing.[10]

There is an early case from the journals of James C. Wyatt, a Tennessee cattleman, detailing encounters in 1888 where he was taken to see a "Crazy Bear," a creature which sounds awfully like a Bigfoot. However, stranger than that was its origin:

> "Crazy Bear," as the creature was called by the Indians, had been brought to the "Big Woods" from the stars. A "small moon" had flown down like a swooping eagle and had landed on a plateau a few miles away from the Indian's encampment. The beast in the cave and two other "crazy bears" had been flung out of the "moon" before the craft had once again soared off to the stars.

> The Indian told Wyatt that other "crazy bears" had been left in the vicinity over the years...The men from the small moon had much shorter hair than the Indians, though, and they wore shiny clothing.[11]

Michael Craft, again in *Alien Impact*, details a strange case from Rome, Ohio.[12] Starting in June 1981 strange stories filtered out of the woods. Amish loggers were attacked by something, and other loggers found an area deep in the forest that had been burned clear – it looked like something had landed there. The family at the center of events had been finding their animals in the woods with their heads bitten off, and it wasn't long before the culprit was sighted. It was a large creature, at least seven or eight feet tall, described as being "like a gorilla with glowing red eyes." They shot it and it screamed and ran off, only to return later. When the family gave pursuit their engine died, a phenomenon often reported with UFOs. A couple of nights later, large figures, lights and glowing red eyes were seen in the trees, and the next day three-toed footprints were found with a six foot stride – oddly they appeared to stop and restart some distance further on. The next night the family came under siege with lights seen above the trees, glowing eyes seen in the woods and dark figures rushing the house. They even saw some kind of ghostly horse in a field. The family shot at what they saw and heard a series of screams. The next day they found more three-toed footprints. Local researcher Dennis Pilichis investigated a few days later, and not only found the family in an agitated state, but witnessed a lot of the reported happenings for himself.

Another case that brings together Bigfoot and UFOs occurred in Greensburg, Pennsylvania:

> Stephen Pulaski and at least fifteen other witnesses saw a bright red ball hovering over a field near them…Stephen's auto headlights dimmed as he neared the object, and as the object descended towards the field, Stephen's German Shepherd, back at the house, became very disturbed. The object was now bright white, and appeared to be about 100 feet in diameter. It was buzzing much like a lawnmower would.

> They stood watching the object on the ground, and then the neighbour boys saw something walking along by the fence. Stephen thought it looked like two bears, and he fired a tracer bullet over the "bears" heads. The creatures were very tall, one 7 feet, the other over 8 feet tall. These measurements were easier than usual to get because the entities were silhouetted against the fence and so could be accurately judged.

> They were hairy and long-armed, with greenish-yellow eyes. They made a noise like a baby whining. A smell like "burning rubber" was present. Stephen, realizing that these creatures were not bears and that they were coming nearer to him, fired over the entities' heads once more and, when they kept on coming, fired directly at the larger creature.

> When the creature was hit, the glowing 150 ft. diameter object disappeared from the field, instantaneously, and the motor noise

stopped. The two creatures turned around and walked back towards the woods. In the field where the object had been was a glowing area about 150 feet in diameter, which was gone by the next morning.[13]

This report is very similar to the "Saltwood Mystery," an odd sighting in 1963 in Kent, where a group of boys saw lights disappear behind a clump of trees, from which one of them saw a large headless bat-winged creature emerge.[14] It should be apparent that, as well as recalling Keel's Mothman encounters, in an earlier age such an encounter would be filed rapidly under some kind of demon attack. In fact, not just demons – as Keel notes, before the Fatima visions, a local woman had reported a "white man without any head floating in the air."[15]

It is noteworthy that although a Bigfoot with wings might seem unlikely, the 1975-1976 flap not only included birdmen and man-apes but also odd mixes including "a huge black bird with red eyes, a sharp beak, and a 'gorilla like' face."[16]

Things can get a lot odder though. Where some people seem to get hit by lightning more often than would seem likely, other people seem to encounter more than their fair share of Bigfoot-like entities. Craig Woolheater calls them "Sasquatch magnets."[17] On very rare occasions an individual seems to report repeated contact, and in at least a couple of cases this led to some very unusual claims, and even further possible insight into the issue.

Jack Lapseritis has reported various contacts with Bigfoot. In addition, he has communicated with them telepathically and witnessed them disappear.[18] He is quoted as saying that Bigfoot "may literally be, as I've discovered, a paraphysical, interdimensional native people that have told me and other people telepathically that they were brought here millions of years ago by their friends, the star people."[19]

However, even more startling is Stan Johnson's story.[20] He claims to have had over a decade of contact with, and eventually befriended, a family of Bigfoot from beyond the stars. They and the "Star People" are said to have taken him on journeys to other worlds, dimensions and inside the Earth, including the famous Mount Shasta. They explained there had been a war between the Bigfoot and an evil, scientifically altered group gaining power and forcing a war with their more gentle brothers and sisters, who took to hiding in our woods.

So, does this mean there is a relatively straightforward solution to this situation – is Bigfoot just one of the hundreds of creatures already known to fly UFOs? John Keel suggested (presumably with his tongue in the general vicinity of his cheek) "it almost seems as if anomalous earthly creatures have been enlisted (or drafted) into service by the saucers to carry out some mysterious missions."[21] As we shall now see, Bigfoot flying around in a flying saucer is actually at the fairly tame end of the weirdness spectrum. So let's delve a little deeper.

How Strange is My Sasquatch?

As we have seen, the "respectable" cryptozoologists (although it may be more accurate to describe them as "respect-seeking") have been accused of ignoring the stranger aspects of unknown animals, and the only way we could fit Bigfoot comfortably into the driving seat of a UFO is by data manipulation that we have already flagged as a cause for concern.

There are plenty of examples of reports that suggest there is more at work than a simple big hairy hominoid. For example, during a UFO flap in Pennsylvania in 1973, a lot of three-toed footprints were found (a common discovery and one suggesting a non-primate ancestry) and "most witnesses reported large ape-like creatures accompanied by a smell like sulfur or rotten eggs or 'rotten meat'. They also reported eyes that glowed "orange-red" in the dark."[22] Harpur says "there is no surer sign, it seems, of a supernatural origin than something strange about the eyes. Many daimonic animals might be mistaken for a natural species were it not for their glowing red eyes – a feature we read about again and again."[23]

While the glowing eyes are the most obvious supernatural element, the strange smell is another important, and common, factor. During the Missouri Monster (Momo) flap in 1972, not only were lights connected with the appearance of the creatures on two occasions[24], but two other reports specifically mentioned an odour so strong it burnt people's nostrils.[25] While one might expect wild animals to smell a bit, the stench of these creatures is often over-powering and is also another widely reported phenomena connected with various strange occurrences, including UFOs.

Strange smells are not the only 'odd' similarity that these encounters share with UFO reports. There are also reported links between Bigfoot and cattle mutilations[26], conjunctivitis and engines stopping.[27] These last two have often been used to suggest some kind of electromagnetic effect emanating from UFOs, but this doesn't make much sense in connection with Bigfoot – especially if we simply class him as just a normal creature we have somehow so far failed to find any solid evidence for. Craft sums it up by saying: "It's highly unlikely that primitive, hairy apes would possess advanced electromagnetic technology. If they did, why would they employ it to halt cars, thereby ensuring a sighting, and then blind the witnesses?"[28] The Bigfoot-related 'swamp ape' has even been reported to glow.[29]

Although later we will hear that Bigfoot is a separate entity from the shapeshifting Skinwalker, a number of reports suggest their identities might be more malleable than previously suspected. A 1964 report from Point Isabel, Ohio, demonstrates this nicely:

> An even stranger confrontation, reminiscent of many "UFO entity" cases occurred to a Mrs. Lister, then eighteen years old, one night in 1964. She was sitting with her husband-to-be in a parked car when they saw in the beam of the headlights a creature hopping and leaping towards them. It passed through a triple-strand barbed wire fence as if

it were as insubstantial as mist. Mrs. Lister screamed as the beast tried to grab her companion through a window. She felt hypnotized by its glowing eyes, as if she had "had a time lapse or like [she] was living in another time..." She could see that the creature was six feet tall, wide-shouldered, covered with yellowish fuzz, with a horrible head that was pointed at the top and narrow at the chin. Its brow was wrinkled, its ears and nose like a pig's, its eyes glowing orange, As she watched, it turned into another form: its hands became paws and it went down on all fours. Then it vanished into thin air.[30]

However, Bigfoot can move in some even more mysterious ways. Their talent at disappearing – especially when shot – is so common we'll skate over it for the sake of brevity (and we'll avoid the "sightings" of invisible Bigfoot for obvious reasons).[31] What I want to touch on are the reports where they gradually disappear. This is best described with a few examples, both of which have been investigated by Sharon Eby from the Texas Bigfoot Research Center, who has found quite a bit of unusual evidence.[32]

Firstly, we have the Three Rivers sighting:

During daylight hours John was traveling east on the dirt road in his truck when he glanced over to his right and noticed a tall hairy ape-like creature walking in the same direction as he was driving. It was taller than the cholla cacti nearby (estimated by John to be at least 8' tall) and it looked toward John as it kept walking...the long-striding creature kept walking eastwardly, still staring at John, for approximately 100' until it seemed to vanish into thin air... Because of this strange aspect John thought it must've walked into an invisible wall of some kind.[33]

The Horizon City sighting also seems to describe similar behaviour, but this time disappearing into the ground (a commonly described feature of UFOs):

The creature did not appear to notice her or her vehicle and walked casually away, swinging its arms naturally while walking up and over a sand mound. Upon going down over the back side of the sand mound it seemed to slightly "jog like a guy" down the hill and keep going down and down until it disappeared. She said that it seemed as if it went down into a cave into the desert even though she (the next day) could not find a cave entrance in the area (she figured perhaps it had a trap door of some kind). Creature was last seen approximately 50 feet or so from original spot before disappearing "into the ground."[34]

What all this means is difficult to tell at the moment but all of this is only small part of the evidence. For example, it seems likely that Bigfoot's Australian cousin the Yowie is equally odd, if not more so. There isn't enough room to go into details but a recent summary covers the relevant bits:

One researcher who does favour a possible paranormal explanation is veteran Australian 'monster hunter' Tony Healy. Healy...believes some accounts point to the creature "being something other than an anthropological or zoological mystery – that is, something other than flesh and blood. If we reject everything about the Yowie that smacks of the paranormal we'd have to sweep 20 per cent of the accumulated data under the carpet," Healy told the Sydney 2001 Myths and Monsters cryptozoology conference...

...How else to explain the vanishing acts, glowing red eyes (in one encounter described as "the size of tennis balls"), superhuman feats of speed and the ability to invoke the so-called "nameless dread" – the inexplicable primal fear that "turns your guts to water" – experienced by so many witnesses?[35]

So Bigfoot can act very oddly, but things only get stranger when he brings his friends to the party too.

Bigfoot and Friends

In regions that I have taken to calling "Hotspots of High Strangeness," Bigfoot is a recurring common element mashed up in the mind-numbing *melange* that makes a mockery of (un)conventional categorization. Although sightings of UFOs, Bigfoot and even higher strangeness are rare, there are places where they seem to occur with higher frequency and are woven together into a very magic carpet.

This kind of area has been most recently and most clearly described at the 'Skinwalker Ranch' in Utah. Bigfoot prints have been found in the vicinity of the ranch[36] and the family living there have reported large shambling shapes.[37] The Uintah Basin, where the ranch is situated, is known for its Bigfoot encounters: Ron Mower, a "Bigfoot magnet," has reported nine encounters in the surrounding hills[38] and police also have recorded a number of sightings in and around the nearest town to the ranch.[39] Interestingly, the local tribe, the Ute, draw a clear distinction between Bigfoot, who they seem to view as being relatively non-threatening, and the much more sinister Skinwalker.[40] This, though, is only a small part of the anomaly avalanche that has engulfed the ranch, and there are more impressive examples where Bigfoot is more involved.

Somewhere at the front of this field is Nick Redfern. He has broad interests in the paranormal field and, while mainly known for his UFO work, he has been involved in cryptozoological investigations galore, as outlined for example in *Three Men Seeking Monsters*.[41] In the case I have followed closest[42], that of the Bigfoot of Cannock Chase (in central England), the large-footed one is joined by big cats, UFOs, black dogs, wolves, underground cannibal tribes[43], weird glowing clouds and ghosts. In fact, Redfern has acknowledged problems with the standard Bigfoot theory for this case, saying "I think that these creatures are some sort of paranormal thing. I think we are looking at something paranormal, rather than a flesh-and-blood animal."[44] It would be difficult to support the hypothesis that there are relic populations of some giant man-ape still living in the UK, especially somewhere so close to urban population centres.

Interestingly, Cannock isn't the only location like this in England. Rendlesham Forest would be best known by most readers for its UFO sighting near the US base there in 1980 – but it has, for a long time, been the source of reports concerning ghosts lights[45] as well as Black Dogs and Alien Big Cats and, most important for this study, the Shug Monkey.[46] This large hairy man-ape seems to align himself more closely with its spooky animal cousins than it does to actual apes. Jon Downes, head of the Centre for Fortean Zoology, says: "…there are still numerous places in those countries [America, Australia and the Himalayas] where large apelike animals could live, relatively free from fear of detection. But in England? Forget it. Of course, the big problem is that people do see man-beasts in the U.K. even though the existence of such things just can't be. So I think that whatever we learn about the Man Monkey, of one thing we can be very certain: the thing is not flesh and blood, whatever it is. It's paranormal."[47]

UFO Trail Signpost in Rendlesham Forest

However, these accounts only show that Bigfoot is one of many oddities in the Hotspots of High Strangeness – which might cast some light on how easily such things seem to intermix, but they still don't really help us understand what Bigfoot's connection with all this is. The following reports get Bigfoot firmly alongside the weirdness.

One of the most remarkable series of accounts emerges from Linda Bradshaw and her family living on a ranch near Sedona, Arizona (the town famous for the sheer number of oddities reported). The accounts of weirdness are as spectacular as you might find at Skinwalker and other sites including, in one afternoon, the family "sighting" four Greys, a herd of invisible pigs and a reptilian.[48] Over a period of time Linda befriended a Bigfoot, "Big Girl," who left drawings in the dirt suggesting a grasp of geometry, mathematics and physics. Not only did they collect hair from Big Girl (a pure white Sasquatch) and her child (a redhead) but they also captured her on video, in a ghostly indistinct form, while filming a UFO.[49] This all led the Bradshaws to suspect she was an interdimensional entity of some sort. It does seem a pity that, with such apparently good evidence, all we seem to get in the book are vague and indistinct photographs...[50]

Equally intriguing are reports from a ranch in Colorado[51]. A series of cattle mutilations was happening in the area and when one was found on the ranch, the boys who found it felt like they were being followed by something. The next morning Bigfoot tracks were found. Twice after that the creatures were spotted and seemed impervious to bullets. Other odd things happened like voices emerging from midair and from radios that weren't switched on. Stranger still were a number of encounters with strange boxes. Previously, a police officer spotted a box with a blinking light on it in a small stand of trees, and when he returned with backup, not only was the box gone but so were the trees. The owner of the ranch, 'Jim', once saw one of the boxes which was buzzing – and then suddenly as they approached "it changed its tone entirely. It sounded like a bunch of angry bees."[52]

Eventually 'Jim' came face to face with his tormentors: they were a fairly average pair of Nordic aliens. The strangest, and most relevant, element of the encounter is that, while they avoided admitting to the cattle mutilations, they did say that they controlled the Bigfoot creatures he had seen. To demonstrate this and how deadly the boxes were, they made a Bigfoot approach one and it keeled over. This case has been thoroughly investigated and the witnesses have been judged to be reliable. What happened to them though is still open to interpretation. However, I won't be offering theories here, just some ways of furthering our understanding of the whole issue.

CONCLUSION

The tide does seem to be turning against the idea that Bigfoot is merely an as yet undiscovered animal, in the same way that the ETH has lost ground in ufology. Curt Sutherly sums up his thoughts on what he calls "para-creatures" which, he suggests, have been the source of our stories of monsters and "were-beasts" over the centuries:

> They sow fear and confusion, and cause havoc wherever they appear. In many cases, they appear in areas frequented by UFOs or odd nocturnal lights, leading some investigators to suspect a connection. Other researchers have gone so far as to suggest that all of those creatures, along with UFOs and similar oddities, are part of a singular global or even cosmic process that we, as humans, barely recognize, let alone understand.[53]

While a conclusion that things are a lot weirder than we might suspect (even if we are actively investigating weirdness) is not unreasonable, it doesn't help explain what is going on. Neither does the fact that more and more researchers are coming to suspect the same thing. We need a way to move the debate forward.

Back to Nick Redfern:

Nick Redfern

> A cryptozoologist has an explanation for why no one has been able to catch elusive creatures like the Loch Ness monster and Bigfoot: Because they're not of this earth. Nick Redfern believes the monsters are not part of the physical world, but instead fall in the paranormal realm…He theorizes cryptozoologists may have to develop new methods of research, similar to the way ghost hunters use infrared photos to detect haunts.[54]

The overarching theme of this piece might help shed some light on the road ahead. The fundamental issue is that our treatment (or, more accurately, mistreatment) of the data is skewing both the conclusions, and even the hypotheses that are being created. The only real way we can move things forward is with an unbiased assessment of the reports and associated phenomena.

As we saw above, 20% of Yowie sightings could be classed as paranormal and, while we don't have similar figures for their relatives, they must be somewhere in that region. This suggests that these elements are not just unusual occurrences, but may be part of the core definition of these big hairy hominoids. The problem is that cryptozoology lacks a framework to examine and classify these occurrences if they work in a purely zoological framework. Luckily, there may be some help from ufology.

In their impressively titled paper "Incommensurability, Orthodoxy and the Physics of High Strangeness: A 6-layer Model for Anomalous Phenomena"[55], Jacques Vallee and Eric Davis discuss the general theories about aliens in general, and UFOs in particular (arising from organizations like SETI as well as ufologists, respectively). They claim that both sides suffer from anthropomorphism and an "assumption of mediocrity," that seems to have partly derailed the debate.

We can see similar things creeping in from the more "respectable", or at least "acceptable," fringes of cryptozoology and it would be right to broaden the scope of inquiry that Vallee and Davis propose to include cryptids. Especially since, as has been shown here, there is no clear dividing line between the two areas – at least not one which doesn't involve some very flimsy assumptions.

Vallee and Davis highlight what they call "anthropomorphic self-selection," in which both the standard ufologist and those in the more sceptical end of the spectrum (like SETI) pre-process the data based on general assumptions stemming from our view of the universe, which by its very nature is rooted in our own humanity. They then propose a six level system designed to examine the underlying properties of the UAP (unidentified aerial phenomena – which they define as stretching from UFOs to religious apparitions, such as those witnessed at Fatima) without imposing any initial assumptions about what these events are.

What is interesting is that Vallee and Davis tend to fall partly into the same trap as the people they criticize. By just focusing on the sky and the UAPs that haunt them, they overlook the rest of the spectrum of high strangeness. This leads them to propose a technological hypothesis as a possible solution (previously Vallee has also suggested it is all part of a control system).

This is a pity as their six level model is flexible enough to cope with the range of Forteana. Most researchers get caught up in Layer I, the physical layer, which deals with the general nature of the encounter. It is Layer II, the anti-physical, which I have attempted to highlight here. This is the area where things start to get weird, and the laws of physics seem to be either ignored or more flexible than we'd like to imagine. Some of the descriptions of phenomena associated with UAP can also apply to the accounts given above, including "sinking into the ground," becoming transparent, and disappearing. Another under-explored area of investigation is Layer IV, the physiological effects. Like Layer II there are similar things reported with Bigfoot (in particular, strange sounds and odours) which might suggest that there is some kind of underlying similarity in what is being reported.

If we are ever to break out of this regime of 'anomaly apartheid', we not only need to examine Layer II and IV phenomena without prejudice, but we also need a cross-disciplinary analysis of them. The evidence suggests that the UFOs and Bigfoot may be less (or more?) real than was suspected a few decades ago. However, they also seem to show an underlying connection, as if they were different expressions of the same force, entity…cosmic brainfart?

Of course, some of the people who make these reports are mad, mistaken or lying (or a mix of three). Jack Lapseritis for one has little credibility amongst the experts – Loren Coleman has said that he "is given no credibility in the ranks of serious cryptozoologists, academic hominologists, or even among most self-styled weekend Bigfoot hunters. He is added to Sasquatch documentaries for comedic relief."[56] However, there are many other sightings along similar lines, and the strange aspects are just too numerous to simply dismiss. Ironically, it is this offhand dismissal that a lot of the researchers have been fighting against themselves.

The thing to bear in mind is that, while a lot of the UFO/Bigfoot accounts are bizarre and contradictory, they are no more so than a lot of other UFO cases, all of which grade into much more straightforward and accepted reports. Equally, the paranormal aspects of Bigfoot are odd, but are also a seamless part of the cryptozoology spectrum. In addition, they also seem to come together in the kind of no-mans-land between the disciplines which one might expect to be empty if more rational explanations applied.

In some ways I am reminded of the analogy of the four blind men describing an elephant by feeling different bits and coming up with different explanations. In a real world example you could imagine three anomaly researchers walking down a forest track out of sight of each other. The ufologist sees a light pass overhead and classifies it as a flying saucer, the cryptozoologist spots a Bigfoot in the woods and notes it down as a cryptid sighting. Meanwhile, an anomalist spots the light land and a Bigfoot emerge and chuckles to himself about how the world is always much stranger than we assume it is.

The Emperor was baptised in the diocese of Jerusalem and the morning after friends "proved" he was the Antichrist, he was nearly killed by two nuns. These facts may not be connected, but what if they are? He has written for *Fortean Times* and a number of British small press magazines and comics. He also blogs at the Cabinet of wonders (www.wunderkabinett.co.uk) and elsewhere. In addition his "Black Hitler" won the Nazisploitation Nanofiction contest.

Enter the
Jaguar

Psychedelics in Ancient Peru

By *Mike Jay*

The monumental ruins of Chavín de Huantar, ten thousand feet up in the Cordillera Blanca of the Peruvian Andes, are, officially, a mystery. The vast, ruined granite and sandstone structures – cyclopean walls, huge sunken plazas and step pyramids – date from around 1000 BC but, although they were refashioned and augmented for close to a thousand years, the evidence for the material culture associated with them is fragmentary at best. Chavín seems to have been neither a city nor a military structure, but a temple complex constructed for unknown ritual purposes by a culture which had vanished long before written sources appeared. Its most striking feature is that its pyramids are hollow, a labyrinth of tunnels connecting hundreds of cramped stone chambers. These might be tombs, but there are no bodies; habitations, but they're arranged in a disorienting layout in pitch blackness; grain stores, but their arrangement is equally impractical. Instead, there are irrigation ducts honeycombed through the carved rock, elaborately channeling a nearby spring through the subterranean maze, and in the centre a megalith set in a vaulted chamber and carved with a swirling, baroque representation of a huge-eyed and jaguar-fanged entity.

The archaeological consensus is that Chavín was some kind of ceremonial focus; some have tentatively located it within a lost tradition of oracles and dream incubation. But the mystery remains profound, and is considerably heightened by the bigger picture that it represents. By most reckonings, and depending on how the term is defined, 'civilization' emerged spontaneously in only a handful of locations around the globe: Mesopotamia, the Indus Valley, China, Mexico, perhaps the Nile. To this short list, especially if civilization is defined in terms of monumental architecture, must now be added Peru. It was only proposed in the 1930s that Chavín is three thousand years old, and it's only recently been recognized that huge ceremonial structures of plazas and pyramids were being constructed in Peru at least a thousand years earlier. The coastal site of Caral, only now being excavated, turns out to contain the oldest stone pyramid thus far discovered, predating those of Old Kingdom Egypt. So the mystery of Chavín is not an isolated one: it was the flowering of a pristine and unique culture, and one which still awaits interpretation.

But there's a salient and largely unexamined feature of the Chavín culture which offers a lead into the heart of the mystery: the presence of a complex of powerful plant hallucinogens in its ritual world. The San Pedro cactus (*Trichocereus/Echinopsis spp.*) is explicitly featured in its iconography; like the Mexican peyote cactus, San Pedro contains mescaline, and is still widely used as a visionary intoxicant in Peru today. Objects excavated from the site also include snuff trays and bone tubes similar to those still used in the Peruvian Amazon for inhaling seeds and barks containing the powerful hallucinogen DMT. The leading Western scholar of the culture, Yale University's Richard Burger – whose *Chavín and the Origins of Andean Civilisation* (Thames & Hudson 1992) is the most authoritative survey of the territory – states plainly enough that "the central role of psychotropic substances at Chavín is amply documented."

It's not special pleading for a drug-centric view of ancient cultures (at least, not necessarily) to observe that the presence of mind-altering plants offers a bridge between remains and ritual, by indicating the state of consciousness in which the latter would have taken place. It also opens up collateral evidence from the deep-rooted traditions of mind-altering plant use which still exist in the region, and from modern understandings of the drugs in question. The combination of mescaline- and DMT-containing plants has been surprisingly little-explored, even in the dedicated fringes of contemporary drug culture, but the preparations in question remain legally obtainable, relatively simple to prepare in high potency doses, and powerfully effective. Such observations may have limited explanatory power, since a state of consciousness is not a belief system and offers little evidence for the content of the ceremonies in which drugs are used. Nevertheless, the effects of these particular drugs set logistical parameters for their use, to which the design of the Chavín complex may have been a practical response.

FISHY BEGINNINGS

For many thousands of years the Pacific coast of Peru has been as it is today: a barren, moonscape desert. Rain never falls except in *El Niño* years; fresh water is only to be found in the few river valleys which punctuate it; for the best part of a thousand miles, rocky shores meet cold ocean in a misty haze. But the harsh terrain has its riches: the Humboldt current, sweeping up from the freezing depths of the southern ocean, is loaded with krill and alive with fish, its biomass a hundred times greater than the balmy Atlantic at the same latitude off Brazil. For ten thousand years a substantial human population has been sustained by this current: rancid industrial fish-meal factories today, but in the Stone Age groups of itinerant hunter-gatherers whose presence is attested by massive shell middens. Some of these hills of organic detritus – oyster shells, cotton twine, dried chillis, crushed bones – are a hundred feet high, and remained in continuous use for five thousand years or more.

It was out of this seasonally nomadic coastal culture, shuttling between the arid coasts and the fertile mountain valleys, that the first monumental sites emerged. Dates are still being revised, but are now firmly set some time before 2000BC. The sites may have been used much earlier as huacas, natural sacred spots, around which ceremonial stone and adobe structures gradually accreted and expanded. Caral, a massive site a hundred miles north of Lima where substantial excavation is finally under way, is perhaps an example of this process. Its sprawling complex of dusty mounds centers on a megalith, perhaps originally upended into the valley by an earthquake; from the vantage point of this stone, the most ancient pyramid precisely mirrors the peak of the mountain which towers over it, suggesting that the megalith may have been the original focus for this alignment. The pyramids, at Caral as elsewhere, seem to have begun as raised platforms for fire-pits, which were subsequently extended upward in layers as the site grew to accomodate increasing human traffic. Below Caral's pyramids is another feature which would endure for millennia and spread from the coast to the high mountains: a sunken circular plaza, large enough for a gathering of several hundred participants, with steps leading up to the platform of the pyramid above.

This plaza-and-pyramid layout, reproduced in dozens of sites spanning hundreds of miles and thousands of years, seems to have evolved for a ceremonial purpose, but there's still little consensus about what this might have entailed. Beyond the general problem of reconstructing systems of meaning and belief from stone, these early sites are sparse in cultural materials. Graves are few, and simple; the early monumental building predates the firing of pottery (hence the archaeological term for the era, 'Preceramic'). There's little general evidence of human habitation, although there are some chambers in the Caral pyramids which may have housed those who attended the site. Some scholars have sought to cast these as a 'priestly elite', the ruling caste of a stratified society, but they may equally have been no more than a class of specialist functionaries without particularly exalted status in the community. Certainly a site like Caral would have been no prize residence: it's not a palace at the centre of a subjugated settlement, so much as a monastic perch on its desolate fringes. Its barren, windswept desert setting overlooks a fertile valley, taking up none of the precious irrigated terrain.

The size of the complex suggests that the fertile valley attracted visitors, and that Caral was a site of pilgrimage for more than its local community. The earliest agriculture on the coast emerged in such valleys, especially cotton and gourds, which were used for making fishing nets and floats: it may be, therefore, that the ceremonial site grew in size as the use of these cultivated commodities spread ever more widely through the loose network of fishing communities up and down the coast. This would suggest a very different picture from the one presented by better-known pristine civilizations, such as Mesopotamia or the Indus Valley, where archaeologists have tended to associate the origins of monumental architecture with the control of complex power relations – a centralized state, coercive labour, irrigation systems, a powerful priestcraft or military might. Peru seems to tell a rather different story: one of structures emerging largely unplanned, piecemeal and over generations, within a shifting, stateless network of hunter-gatherers.

A further clue to the culture of these Preceramic coastal sites is provided by Sechin, a complex a few centuries later than Caral (around 1700 BC) and couple of river valleys to the north. Here, for the first time, the temple is adorned with figurative carvings. But if these are a clue, they're an oblique one: graphic but inscrutable representations carved in relief on stone blocks. Most are of human forms, some of them dismembered, but their most distinctive motif is wavy trail lines, often ending in finger-like tips, emanating from various parts of the bodies. Some of these seem to be intestines, and some emerge from the mouths of the carvings, but others coil from heads, hands and ears, suggesting they aren't literal representations of blood, guts or bodily fluids. Their significance remains disputed. Early interpretations of them tended to claim that they were savage warrior figures commemorating tribal battles, victories and annihilated populations, but many of the figures are hard to fit into such a scheme. Recent interpretations, by contrast, have tended to focus on visionary, perhaps shamanic states, just as the Palaeolithic cave art of Europe is now increasingly interpreted not as realistic representations of 'hunting scenes' but of an imaginal dreamtime previously visited in a heightened state of consciousness – see, for example, David Lewis-Williams' *The Mind in the Cave* (Thames & Hudson 2002). Within this reading, the numinous swirls and haloes would commemorate not military victories but the mysteries which the ceremony at Sechin engendered.

There's circumstantial evidence for interpolating the use of plant drugs into this ceremonial world. Part of this comes from Chavín, where the same structures would emerge later with images of these plants explicitly represented. Part of it comes from nearby archaeological finds of chewed coca leaf quids and rolls of plant material which may be cored, skinned and dried San Pedro cactus. The coca, along with other plant remains, implies a trade network which connected the coast and the mountains – a symbiosis which would later characterize the Chavín culture. Coca doesn't grow on the coast, but at an altitude of 1000-2000m up the mountain valleys; San Pedro begins to colonize the steep mountain cliffs at the upper

San Pedro Cactus (© Mike Jay)

end of this belt, continuing up to 3000m. Given that more bulky mountain plant foodstuffs were being supplied to the barren desert coast two or three days' journey away, and dried and salted fish traded in return, fresh or dried San Pedro could have been brought down in quantity, as it still is today.

Chavín culture, when it emerged, would testify to the existence of such cross-cultural contact, and more besides. Yet Chavín wasn't the first ceremonial centre in the mountains. The Preceramic site of Kotosh, a hundred miles away across the inland ranges, dates from a similar period to Sechin, and its remains show similar structures: altar-like platforms around stone-enclosed fire pits, stacked on top of each other through several layers of occupation. One gnomic Preceramic symbol also survives: a moulded mud-brick relief of a pair of crossed hands, now housed in the national museum in Lima. Centuries before Chavín, perhaps as early as 2000BC, Kotosh demonstrates that trade links between the mountains and the coast had also generated some commonality of worship.

THE LABYRINTH AND THE LANZON

The emergence of Chavín as a ceremonial centre, probably around 900BC, adds much to this earlier picture: it's more complex in construction than its predecessors, and far richer in symbolic art. It's set not on a peak or commanding ridge, but in the narrow valley of the Mosna river, at the junction of a tributary, with mountains rising up steeply to enclose it on all sides. Similarly, the temple structure itself isn't designed to be spectacular or visible from a distance, but is concealed from all sides behind high walls. The approach to the site would have been through a narrow ramped entrance in these walls, whose distinctive feature was that they were studded with gargoyle-like, life-size heads: some human, some distinctly feline with exaggerated jaws and sprouting canine teeth, and some – often covered in swirling patterns – in the process of transforming from one state to the other. This process of transformation is clearly a physical ordeal: the shapeshifting heads grimace, teeth exposed in rictus grins. In a specific and recurrent detail, mucus emanates in streams from their noses.

Inside these walls – now mostly crumbled, and with the majority of the heads housed in the on-site museum – there are still substantial remains of a ceremonial complex which was reworked and expanded for nearly a thousand years, its last and largest elements dating to around 200BC. The basic arrangement is the traditional one of plaza and step pyramid, but these are adorned with far more complexity than their predecessors. Many lintels, columns and stelae are covered with relief carvings, swirling motifs featuring feline jaws, eyes and wings. The initial impression is amorphous and chaotic, but on closer inspection these motifs unfurl into composite images, their interleaved elements in different scales and dimensions, the whole often representing some chimerical entity composed of smaller-scale entities roiling inside it. As the architecture develops through the centuries it becomes larger in scale, reflecting the increased scale of the site; at the same time, the reliefs gradually become less figurative and more abstract, discrete entities melting into a mosaic of stylized patterns and flourishes.

It was only in 1972 that the most striking of these reliefs were uncovered, on faced slabs which line the oldest of the sunken plazas, running like a frieze around its circle at knee height. These figures are presumably from the site's formative period; the most remarkable is a human figure in a state of feline transformation, bristling with jaws, claws and snakes, and clutching an unmistakable San Pedro cactus like a staff or spear. Beneath this figure – the 'Chaman', as he's become informally known – runs a procession of jaguars carved in swirling lines, with other creatures, birds of prey and snakes, sometimes incorporated into the whorls of their tails.

These reliefs are all carved in profile, and all face towards the steps which lead up from the circular plaza to the old pyramid, at the top of which is the familiar altar-like platform. But at the back of this platform is something entirely unfamiliar: a pair of stone doorways disappearing into the darkness inside the pyramid itself. These lead via steps down into tunnels around six foot high and constructed, rather like Bronze Age long barrows, from huge granite slabs and lintels. The tunnels take sharp, maze-like, usually right-angled turns, apparently designed to disorient and cut out the daylight, zig-zagging into pitch blackness. Opening out from these subterranean corridors are dozens of rock-hewn side chambers, some large enough for half a dozen people, others seemingly for solitary confinement. There are niches hacked in some of the chamber walls which might have housed oil lamps, and lintels which extrude like hammock pegs. Running through the bewildering network of tunnels and chambers are smaller shafts, some of them air vents, others water ducts which allowed the nearby spring to gush and echo through this elaborately constructed underworld.

Right in the heart of the labyrinth is a stela carved in the early Chavín style, a clawed, fanged and rolling-eyed humanoid form,

boxed inside a cramped cruciform chamber which rises to the top of
the pyramid. The loose arrangement of stones in the roof above, which
form a plug at the crown of the pyramid, have led to speculation that
they might have been removable, allowing the Lanzon, as the carved
stela is known, to point up like a needle to a gap of exposed sky. Other
fragments of evidence from the site, such as a large boulder with
seven sunken pits in the configuration of the Pleiades, suggest that
an element of the Chavín ritual – perhaps, given the narrow confines
around the Lanzon, a priestly rather than a public one – might have
involved aligning the stela with astronomical events.

This plaza and pyramid complex was Chavín's original structure,
but over the centuries more and grander variants were added. There
are several shafts, some still unexcavated, which lead down into larger
underground complexes, their stonework more regular than the old
pyramid and their side-chambers typically more spacious. There is a
far larger sunken plaza, too, square rather than circular and leading
up to a new pyramid and surrounding walls on a more massive
scale. Whatever happened at Chavín, the architecture suggests that
it carried on happening for centuries, and for an increasing volume
of participants.

Technologies of Transformation

The term most commonly applied to what went on at Chavín is 'cult',
although elements of meaning might perhaps be imported from other
terms like pilgrimage destination, sacred site, oracle or, in its classical
sense, temple of mysteries. This is a conclusion partly drawn from
the lack of evidence that it represented an empire, or a state power:
there are no military structures associated with it, nor centralized
labour for major public works like irrigation or housing. During the
several centuries of its existence, tribal networks would have risen and
fallen around it, changes in the balance of power apparently leaving

its source of authority untouched. Its cultic – or cultural – influence, though, spread far and wide. Throughout the first millennium BC, 'Chavínoid' sites spread across large swathes of northern Peru, and pre-existing natural *huacas* began to develop Chavín-style flourishes: rock surfaces carved with snaky fangs and jaws, standing stones decorated with bug-eyed, fierce-toothed humanoid forms. People were clearly coming to

Chavinoid Stela (© Mike Jay)

Chavín from considerable distances, and carrying its influence back to far-flung valleys, mountains and coasts.

Was Chavín, then, a religion? There's been some speculation that the carvings on the site represent a 'Chavín cosmology', with eagle, snake and jaguar corresponding to earth and sky and so forth, and the humanoid shapeshifter, as represented on the Lanzon, a 'supreme deity'. But Chavín was not a power base which could coerce its subjects to replace their religion with its own: the spread of its influence indicates that it drew its devotees from a wide range of tribal belief systems with which it existed in parallel. It's perhaps better understood as a site which offered an experience rather than a cosmology or creed, with its architecture conceived and designed as the locus for a particular ritual journey. In this sense, the Chavín figures would not have been deities competing with those of the participants, but graphic representations of the process which took place inside its walls.

The central motif of this process is signalled clearly enough by the shapeshifting feline heads which studded its portals: transformation from the human state into something else. It's here that Chavin displays the influence of a new cultural element not conspicuous in the sites which preceded it. The prominence of the jaguar and shapeshifting motifs suggest the intertwining of traditions not just from the coast and the mountains, but also from the jungle on the far side of the Andes. While the monumental style of Chavín's architecture builds on earlier coastal models, its symbolism points towards the feline transformations which still chararacterize many Amazon shamanisms. The trading networks on the Pacific coast had long ago joined with those in the mountains; at Chavín, where the river Mosna runs east into the Rio Marañon and thence into the Amazon, it seems that these networks had also reached down the humid eastern Andean slopes into the jungle, and had transmitted the influence of another hunter-gatherer culture: one characterized by powerful shamanic technologies of transformation, in many cases with the use of plant hallucinogens.

These twin influences – the coastal mountains and the jungle – are mirrored by the presence at Chavín not of one hallucinogenic plant but two. The San Pedro cactus, as depicted on the wall of Chavín's old plaza, may have been an element of the earlier coastal tradition, but is in any case native to Chavín's high valley: a magnificent specimen, which must be at least 200 years old, towers over the site today. Local villages still plant hedges with it, and traders to the *curandero* markets down in the coastal cities still source it from the area. But the mucus pouring from the noses of the carved heads, combined with material finds of bone sniffing tubes and snuff trays, all point with equal clarity to the use at Chavín of plants containing a second drug, DMT, and a tradition with a different source: the Amazon jungle.

Today, the best-known ethnographic use of DMT-containing snuffs is among the Yanomami people of the Amazon, who traditionally blow powdered Virola tree bark resin up each others' noses with six-foot blowpipes, a practice which produces a short and intense hallucinatory burst accompanied by spectacular streams of mucus. But there are various other DMT-containing snuffs used in the region, including the powdered seeds of the tree *Anadenanthera colubrina*, whose distribution – and its artistic depiction in later Andean cultures – makes it the most likely ingredient in the Chavín brew. *Anadenanthera*-snuffing has been largely replaced in many areas of the Amazon by *ayahuasca*-drinking, a more manageable technique of DMT ingestion, but this displacement is a recent one, and *Anadenanthera* is still used by some tribal groups in the remote forest around the borders of Peru, Colombia and Brazil. Even today, the tree grows up the Amazonian slopes of the eastern Andes and as far west as the highlands around Kotosh. The transformation offered at Chavín was, it seems, mediated by the combination of these two extremely potent psychedelics.

The presence of these two plants at Chavín, without necessarily illuminating the purpose or content of the rituals, has certain implications. The effects and duration of San Pedro and *Anadenanthera* are very distinct from one another, and characterized by quite different ritual uses. San Pedro, boiled, stewed and drunk, can take an hour or more before the effects are felt; once they appear, they last for at least ten. The physical sensation is euphoric, languid, expansive, often with some accompanying nausea; in many Indian traditions, such effects are dealt with by setting the participants to slow, shuffling three-step dances and chants. The effect on consciousness is similarly fluid and oceanic, including visual trails and a heightened sense of presence: the swirling lines which surround the figures at Sechin could perhaps be read as visual representations of this sense of energy projecting itself from the body – particularly from the swirling, psychedelicized intestines – into an immanent spirit world.

Anadenanthera, by contrast, is a short sharp shock, and one that's powerfully potentiated by a prior dose of San Pedro. About a gramme of powdered seed needs to be snuffed, enough to pack both nostrils. This process rapidly elicits a burning sensation, extreme nausea and often convulsive vomiting, the production of gouts of nasal mucus and perhaps half an hour of exquisite visions, often accompanied by physical contortions, growls and grimaces which are typically understood in Amazon cultures as feline transformations. Unlike San Pedro, which can be taken communally, the physical ordeal of *Anadenanthera* tends to make it a solitary one, the subject hunched in a ball, eyes closed, absorbed in an interior world. This interior world is perhaps recognizable in the new decorative elements which emerge at Chavín. Images like the spectacular glyph that covers the Raimundi stela – a human figure which seems to be flowering into other dimensions and sprouting an elaborate headdress of multiple eyes and fangs – are reminiscent not just of *ayahuasca* art in the Amazon today but also of the fractal, computer-generated visual work associated with DMT in modern Western subcultures.

The distinct effects of these two drugs suggests a functional division between two elements or phases of the ritual which is mirrored in Chavín's contrasting architectural elements. Like the *kiva* in Southwestern Native American architecture which it so closely resembles, the circular plaza is readily interpreted as a communal space, used for gathering and mingling, and thus perhaps for dancing and chanting through a long ritual accompanied by group intoxication with San Pedro: it may be that the cactus was already a traditional element of the coastal ceremonies where the form of the plaza originated. The innovative addition of chambers inside the pyramid, by contrast, seems designed for the absorption in an interior world engendered by *Anadenanthera*, an incubation where the subject is transformed and reborn in the womb of darkness.

ARCHITECTURAL ENHANCEMENT

Chavín's architecture, in this sense, can be understood as a visionary technology, designed to externalize and intensify these intoxications and to focus them into a particular inner journey. This in turn offers an explanation for why so many might have made such long and arduous pilgrimages to its ceremonies. It wasn't necessary to visit Chavín simply to obtain San Pedro or *Anadenanthera*. Both grow wild in abundance in the Andes; there could hardly have been, as in some cultures ancient and modern, a priestly monopoly on their use. Those who came to Chavín weren't coerced into doing so; it drew participants from a wide area over which it exercised no political or military control. The Chavín ceremony, rather, would have offered a ritual on a spectacular scale, where the effects of the plants could be experienced *en masse* within an architecture designed to enhance and direct them.

Within this environment, participants could congregate to enter a shared otherworld, and also submit themselves to a highly charged individual vision quest. The sunken plaza might, as the reliefs suggest, have harnessed the heightened consciousness of San Pedro to a mass ritual of dancing and chanting; the participants might subsequently have ascended the temple steps individually to receive a further sacrament of powdered *Anadenanthera* seeds administered to them by the priests via bone snuffing tubes. As this was taking hold, they would be led into the chambers within the pyramid where they could experience their DMT-enhanced visions in solitary darkness. Here, the amplified rushing of water and the growls and roars of the unseen participants around them would enclose them in a supernatural world, one where ordinary consciousness could be abandoned, the body itself metamorphosed and the world seen from an enhanced, superhuman perspective – analogous, perhaps, to the uncanny night vision of the feline predator. The development of the subterranean chambers over centuries would reflect the logistical demands of ever greater numbers of participants willing to enter the jaguar portal and submit themselves to a life-changing ordeal that offered a glimpse of the eternal world beyond the human.

So Chavín remains a mystery, but perhaps in a more specific sense. If we want an analogy for its function drawn from Western culture, it might be the Eleusinian Mysteries, originating as they did in subterranean chambers near Athens a little later than Chavín, around 700BC. Like Chavín, Eleusis persisted for nearly a thousand years, under different empires, in its case Greek and Roman; like Chavín – and like the Hajj at Mecca today – it was a pilgrimage site which drew its participants from a diverse network of cultures spanning virtually the known world. Classical written sources attest to some of the exterior details of the Eleusinian mysteries: its seasonal calendar, its processions, the ritual fasting and the breaking of the fast with a sacred plant potion, the *kykeon*. But over the thousand years that these mysteries endured, the deepest secrets of Eleusis – the visions that were revealed by the priestesses in the chambers in the bowels of the earth – were never revealed, protected under penalty of death. At Chavín the only surviving records are the stones of the site itself, but the mystery is perhaps of the same order.

Mike Jay is the author of *Emperors of Dreams: Drugs in the Nineteenth Century*. His most recent book is *The Air Loom Gang: The Strange and True Story of James Tilly Matthews and his Visionary Madness* (Bantam Press, 2003).

The Beatific

VISION

Evidence for an afterlife from the moment of death

By *Michael Grosso*

n 1878, Edward H. Clarke, M.D., published *Visions: A Study of False Sight*. It contains, as far as I know, one of the earliest discussions of visions of the dying. "There is scarcely a family in the land, some one of whose members has not died with a glorious expression on the features, or exclamation on the lips, which, to the standers by, was a token of beatific vision. History is full of the detailed accounts of the deathbeds of great men, warriors, statesmen, martyrs, confessors, monarchs, enthusiasts, and others, to whom, at the moment of death, visions of congenial spirits, or of heavenly glories were granted."

Consider a story that a college professor told me in September 2001: "I had never thought much about life after death until an experience

I had some years ago. I was living in a two family house when my landlady took ill. It's important to emphasize that this woman was extremely unpleasant with me. She lived alone and generally gave the impression of being almost always angry and complaining. Her condition rapidly got worse. On the night of her death I was the only person present in the house with her. Toward evening, I witnessed something that to date sends shivers running up and down my spine. Suddenly, my landlady looked up at the ceiling and began to talk to what seemed like several different people."

"She continued like this for an hour or so; at one point, she turned toward me, and gently asked: 'Have we been fighting?' What shocked me, and made me tremble like a leaf, was that this woman, whom I had known only for a few months and never saw smile, suddenly looked at least twenty years younger. She literally *glowed* with health, warmth and joy. Something she saw just before she died completely transformed her. I'll never forget this till my dying day."

I See Dead People

The first attempts to compile critical reports of deathbed visions were produced early in the twentieth century. Italian parapsychologist Ernesto Bozzano was the first to notice that dying people mainly see visions of dead folk.[1] He reasoned that if such visions were merely subjective hallucinations produced by dying brains, why not see living as well as dead people? They see people until that moment forgotten, one not especially dear, or even somebody not known to be dead, but almost invariably the dying see visions of the dead.

Deathbed visions are noted for the sudden elevations of mood they induce and the occasional *shared* vision. (See the account that follows shortly of Walt Whitman's apparition.) Nobel Prize-winning physiologist, Charles Richet, a nonbeliever in post-mortem survival, said this about deathbed visions: "Among all the facts adduced to prove survival, these seem to me to be the most disquieting, that is, from a materialistic point of view."[2]

British physicist Sir William Barrett wrote a book on deathbed visions. Barrett, one of the founders of psychical research, submitted a paper in 1876 to the British Association for the Advancement of Science on his experiments in telepathy. At first rejected, the paper was later accepted, thanks to the intervention of Alfred Russel Wallace, the great naturalist and coworker of Charles Darwin. Barrett collaborated with his wife, Lady Florence Barrett, a nurse and obstetric surgeon, on his book about deathbed visions. Lady Barrett's introduction states that her husband also noticed what Bozzano had: The dying consistently see apparitions of the dead who come to take them away.

Sometimes they see people they didn't know had recently died. An anonymous vicar wrote: "On November 2nd and 3rd, I lost my two eldest boys, David Edward and Harry, from scarlet fever, they being three and four years old respectively. Harry died at Abbot's Langley on November 2nd, fourteen miles from my vicarage at Aspley, David the following day at Aspley. About an hour before the death of this latter child he sat up, and pointing to the bottom of the bed said distinctly, 'There is little Harry calling me.'"[3] The nurse also heard the child say this. The vicar stated that he took care not to let David know of his brother's death. The puzzle here is why David saw his brother Harry, about whose death he knew nothing.

In a book called *The Peak in Darien* by Frances Cobbe, we read: "A dying lady, exhibiting the aspect of joyful surprise, spoke of seeing, one after another, three of her brothers who had been long dead, and then apparently recognized last of all a fourth brother, who was believed by the bystanders to be still living in India." A while later the family received letters from India announcing the death of the brother, which occurred before his sister's deathbed vision. Everything looks as if the fourth brother died, joined his three dead brothers, and that all together they escorted their dying sister into the next world.

The circumstances for "Peak in Darien" cases are rare, but reports continue. In a 1982 George Gallup Jr. book on death experiences we read: "...a woman who was in the last seconds of life looked up and in the presence of witnesses said, 'there's Bill,' and then she passed away. As it happened, Bill was her brother and he had died just the week before – but she had never been informed of his death."[4]

In reading accounts of deathbed visions, I'm struck by a difference between the twenty-first-century way of dying, which is hospital-centered, and that of the late nineteenth century, which was home- and family-centered. Narratives were then set in the home of the dying person, with family members, physicians, and ministers all present, gathered in a quiet, solemn mood. Opportunities for having, noting, and recording these phenomena surely were greater then than they are now. Our more efficient, but less human, style of dying in high-tech hospitals may be cheating us of deeply enriching experiences.

Sharing the Experience

Doubters will dismiss deathbed visions as a form of denial or wish fulfillment. But what if more than one person perceives the vision? It would be cavalier to dismiss these stories as mere illusion.

Horace Traubel was a poet, a friend and disciple of Walt Whitman. Mrs. Flora McDonald Dension was present at Traubel's death in 1919, and reported:

> All day on August 28th, Horace was very low spirited...Mildred was with him a good deal and we decided not to leave him a minute. He had been brought in from the veranda and on seeing me, he called out, "Look, look, Flora, quick, quick, he is going."
>
> "What, Horace," I said, "what do you see?"

"Why just over the rock, Walt appeared, head and shoulders and hat on in a golden glory – brilliant and splendid…I heard his voice but did not understand all he said, only 'Come on.'"

After the vision, Traubel's mood soared but soon sank again. Several days passed. "On the night of September 3rd Horace was very low. I stayed for a few hours with him. Once his eyes rolled. I thought he was dying, but he just wanted me to turn him. As I did so, he listened and seemed to hear something. Then he said: 'I hear Walt's voice; he is talking to me…Walt says, 'Come on, come on.'"[5]

Especially intriguing is what Dension adds:

Colonel Cosgrave had been with Horace in the afternoon and had seen Walt on the opposite side of the bed, and felt his presence. Then Walt passed through the bed and touched the Colonel's hand, which was in his pocket. The contact was like an electric shock. Horace was also aware of Walt's presence and said so.

Cosgrave gave written testimony of his remarkable experience. The vision of Whitman not only elevated the dying Traubel's mood but also made itself visible *and tangible* to another witness. Cases like this pop up in the *Census of Hallucinations*; a deceased person appears to different people through different senses.

The Elation of Death

In 1961, Karlis Osis of the American Society for Psychical Research undertook a scientific study of deathbed visions.[6] Osis reasoned that a more objective way to study deathbed visions would be to obtain descriptions of them from medical professionals. He sent a detailed questionnaire to 5000 physicians and 5000 nurses; he received in return 640. This was followed by telephone interviews and written correspondence. Nurses, by the way, turned in three times the observations that physicians did.

The questionnaire was designed to find out what caused the experiences. Were there cultural (religious beliefs), psychological (expectation), or medical factors (drugs) causing patients' visions? Or did they occur independently of such factors, thus suggesting an *external source*? As usual, the method is to try to infer the best explanation of the phenomenon.

Fear apparently is not the main emotion at the time of death; indifference is more common. What was surprising was the number of terminal patients becoming *elated* at the hour of death. The exaltation of dying persons is often observed to occur suddenly; the external behavior of the dying person clearly suggests they have *seen* something. This sudden elation is unlike drug-induced euphoria. One physician commented: "There is such a resigned, peaceful, almost happy expression which comes over the patient – it is hard to explain but it leaves me with the feeling that I would not be afraid to die."[7]

The data showed a strong relationship between deathbed elation and religious belief. There are two ways you can interpret this. Religious belief may cause the hallucination or sensitize the patient to transcendent experiences. Other puzzling observations: Some patients display "extreme strength just before death," and two patients, a schizophrenic, the other senile, recovered their normal mental functions just before death. This is a classic anomaly, not easy to explain in terms of the prevailing medical paradigm.

Osis harvested 884 cases of dying people who had visionary experiences. What did all this data tell him? Were there discernible trends pointing toward destruction or toward the afterlife? First of all, this work confirmed earlier findings. Dying people mainly hallucinate the dead. In other types of hallucination, the living, not just the dead, are "seen." The young – not just the old – hallucinate the dead. The dying hallucinate close relatives, a fact consistent with the afterlife hypothesis. Close relatives, if they 'survived', would be motivated to visit the dying. (In nondeathbed hallucinations, close relatives are *not* typically seen.)

Patients who saw deathbed figures perceived their surroundings in a normal way. Again, this differs from psychotic hallucinations where patients see their surroundings as distorted. Deathbed visions have a clear purpose: It is to take the dying person to another world. Traubel sees Walt Whitman, who keeps saying, "Come on, come on."

Osis found four cases where the apparitions were collectively perceived. Could these visions be explained by disease, toxicity, or pharmaceutical intervention? Nothing in the data supports these explanations. No correlation between deathbed visions and being medicated or delirious was found, and in fact sedatives were found to *suppress* deathbed visions. An intact consciousness is best for having a deathbed vision. "Deathbed patients see apparitions more often when fully conscious and having proper awareness and capability of responding to their environment." In other words, the patient's consciousness is not impaired at the moment of having the vision.

Could the visions reflect a superstitious lack of education? It turns out that the majority of dying visionaries were educated. Another finding was that "...calm and radiant peace emerge in the death situation without any apparent external cause." The immediate impression, especially when the patient suddenly gazes fixedly, rapturously, at a specific spot in the room, is that the exaltation is externally caused. According to Osis, this unexplained elation confirms the afterlife hypothesis.

Not a Soothing Illusion

In 1977, Osis and Icelandic psychologist Erlendur Haraldsson published a *cross-cultural* study of deathbed visions.[8] They compared deathbed observations of Indian and American medical professionals, and sought to determine whether the visions depended on cultural, medical, and psychological influences. For the most part, this new survey confirmed the earlier work, adding new observations to an already strange picture.

In one case, a frightened four-year-old girl was admitted to a hospital in Delhi; for three days a god was loudly telling her she was about to die. Physicians examined her and found her in perfect health. The girl stared fixedly at something invisible, shouting, "God is calling and I am going to die," so the distraught parents left her in the hospital for observation. The following day she died from circulatory collapse without apparent cause.

Could this have been caused by autosuggestion? The girl may have come to believe she was going to die, and died as a result of autosuggestion. Physiologist Walter Cannon studied cases of voodoo death, and found that some people, in perfect health, who believe they're under a spell, can indeed die by autosuggestion.[9] So it is physiologically possible; however, the Hindu child wasn't under any spell, and no one planted the idea of death in her head. Nor is there any explanation of why she might have planted the expectation herself.

Most reported visions dispel fear and facilitate dying. But what of visions that call (Whitman's "come on!") but cause fear and exacerbate dying? These are the "no-consent" cases. No-consent cases strengthen the impression that the caller is external, not part of the dying patient's subconscious fantasy life. For example, a nineteen-year-old woman saw her father coming to take her away, but she was terrified. "Edna, hold me tight," she said to the nurse, and died in her arms.

This brings us to how Indian and American samples differ. Indians seem less inclined to go gentle into the night; the afterlife retains its frightful side; Americans seem less cowed by fantasies of hell and the devil. There is another difference. Along with the usual deceased relatives, gods and goddesses show up more frequently in Indian deathbed visions. Hindu visions include nasty *Yamdoots*, angels of death who terrify and rudely drag the dying person away. These invasive *Yamdoot* epiphanies certainly look as if they're coming  from an external agent. I thought the Freudian id was supposed to shower us with soothing illusions of uterine bliss? Consider this laconic report. A young college-educated Indian is recovering from mastoiditis; he and his doctor expect prompt recovery: "He was going to be discharged that day. Suddenly, at 5 a.m., he shouted: 'Somebody is standing here, dressed in white clothes. I will not go with you!' He was dead in ten minutes." That was not a soothing illusion.

Osis and Haraldsson used a model to interpret their data. Are deathbed visions consistent with an afterlife – or with destruction of the personality? The trend of the data supports survival, according to the researchers. It showed that visions of the dying are consistent with the way ESP works, but not with the way malfunctioning brains work; the visions did not correlate with hallucinogenic or other medical factors; they were coherent, not confused or jumbled; they occurred in clear consciousness and sometimes independently of expectation; and they showed little variability. Whereas, if the data were pointing to destruction, we should see clear evidence of subjective influence. The experiencer's belief-system would stick out like a sore thumb.

This last is key to the whole model. The more variability, the more likely you have subjective and cultural differences shaping the experience. If, on the other hand, the visions show few variations, and aren't shaped by age, sex, brain malfunction, drugs, and culture, it would say something positive about their autonomous status.

I agree that it's suggestive when the "apparitions show a purpose of their own, contradicting the intentions of the patients." More telling is when they contradict the medical prognosis. "Especially dramatic were apparitions that called a patient for transition to the other world, and the patient, not willing to go, cried out for help or tried to hide. Fifty-four of these 'no-consent' cases were observed, nearly all in India. Such cases are not easily seen as wish-fulfillment, and they are even more impressive when the apparitions' prediction of death was not only correct but contradictory to the medical prognosis of recovery." No-consent cases, occurring in unimpaired consciousness, point to external causes.

Anomalous Deathbed Recoveries

Philosopher Paul Edwards thinks that diseases of aging brains like Alzheimer's and dementia testify against consciousness surviving death.[10] They seem to prove that consciousness is hopelessly wed to the brain. As the brain decays, it appears, mental function decays in tandem. Once our brains are destroyed by death, could there be anything left of us to survive?

Many of us know from experience how people, sometimes our parents or grandparents, begin to lose their memories. We can see how the personality is gradually lost, until the day comes when your own mother or father no longer recognize you.

"Mom," I used to say to my mother, "it's me, Michael, your son." She'd look straight into my eyes, and turn away without recognizing me. Isn't this a sign of irreparable loss? Unmistakable proof of the victorious onset of death?

Perhaps. On the other hand, there remains an unanswered question: Were my mother's lost memories destroyed forever by her malfunctioning brain, or have they become temporarily, not irreversibly, inaccessible? As it turns out, there is evidence of the latter, reports of brain-impaired people who recover their memories, and other mental functions, hours or sometimes moments before they expire. These reports suggest that memories aren't annihilated by brain disease, but put out of commission, temporarily out of reach. The radio on your kitchen table is broken, but radio waves still flood the atmosphere.

A pioneer study of hallucinations states: "...at the approach of death we observe that the senses acquire a wonderful degree of sensitivity. The patients astonish those who are around them by the elevation of their thoughts, and the intellect, which may have been obscured or extinguished during many years, is again restored to all its integrity."[11]

There are contemporary reports of this. A patient with meningitis, after a deathbed vision, recovered the use of his mind and body. Osis also mentioned two sudden recovery cases, a schizophrenic and a victim of dementia. In a personal communication, philosopher Jean Houston described her grandmother before she died. The demented grandmother no longer recognized family members; but before she died she became mentally clear and spoke coherently in Italian (her native tongue), recognized Jean Houston, and addressed her by name.

A nurse, C.X., working with dying patients in a New Jersey hospital, responded to my questions about deathbed mental recoveries. "A 92-year-old woman had been diagnosed with Alzheimer's for nine years. She no longer recognized her son, daughter-in-law or grandchildren. She believed that people were coming to her home at night, knocking over chairs and lamps. In reality, she was doing it. Twenty-four hours before she died, she recognized her family members. She also knew where she was and how old she was, which she had not known for many years."

C.X. sent me observations on other cases, in which dying patients recovered lost mental functions. "A male resident had been on the unit for five years. Had to be fed by staff. Would call out obscenities linked to his wife's name, although wife visited daily. Wife informed staff that her relationship with her husband was a loving one, and that he never swore at her. Resident never regained awareness of surroundings or family members. Apart from tactile stimuli, the patient sank deeper and deeper into unresponsiveness. On the night before he died, his wife stated: 'He was more alert and he recognized me. He smiled, squeezed my hand and when I kissed him goodnight, my husband turned his head toward me and his lips touched my face.' Resident's sister-in-law was present and verified wife's statement."

These and similar observations weaken the force of one argument against life after death. It is true that if a person has brain disease, mental abilities are lost, but whether the losses are absolute and substantial, or temporary and functional, remains an open question, along with the question of life after death.

Michael Grosso is a teacher, author, and painter, whose interests span psychical research, metaphysical art, the parapsychology of religion, and, primarily, philosophy. He received his Ph.D. in philosophy, and studied classical Greek, at Columbia University. He has published books on topics ranging from life after death to the mythologies of endtime. Michael's most recent book is *Experiencing the Next World Now*, which surveys the evidence for life after death and shows how personal experience can convince you it is real. More information and some of his writings can be found at his website, www.parapsi.com.

This article is a modified excerpt from Michael's book *Experiencing the Next World Now* (Paraview Pocket Books, 2004), reprinted with permission.

Were the
UFO Contactees
RITUAL MAGICIANS?

Someone opened a door
and
something flew in...

by *Adam Gorightly*

 letter I wrote to a respected UFO researcher, some two decades ago:

12-12-86
Dear Ms. Jenny Randles,

I would like to relate an experience that happened to myself and a colleague in 1979 in Fresno, CA. Let me preface this statement by saying that we were under the influence of the hallucinogenic drug, LSD. But hear me out: these are not the ravings of a drug-saturated fruitcake; I am not an habitual drug user, nor have I used LSD for several years. But to deny that I was not under its influence when this incident occurred would be to give an incomplete account of what transpired on that fateful night.

On the night in question – fully under the influence of said drug – we observed several 'flying saucers', in several shapes, sizes and multicolored variations. I am not denying that what we saw were hallucinations, but if they were, then they were 'dual hallucinations', for we both saw the same sights and sounds.

Now, a brief description of this event: The sighting occurred along a levee located in a residential section of town. Before we arrived at the levee (we were on foot) we joked to ourselves about how we might see a UFO during our little 'trip'. We laughed to ourselves (somewhat uncontrollably) how no one would ever believe us due to the condition we were in. Anyway, after walking a short time on the levee, we saw our first 'UFO'. The sight of this made me fall to one knee and we were both astounded by its sight. During the course of the night we saw several, anywhere from six to eight. One was cigar shaped, some saucer shaped, one with a multi-colored propeller. This all occurred in the span of not more than an hour and a half, I think, though the passing of time was hard to estimate due to the effects of the drug.

The last one we saw appeared like a falling star in the sky that seemed to stop in mid-descent, then turned into a space ship, or whatever it was. After the sighting of this 'UFO' we turned around and headed back, the way we came.

Now I realize the descriptions I am giving are sketchy, but in retrospect it seemed almost like a dream, everything happening so fast. If I were to describe every little detail, I'd be here all night. So I'll try to wrap it up and sum up the experience in a few more words.

When we arrived back at the point where we saw the first UFO, a beam of light shot down directly in front of us some 50 yards away, emanating from nothing we could see. I said, "Wow, did you see that?" and my colleague responded that he saw it too. Of course, we said things like, "Wow, did you see that?" and, "Oh, my God!" many times that night. Through the whole experience, we felt a presence communicating non-verbally to us. Obviously, we were the only ones who saw 'them'. There were many houses in the vicinity, with many people living there who could have seen 'them', but it appears that 'they' were for our eyes only. Perhaps 'they' were hallucinations, but if they were, it was a 'dual hallucination', for we both saw the same thing.

If you get the chance, write me and comment upon these 'dual hallucinations'.

Best Wishes,
Adam Gorightly

And Something Flew In...

Following my aforementioned psychedelic UFO encounter, I attempted to come to terms with the experience, and over the years have entertained a number of different theories to explain what occurred. Now, it's only natural that some may write off this experience to drugged delusions. However, I don't believe this to be the case. But what I do suspect is that LSD opened a doorway that allowed my friend and I to see into a realm that UFO researcher John Keel has referred to as the *Superspectrum*; a realm, or alternate dimension that is all around us, although hidden from everyday or normal modes of perception. Keel has suggested that one method of accessing this realm is through the use of hallucinogenic drugs. This is not to suggest that Keel endorses the willy-nilly use of said drugs.

Perhaps this Superspectrum is what those who have dabbled in the magical traditions have gained access to over the millennium, allowing a portal of entry to the beings who exist within these realms. We'll explore this theory of the Superspectrum in more depth later, but what I'm suggesting is that – in order to observe UFO's – one must often enter into a more receptive state, like a psychic or channeler tuning into voices or subtle energies. Channelers must first induce in themselves a trance state before being able to invoke spirits. There are a number of methods that can be used to induce altered states; these include drugs, sensory deprivation, sex magic rituals, hypnosis and chanting.

Many of these practices were used by the notorious occultist and magician, Aleister Crowley. In 1918 Crowley performed a magical ritual called the Amalantrah Working, which consisted of a series of visions he received through one of his many "Scarlet Women" who worked as his mediums. Throughout his life, Crowley had a number of Scarlet Women, such as his wife Rose Kelley, who acted as channels for otherworldly transmissions. The Scarlet Woman also played a large part in Crowley's notorious sex rituals, which incorporated the use of hallucinogenic drugs. The intent of these rituals was to invoke certain intelligences into physical manifestation. To this end, Crowley and his Scarlet Woman presumably created a magickal portal to allow entrance to ultradimensional entities.

It was through Crowley's 1918 magical working that he came into contact with an otherworldly being named Lam, who

'LAM'

looks strikingly similar to the grey alien on the cover of Whitley Strieber's *Communion*. Crowley referred to Lam as an "Enochian entity," because he contacted Lam using the "Enochian calls" – a Cabalistic language devised by 17th century Elizabethan magician Dr. John Dee, and his assistant Edward Kelley. Kelley worked as a scryer in these rituals, the scryer being the vehicle through which the channeled messages are received, similar to Crowley's Scarlet Woman. Although Kelley is quite a common name, it's interesting to note that both these magicians, Crowley and Dee, had scryers with the same last name Kelley.

Enochian language refers to the biblical books of Enoch, which were removed from the Bible around 400 AD and banned by the early church. The original texts were discovered in Ethiopia in 1768. The *Book of Enoch* describes trips Enoch took to other worlds, where he encountered wondrous beings and was given information by them to take back to Earth. The narrative tells the story of wicked angels who abducted and mated with human women, which was also related in Genesis Chapter 6. The Old Testament says "The sons of God came in unto the daughters of man." This intercourse and interaction resulted in a hybrid race known as the *Nephilim*. Some have interpreted this 'myth' as telling the story of invading aliens, who came to Earth to practice genetic manipulation. *Nephilim* comes from ancient Hebrew meaning "the Fallen Ones."

The offspring of this mating between the Earth Women and these wicked angels, as noted, was the *Nephilim* who, in turn, went on to commingle with the earth gals, and –as taken from Genesis – taught them "sorcery, incantation, and the dividing of roots and trees." According to UFO researcher Guy Malone, the dividing of roots refers to the use of shamanic drugs. Shamanic drugs, or hallucinogens, as I have discovered, are an integral link between ritual magic and the UFO phenomenon. To quote Crowley chronicler Kenneth Grant:

Crowley was aware of the possibility of opening the spatial gateways and of admitting an extraterrestrial Current in the human life-wave...It is an occult tradition – and Lovecraft gave it persistent utterance in his writings – that some transfinite and superhuman power is marshalling its forces with the intent to invade and take possession of this planet...This is reminiscent of Charles Fort's dark hints about a secret society on earth already in contact with cosmic beings and, perhaps, preparing the way for their advent. Crowley dispels the aura of evil with which these authors (Lovecraft and Fort) invest the fact; he prefers to interpret it...not as an attack upon human consciousness by an extra-terrestrial and alien entity but as an expansion of consciousness from within, to embrace other stars and to absorb their energies into a system that is thereby enriched and rendered truly cosmic by the process.

To this end, many in occult circles believe that Crowley intentionally opened a portal of entry, or a Stargate, by the practice of ritual magick which allowed the likes of Lam and otherworldly beings a passageway onto the earth-plane. In Enochian magick, the intent is to gain access to different *aethers*, as they are called. And each of these *aethers* is inhabited by a certain entity who exists in, and guards over, that particular aether. Perhaps one such entity was Lam. *Aethers* themselves are perhaps just another name for dimensions.

A noted protégé of Crowley was Jack Parsons, a renowned rocket scientist and founding member of Jet Propulsion Laboratories. In 1946, with the aid of the future founder of Scientology, L. Ron Hubbard, Parsons contacted beings not unlike Crowley's Lam. During that period, Parsons and Hubbard conducted a series of rituals called the Babalon Working in California's Mojave Desert, a hotbed of UFO activity throughout the early days of UFO sightings.

During this period, a young lady named Marjorie Cameron showed up at Parsons' house, and a couple weeks after arriving there claimed she saw a silver cigar-shaped UFO. To Parsons this incident was a sign that Cameron was the chosen one with whom to conduct the Babalon Working, the intent of which was to create a "child" in the spiritual realms, who would be "called down" and directed into the womb of a female volunteer. When born, this child would incarnate the forces of Babalon, and become the Scarlet Woman of Revelations, symbolizing the dawning of the Age of Horus, the coming new age.

Some have speculated that the portal of entry for alien beings that Crowley opened may have been further enlarged by the rituals of Parsons, Hubbard and Cameron, and that these rituals also increased the intensity of this portal and made it highly unstable, thus facilitating a monumental paradigm shift in human consciousness.

The Babalon Working rituals ended just before the "Great Flying Saucer Flap" of 1947 when the modern age of UFO sightings began. In this regard, some have suggested that Parsons and Hubbard opened a door – and something flew in. Curiously enough, conspiracy researcher John Judge claims that Jack Parsons and Kenneth Arnold were flying partners and colleagues.

In addition to the Arnold sightings, 1947 was the year of the famous and alleged Roswell saucer crash and also marked the passing of Aleister Crowley. Also in 1947, the Dead Sea Scrolls were discovered, containing multiple copies of the Books of Enoch, which as previously noted, detailed interactions between otherworldly angels and the fair maidens of Earth.

SPACE BROTHERS...SIRIUSLY

On June 17th 1952, Jack Parsons met a fiery death when he blew himself up with explosives at his house in Los Angeles. Crowley chronicler Kenneth Grant believed that Marjorie Cameron, during the course of the Babalon Working, became possessed by alien entities – and this somehow led to Jack Parsons' demise. There have been numerous rumors over the years about Parsons' death, one which suggests that he was conducting a homunculus experiment when he blew himself up – basically trying to make matter out of energy, to create a living being through magic ritual, like the alchemists of old.

This theory may relate to what was going on with UFOs, then and now; that they are in fact energy critters, and what the likes of Parsons were playing around with was creating a way of taking etheric energy and giving it form, which is perhaps what the whole UFO phenomenon is about; humans interacting with subtle energies, in essence tuning into these subtle energies, then taking this energy – and with conscious will and intent – giving it a shape. The shape it took with the early UFO contactees was the UFO, the flying saucer.

A month after Jack Parsons' death, a squadron of UFOs buzzed the White House, the Capitol and the Pentagon, sightings that were confirmed by photographs, radar and pilot testimony, putting the nation on alert.

It was onto this backdrop that George Adamski invoked his own brand of cosmic messengers. Adamski's first encounter with the Space Brothers occurred in the Mojave in 1952, when – in the company of six other witnesses, who included George Hunt Williamson – he witnessed a flying saucer, followed by a man with long blond hair who exiting the ship. Telepathically, the "man" informed Adamski he was from Venus, and that he was concerned about the human race detonating atomic bombs. According to Adamski, he was then taken aboard the alien ship and flown around the universe.

Interestingly, Adamski had a long history of involvement in mysticism. In 1934, he founded "The Royal Order of Tibet," where he gave lectures on "The Universal Laws" and the teachings of ascended masters. So Adamski was entertaining ideas concerning evolved beings from higher planes interacting with humans many years before his contact with UFOs.

Also in 1952, George Van Tassel, while meditating under 'Giant Rock' in the Southern California desert, came into contact with

Venusians who took him aboard their spaceship and gave him instructions on how to build an otherworldly rejuvenation machine called the Integratron. So in essence, Van Tassel entered into a self induced trance prior to coming into contact with the space people. The key, once again, is altered states as a mechanism for contacting entities from other realms or dimensions.

Delving deeper into the modern era of UFOs, 1952 appears to be a pivotal year. It was in 1952 – in a Mayan temple in Palenque – that a sarcophagus was discovered, the design of which depicts what appears to be a man at the controls of an intricate piece of machinery that some have contended is a spacecraft. Also in 1952, President Eisenhower was allegedly debriefed on MJ-12, the super secret government group that had been formed in 1947 (another pivotal year) to investigate UFOs, and that this group had presumably made contact with extraterrestrials.

Through a channeled message, the space brothers informed Adamski's colleague, George Hunt Williamson, that the secret of their mission on earth was revealed in a Bugs Bunny cartoon (of all things) which premiered in 1952, co-starring the lovable Marvin Martian. The episode was entitled *The Hasty Hare*. Author Robert Anton Wilson claimed that this cartoon documented the first alien abduction, that of Bugs Bunny. Williamson authored *Other Tongues, Other Flesh*, which presented the idea of a cosmic battle between the "good guys" from the star system Sirius versus the evil meanies from the planet Orion. Williamson experimented with some novel methods to contact the Space People, which included channeling. In addition, Williamson developed something similar to an Ouija Board with a glass tumbler that he used as a method to channel his otherworldly benefactors. This eventually put him in contact with these beings from Sirius, who he conversed to in an Enochian language similar to that used by Dee and Crowley.

Robert Temple's *The Sirius Mystery*, published in 1977, documents the history of the Dogon tribe of Africa, and their meetings in 3200

B.C. with a race of beings from Sirius. At that time, Temple says, these creatures appeared in space ships and revealed mysteries which were passed on to initiates in various secret societies in Egypt and the Near East. These contacts, Temple contended, planted the seeds for the various mystery religions that sprang up across the planet. The adepts of these mystery religions have referred to themselves – in one form or another throughout history – as 'the Illuminati'. The Dogon tribe allegedly produced advanced astronomical charts, which revealed the hidden dual star of Sirius centuries before it was actually discovered by astronomers in the 20th century.

The brightest star in the heavens, Sirius is regarded in occult circles as the "hidden god of the cosmos," the sun behind the sun. Sirius has long been an object of worship and veneration. The ancient Egyptians equated their chief goddess, Isis, with Sirius, which they called Set. According to Kenneth Grant, "Crowley unequivocally identifies his Holy Guardian Angel with Sirius, or Set-Isis." Another secret society adept, the American Masonic leader Albert Pike, wrote that "Sirius still glitters in our Lodges as the Blazing Star." The emblem of the all-seeing eye, hovering above the unfinished pyramid, is a depiction of the Eye of Sirius, a common motif found throughout Masonic lore. It is no secret that many of our nation's founding fathers were Freemasons, which explains the odd appearance of the Eye of Sirius on the dollar bill. George Hunt Williamson as well spoke of a secret society on Earth that has been in contact with Sirius for thousands of years, and that the emblem of this secret society was the all-seeing eye.

Around the turn of the century, an occultist named Lucien-Francois Jean-Maine in Haiti claimed contact with the Sirius star system, which was made possible by performing Crowleyean rituals. In 1922, Jean-Maine combined these Crowleyean rituals with voodoo practices to form the Cult of the Snake in his native Haiti. Jean-Maine also claimed to be in contact with a disembodied being named Lam.

A rash of Sirius contacts continued on into the 1970s. In 1974, science fiction author Phillip K. Dick had some sort of "mystical experience" involving three-eyed, crab-clawed beings from Sirius. During this same period (1973-74) – authors Robert Anton Wilson and Doris Lessing also had contact with Sirius, both independent from one another. Robert Anton Wilson, it should be noted, was dabbling in Crowleyean magic and the ritualistic use of hallucinogens during this period. After conducting a Crowleyean ritual known as the Conversation with the Holy Guardian Angel, Wilson encountered an ascended master who instructed him on the importance of Sirius. This experience happened to Wilson on July 23rd, 1973. Wilson later discovered that July 23 is the day when Sirius rises behind the sun, known as the Dog days.

In the *Book of Enoch*, the *Nephilim* were referred to as the Watchers, which equates to angels in the biblical texts. And an angel who watches over someone is called a holy guardian angel. So perhaps, when Wilson was conducting the ritual of the Holy Guardian Angel, what he summoned forth, in the guise of an ascended master, was really a Watcher, or a *Nephilim*. It should come as no surprise that Crowley oversaw a mystical order known as the *Argenteum Astrum*, also know as the Order of the Silver Star, which was named after the dual stars of Sirius.

One of the more bizarre Sirius-related theories I've heard comes courtesy of renowned conspiracy researcher James Shelby Downard, who described a ritual conducted at the Palomar Observatory by a "Sirius-worship cult," as he termed it, who performed sex magick rituals there immersed under the telescopically focused light of Sirius, beamed through a Palomar telescope. George Adamski, during the 1950s and early 1960s, lived at the base of Palomar Observatory. In *The Stargate Conspiracy*, authors Picknett and Prince claimed that Parsons' OTO Lodge once had a temple located atop Mount Palomar, long before the Observatory was built.

CROWLEY'S CONTACTS

Lam wasn't the first otherworldly entity with whom Crowley came into contact. A perhaps more significant encounter occurred a decade before, with a being named Aiwass, who was channeled through Crowley's wife and Scarlet Woman, Rose Kelley. It was through Rose that Aiwass dictated Crowley's own bible, *The Book of the Law*, which set down the precepts of his religion, Thelema. The physical description of Aiwass is particularly creepy, because it matches the classical Men In Black descriptions: oriental features, angular face, and a strange pallor to the skin.

According to UFO researcher Allen Greenfield in *Secret Cipher of the UFOnauts*, Crowley's *The Book of the Law* is much more than a blasphemous bible, as some have perceived it, but is in essence an instruction manual on how to contact alien beings, and within its contents presumably are secret codes that can be used to summon forth these aliens or ultradimensional critters. According to Greenfield, Crowley himself never quite figured out how to interpret the code contained within *The Book of the Law*. However, his prodigy, Charles Stansfeld Jones (also known as Frater Achad) – who was proclaimed by Crowley to be his magical child – supposedly deciphered the code, and passed on this arcane knowledge to other initiates and magic adepts.

Crowley's portrait of Lam was passed into the hands of Kenneth Grant in 1945 following a joint magical working in which he and Crowley were involved. Since that time, several occultists under Grant's influence have carried on similar magical workings, with the intent of contacting Lam. This has spawned an unofficial Cult of Lam, known more popularly as the Typhonian OTO.

Aleister Crowley

The most notable practitioner in this regard is Michael Bertiaux, who throughout the 1960s and 1970s carried out magical workings in this vein. And, if we are to believe OTO propaganda, Bertiaux and others have been quite successful in their endeavors.

CURIOUS CONNECTIONS

In the 1930s and early 1940s there was a group known as the Choronzon Club, with lodges located throughout the U.S. Later membership of the Choronzon Club would overlap with Jack Parsons' OTO Lodge. Choronzon is a demon or devil that originated in the writings of Dr. John Dee and Edward Kelley as part of their practice of Enochian Magick, and later became an important element in Aleister Crowley's magickal system. Meade Layne, a resident of Southern California, was associated with the Choronzon Club. Layne was also a student of Frater Achad (aka Charles Stansfeld Jones), Crowley's prodigy and 'Magical Child'.

In 1946 – the same year that Parsons and Hubbard were conjuring ultradimensional somethings in the Southern California desert – Layne and a psychic channeler, Mark Probert, came in contact with what they called The Inner Circle. This alleged group of discarnate beings were said to be in touch with aliens visiting the earth in Ether Ships, presumably from the fourth dimension. Layne referred to these beings as the Ethereans; entities that exist all around us, but which we cannot see with our normal senses.

Layne went on to form Borderlands Sciences Research Foundation (BSRF). BSRF published some of the first info on UFOs – predating the Kenneth Arnold sighting of 1947 – and was one of the first groups to combine mediumship with a belief in extraterrestrials, with Probert questioning his spirit guides on the emerging mystery of flying saucers. Once again, the connection linking Aleister Crowley to the modern era of UFOs appears quite evident.

From 1948-1958, paranormal researcher Dr. Andrija Puharich ran a research center called the Round Table Foundation, carrying out experiments over the years with several famous psychics. In that pivotal year 1952, Puharich brought an Indian mystic named Dr. D.G. Vinod to his lab where Vinod channeled 'The Nine'. The Nine presented themselves as a collective intelligence, consisting of nine entities that were presumably in touch with a cosmic intelligence.

A number of psychics and channelers worked with Puharich in the years to follow, many of them allegedly contacting The Nine, the most famous being Uri Geller in the early 1970s. These otherworldly communications led to a group which Puharich oversaw called "Lab Nine" that included cutting edge scientists, multi-millionaire industrialists and leading politicians of the day – among them *Star Trek* creator Gene Roddenberry, who actually wrote a screenplay based upon The Nine. At a conference at Esalen in Big Sur, California, one of the Lab Nine channelers divulged that The Nine originated from Sirius. Puharich talked about opening a gateway through The Nine, which he later termed as a Stargate.

After having a vision featuring Enoch of the Bible, James Hurtak claims to have come in contact with extraterrestrials in 1973, the same period that Phil Dick, Robert Anton Wilson and Doris Lessing were contacted by certain beings from Sirius. Like 1947 and 1952, 1973 is another key year in Contactee lore. In the wake of his visions and purported extraterrestrial contacts, Hurtak went on to author *The Keys of Enoch*, which embodies the spiritual teachings of his otherworldly benefactors. In the Lab Nine earthly hierarchy, James Hurtak was Puharich's second-in-command, a key player in the Lab Nine scene.

Also in 1973, LSD guru Dr. Timothy Leary claimed telepathic contact with extraterrestrials. During July and August of that year, while serving time at Folsom Prison, Leary formed a four-person telepathy team. Synchronistically, these communications happened during the 'dog days' of Sirius. At the same time Leary was receiving his Starseed Transmissions, another psychedelic pioneer, Dr. John Lilly, started having his own series of interstellar communications with a network of entities known as ECCO: "Earth Coincidence Control Office." These communications were achieved through the use of the drug Ketamine.

UFO FLAPS AND WINDOWS

According to The Temporal Doorway, a website dedicated to statistical UFO analysis (www.temporaldoorway.com), the most significant historical years for UFO sightings – referred to as 'flaps' – occurred in 1947, 1952, 1954, 1967, 1973 and 1979.

1947, the first spike, was the year of the fabled Kenneth Arnold sighting, the reported Roswell crash and many other noteworthy UFO events. The next spike was 1952, a year when many UFO Contactees garnered attention with extraordinary claims, the most famous among them George Adamski. 1954 stands on record as the greatest year of UFO sightings, however a majority of these occurred in France. The next significant year was 1967, the dawning of the Age of Aquarius, the Summer of Love and rampant psychedelic drug experimentation

Continuing on, the next significant spike occurred in 1973, the year that Leary, Wilson, Phil Dick and the others I have mentioned were experiencing their own otherworldly contacts with the star system Sirius. And the next spike was 1979, the year I had my own UFO freakout.

Paranormal researchers have long noted unusual electromagnetic activity in areas where UFOs are encountered. These areas are called "UFO windows" where UFOs and other weird sightings occur. Occultists described these areas as "Gateways" – weak spots in the Earth's magnetic field through which beings from other space time continuums enter into our reality. It is within these "UFO windows" that a Superspectrum exists, according to the theory of UFO researcher John Keel. These areas have also been called 'hot spots'. Loch Ness, presumably, is one such area where the fabled Loch Ness monster has been rumored to exist. Loch Ness was also the home, for a period, of Aleister Crowley.

A common description of UFOs is that they often change colors, which suggested to Keel that they are specters traveling through our visible light spectrum. And this is exactly the type of phenomenon I saw during my own UFO sighting, this changing of colors. The Superspectrum Theory contends that UFOs exist at frequencies beyond visible light, but that they can also adjust their frequency and descend into the electromagnetic spectrum – just as you can turn the dial of your radio up and down the scale of radio frequencies. When a UFO frequency nears that of visible light, it will first appear as a purplish blob. As it moves further down the scale, it changes to blue, and then to blue-ish green and so on, finally to white. This is how many UFO sightings unfold.

UFOs, Mr. Keel suggested, are energies of a different frequency. Like tuning a radio, you pick up and amplify only the signal coming in at a certain point, or frequency, of the electromagnetic spectrum. Your eyes are also receivers tuned to very specific wavelengths, as your brain is also a receiver.

Paranormal investigators often use infrared detection systems which reveal otherwise "invisible" activity. Altered states – such as those produced by ritual magick or the use of mind altering drugs – are other possible methods of seeing into the Superspectrum, which is akin to someone using infrared goggles at night to see what the naked eye cannot. This, in essence, is what psychics claim to do. They have simply fine-tuned this ability to pick up waves and frequencies that normal people can't see. Interestingly enough, George Van Tassel described the way he communicated to the aliens as "channeling" and said it was like tuning in a television to decode an electromagnetic signal.

The Superspectrum Theory contends that once these waves and frequencies are filtered through a person's consciousness and belief system, then what comes out on the other end of perception may be an angel if someone is religiously inclined, or alien beings in flying saucers, or whatever we view them to be through the filters of our belief systems. So, in essence, these entities appear to be temporary manipulations of energy. Keel likes to use the word "transmogrifications" to describe them. A transmogrification is reminiscent of what the Native Americans called a shapeshifter, or what the Tibetans call tulpas – entities that can change shape and form. And this is how I view the UFO phenomenon: as an intelligence that can take many shapes, not only flying saucers, but a vast spectrum of shapes, sizes and colors.

WHO MAKES THE GRASS GREEN?

So in finishing, to answer my own provocative question, "Were the UFO Contactees Ritual Magicians?", I would answer a resounding YES, in the sense that we all create our own reality. "*Who is the Master that makes the grass green?*", as the Buddhist saying goes. We are, of course – through the lenses of our perception.

And to take this theory one step further, I would contend that the electromagnetic spectrum also plays a part in the creation of this enigma, acting in a symbiotic manner, interacting with human consciousness. The UFOs I saw indeed behaved like critters moving through a light spectrum, changing colors and size, each one different from the other, some even cartoonish looking with multicolored propellers, spinning in the air. Perhaps, what I call "The Magician's Intent" opens the door to the Superspectrum.

As recounted in my own psychedelic UFO encounter, I mentioned a pivotal moment leading up to the event, when my friend and I said to each other "What if we saw a UFO right now – no one would ever believe because we were under the influence." In essence what we did, I believe, was plant the seeds for a magical ritual to unfold, however unwittingly. Prior to his famous UFO sighting, George Adamski went out intentionally hunting UFOs, which brings to mind the concept of 'The Magician's Intent'. That Adamski was first forming the intent in his mind that he wanted to see UFOs is key here. Seek and ye shall find.

Now just think what can happen if you intentionally planted that seed, and then used various methods to alter your consciousness with the intent in mind of conjuring UFOs. You too might then be able to see beyond the veil and inside the Superspectrum, and the appearance of UFOs might be the end result.

But be careful what you wish for, and how you tend the garden of your consciousness...

Adam Gorightly is a self-described "crackpot historian" who has been chronicling fringe culture and conspiracy politics in an illuminating manner for more than two decades. He has authored a number of books, including *The Shadow Over Santa Susana: Black Magic, Mind Control and the Manson Family Mythos*, and *The Prankster and the Conspiracy: The Story of Kerry Thornley and How He Met Oswald and Inspired the Counterculture*. You can visit his website at: www.adamgorightly.com

ENDNOTES

Michael Prescott - Hungry Ghosts (p. 3)

Notes

1. Quoted from www.worlditc.org/c_04_s_bridge_28.htm
2. *The Trickster and the Paranormal*, George P. Hansen. pp. 264-266

Sources

Books:
Hungry Ghosts, Joe Fisher; reissued in 2001 as *The Siren Call of Hungry Ghosts: A Riveting Investigation Into Channeling and Spirit Guides*
Flim-Flam! Psychics, ESP, Unicorns, and Other Delusions, James Randi
Teller of Tales: The Life of Arthur Conan Doyle, Daniel Stashower
To Your Scattered Bodies Go, Philip Jose Farmer
The Trickster and the Paranormal, George P. Hansen
Miracles in the Storm, Mark Macy

Websites:
American Association of Electronic Voice Phenomena site - aaevp.com/
Cottingley fairies articles - www.lhup.edu/~dsimanek/cooper.htm and www.chriswillis.freeserve.co.uk/cottfair.htm
Joe Fisher obituary - www.anomalist.com/milestones/fisher.html
George P. Hansen's site - www.tricksterbook.com/
Mark Macy's site - www.worlditc.org

Greg Taylor - Her Sweet Murmer (p. 15)

Notes

1. Dr George Ritchie, *Return From Tomorrow*
2. Dr Raymond Moody, *Life After Life*
3. NDE of Lorraine Tutmarc, cited on Near-Death.com (http://www.near-death.com/experiences/research29.html)

4. NDE of Vicki Umipeg, cited on Near-Death.com (http://www.near-death.com/experiences/research29.html)

5. E.M. Butler, *Ritual Magic*, pp. 11-12

6. Terence McKenna, *True Hallucinations*

7. Dr Rick Strassman, *DMT: The Spirit Molecule*, p. 212

8. "The Sound of Rushing Water", Michael Harner, from *Hallucinogens and Shamanism*, p. 15

9. Gerardo Reichel-Dolmatoff, *Amazonian Cosmos*

10. "Listening for the Logos: A Study of Reports of Audible Voices at High Doses of Psilocybin", Horace Beach, Ph.D.

11. Edward Sell, *The Faith of Islam*

12. Jacques Vallee, *The Invisible College*, p. 163

13. Graham Hancock, *Supernatural*, p. 507

14. Jacques Vallee, *The Invisible College*, pp. 149, 156

15. While researching this article, I came across some parallel research done by Jeff Wells on his blog 'Rigorous Intution', posted under the title 'Spirit of the Beehive' (see http://rigorousintuition.blogspot.com/2005/12/spirit-of-beehive_04.html). I am indebted to a comment left by poster 'owlindaylight', which directed me towards a new line of investigation, namely into the Eastern religions and their documentation of sounds heard while in altered states of consciousness. I would therefore like to point out that credit for this particular discovery is due to 'owlindaylight' and Jeff Wells, not myself.

16. "Effects of UFOs on People", James McCampbell

17. Stanton Friedman and Kathleen Marden, *Captured*, p. 169

18. "1920-1919 Humanoid Reports", compiled by Albert Rosales (http://www.ufoinfo.com/humanoid/humanoid1910.shtml)

19. Brad Steiger, *Revelation: The Divine Fire*, p. 148

20. "Return to Point Pleasant", Rick Moran, *Fortean Times #156* (also online at http://www.forteantimes.com/features/articles/251/return_to_point_pleasant.html)

21. "You Can Explore Paranormal Habitat", Robert A. Goerman (http://www.book-of-thoth.com/article_submit/paranormal/phenomena/you-can-explore-paranormal-habitat.html)

22. "1975 Humanoid Reports", compiled by Albert Rosales (http://ufoinfo.com/humanoid/humanoid1975.shtml), cited on "Spirit of the Beehive", Jeff Wells (http://rigorousintuition.blogspot.com/2005/12/spirit-of-beehive_04.html)

23. "Does Recurrent Isolated Sleep Paralysis Involve More Than Cognitive Neuroscience", Jean-Christopher Terrillon and Sirley Marques-Bonham, *Journal of Scientific Exploration 15:1*)

24. Jacques Vallee, *Passport to Magonia*, p. 120

25. Janet Bord, *Fairies: Real Encounters with Little People*, p. 75

26. The two books are actually Volume 1 and 2 of D. Scott Rogo's *Paranormal Music Experiences*, (see http://www.anomalistbooks.com/rogo.html). My thanks must go to Patrick Huyghe of Anomalist Books for sending me these titles, as they offered a new line of investigation at just the right time, similar to note 14 above. In fact, the 'library angel' factor and additional synchronicities which occurred during research of this article are worth a separate article in themselves!

27. Recounted in *Heyday of a Wizard*, A.A. Knopf. My thanks to commenter 'Darryn' on Michael Prescott's blog for pointing this out (see: http://michaelprescott. typepad.com/michael_prescotts_blog/2007/07/the-psychic-lif.html)

28. "Temporal Lobe Epilepsy", J.S. Duncan (http://www.e-epilepsy.org.uk/pages/articles/show_article.cfm?id=36)

Robert Schoch - Life with the Great Sphinx (p. 39)

For Further Reading

Schoch, Robert M., with Robert Aquinas McNally. *Voices of the Rocks: A Scientist Looks at Catastrophes and Ancient Civilizations*. New York: Harmony Books, 1999. [See especially Chapter 2, "A Shape with Lion Body and the Head of a Man," pp. 33-51.]

Schoch, Robert M., with Robert Aquinas McNally. *Voyages of the Pyramid Builders: The True Origins of the Pyramids from Lost Egypt to Ancient America*. New York: Jeremy P. Tarcher/Putnam, 2003. [See especially the appendix, "Redating the Great Sphinx of Giza," pp. 278-298.]

Schoch, Robert M., and Robert Aquinas McNally. *Pyramid Quest: Secrets of the Great Pyramid and the Dawn of Civilization*. New York: Jeremy P. Tarcher/Penguin, 2005. [See especially Chapter 4, "A Certain Age," pp. 61-81, and the section of the appendices titled "Seeking Wisdom on the Giza Plateau," pp. 327-331.]

Nick Redfern - Who is Flying the Triangles? (p. 57)

Sources

1. *Project Sign, Subversive Activity*, May 26, 1949. Prepared by Special Agent Bernard A. Price, Air Force Office of Special Investigations.

2. Records pertaining to the history of Mainbrace made available to Nick Redfern in 1990 by Bernard F. Cavalcante, Head, Operational Archives Branch, Naval Historical Center, Washington, D.C., 20374-0571. Project Blue Book Report 2087.

3. *Flying Triangle UFOs – The Continuing Story*, Omar Fowler, self-published.
4. *Newcastle Evening Chronicle*, September 9, 1960.
5. The document in question is contained within Ministry of Defense file reference: AIR 2/17527 and can be viewed in-person at the National Archive, Kew, England. Interview with Jeffrey Brown, September 11, 1999.
6. *Report – Extra!*, Norman Oliver, *Bufora Journal*, Vol. 7, No. 3, 1978. *Bufora Journal*, Vol. 6, No. 6, 1978.
7. Interview with source, January 12, 1993.
8. British Ministry of Defense files, 1984. Letter from Mark Birdsall to the Ministry of Defense, March 27, 1984.

Susan B. Martinez – *The Authors are in Eternity (p. 83)*

Notes

1. Guy Clinton Harwood, *The Geniuses*.
2. Wilma Davidson, *Spirit Rescue*. MN: Llewellyn Publications, 2006, 25.
3. Oahspe, NY: The Oahspe Publishing Co., 1882; Book of Judgment, 6:10.
4. Andrew Mackenzie, *A Gallery of Ghosts*. NY: Taplinger, 1973, 60.
5. Editors at Psychics, *Psychics*. NY: Harper & Row, 1972.
6. M.L.H., "Uncle Tom's Cabin. Was it written by spirit aid or Inspiration?", *Religio-Philosophical Journal*. Chicago, IL: July 30, 1887, 7.
7. Ibid.
8. Edward Wagenknecht, *Harriet Beecher Stowe*. NY: Oxford University Press, 1965.
9. Harriet M. Shelton, *Abraham Lincoln Returns*. NY: The Evans Publishing Co., 1957, 32.
10. N.R. Stuart, "Spiritualism's Unlikely Founders," *American History Magazine*, August, 2005.
11. Raymond Moody, *Reunions*. NY: Villard Books, 1993, 21.
12. Ruth Brandon, *The Spiritualists*. NY: Prometheus Books, 1984, 309.
13. Ibid., 57.
14. Joel Martin & William J. Birnes, *The Haunting of the Presidents*. NY: New American Library, 2003.
15. Nandor Fodor, *Encyclopedia of Psychic Science*. NY: University Books, 1966, 382. ("Thoughtforms")
16. Thackery, in his "Roundabout Papers," *Cornhill Magazine*, London, August, 1862.
17. Martin Ebon, *They Knew the Unknown*. NY: The World Publishing Co., 1971, 69.
18. Mackenzie, op. cit., 59-60.
19. J.B. Newbrough, *Spiritalis*, NY: 1874, 43.

20. Carl Sandburg, *Abraham Lincoln: The War Years I*, NY: Scribner's Sons, 1936, 261.

21. http.//womenshistory.about.com/library; "Julia ward Howe – writing the Battle Hymn of the Republic."

22. Martin Ebon, *Beyond Space and Time*. NY: New American Library, 1967, 195-7.

23. Gore Vidal, *Point to Point Navigation*. NY: Doubleday, 2006, 142.

24. The problem is discussed at length (Chapter 5) in my work-in-progress, *The Myth of Reincarnation*.

25. Isabel Allende, *Paula*, Avon, UK: G.K. Hall & Co., 1995, 280.

26. Troy Taylor, *The Haunted President*. IL: Whitechapel Press, 2005

Picknett and Prince – Templar Revelations (p. 183)

Notes

1. J.M. Upton-Ward, *The Rule of the Templars*, Boydell Press, Woodbridge, 1992, p. 2.

2. Evelyn Lord, *The Knights Templar in Britain*, Longman, Harlow, 2002, p. 10.

3. Michel Lamy, *Les templiers: Ces grands seigneurs aux blancs manteaux*, Aubéron, Bordeaux, 1994, pp. 117-9

4. Hugh J. Schonfield, *The Essene Odyssey*, Element, Shaftesbury, 1984, pp. 162-4.

5. See Edward Burman, *Supremely Abominable Crimes: The Trial of the Knights Templar*, Allison & Busby, London, 1994, pp. 226-8.

6. Malcolm Barber, *The Trial of the Templars*, Cambridge University Press, Cambridge, 1978, pp. 224-5.

The Emperor – The Unbelievable Strangeness of Bigfoot (p. 217)

Sources

Bowen, Charles (ed.) (1977a) *Humanoids*. Futura Publications.

Bowen, Charles (1977b) *Few and Far Between: Landing and occupant reports a rarity in the British Isles*. In Bowen (1977a). Pages 13-26.

Coleman, Loren (1989) *The Menehune: Little People of the Pacific*. Fate. 4 (7).

Craft, Michael (1996) *Alien Impact*. St. Martin's Press.

Creighton, Gordon (1977) *The Humanoids in Latin America*. In Bowen (1977a). Pages 84-129.

The Desert News (7th June 1997) *Utah man says he's seen Bigfoot 9 times*. http://www.bigfootencounters.com/articles/deseret.htm

Dongo, Tom & Bradshaw, Linda (1995) *Merging Dimensions: The Opening Portals of Sedona*. Hummingbird Publishing.

Good, Timothy (1993) *Alien Contact: Top-Secret UFO Files Revealed.* Quill, William Morrow and Company.

Elkins, Don and Rueckert, Carla (1977) *Secrets of the UFO.* L/L Research.

Harpur, Patrick (2003) *Daimonic Reality.* Pine Winds Press

Johnson, Stan (1996) *Bigfoot Memoirs: My Life with the Sasquatch.* Blue Water Publishing

Keel, John (2002) *The Complete Guide to Mysterious Beings.* Tor.

Kelleher, Colm and Knapp, George (2005) *Hunt for the Skinwalker: Science Confronts the Unexplained at a Remote Ranch in Utah.* Paraview

Lapseritis, Jack (1998) *The Psychic Sasquatch: And Their UFO Connection.* Wild Flower Press

Murdie, Alan and Halliday, Robert (2005) *Magic Lanterns. Fortean Times #204.* 40-42.

Redfern, Nick (2004) *Three Men Seeking Monsters: Six weeks in pursuit of werewolves, lake monsters, giant cats, ghostly dogs, and ape-men.* Paraview.

Steiger, Brad (1974) *Mysteries of Time and Space.* Sphere Books.

Sutherly, Curt (1996) *Fate Presents: Strange Encounters: UFOs, Aliens & Monsters Among Us.* Llewellyn Publications.

Vallee, Jacques (1990) *Confrontations: A Scientist's Search for Alien Contact.* Ballantine Books.

Vallee, Jacques and Davis, E.W. *"Incommensurability, Orthodoxy and the Physics of High Strangeness: A 6-layer Model for Anomalous Phenomena"* NIDS http://www.nidsci.org/pdf/vallee_davis.pdf

Notes

1. Vallee and Davis, page 2
2. Vallee (1990) page 54
3. Craft (1996) page 66
4. Harpur (2003) page 68
5, Kelleher and Knapp (2005) page 157
6. Keel (2002), page 62-63. ABSM is his abbreviation of Abominable Snowman
7. Coleman (1989)
8. Creighton (1977) cases 9, 12, 14. 18 (the first 3 are from 1954 and describe immensely strong hairy dwarves in close proximity to flying vehicles attacking people – the same year saw similar reports of very strong dwarves in connection ot UFOs but their hairiness is unreported: 11 and 15)
9. Sutherly (1996) page 147
10. Sutherly (1996) page 143-146
11. Steiger (1974) page 118
12. Craft (1996) page 66-70

13. Elkins and Rueckert (1977) reproduced at http://tinyurl.com/2q5rxe

14. Bowen (1977) pages 19-30. Worth noting this has been re-investigated and there is the suggestion it might have a more mundane explanation, although other sightings, large footprints from the same area at the same time can't be so easily explained: http://www.virtuallystrange.net/ufo/updates/2002/feb/m03-012.shtml

15. Keel (2002) page 234

16. Sutherly (1996) 147

17. Coleman, Loren. Bigfoot Contactees. (19th March 2006) http://www.cryptomundo.com/cryptozoo-news/bf-contactees/

18. Lapseritis (1998)

19. The Desert News (1997)

20. Johnson (1996)

21. Keel (2002) page 62

22. Sutherly (1996) note 64, page 153

23. Harpur (2003) pages 272-273

24. Steiger (1974) page 115

25. Steiger (1974) page114

26. Kelleher and Knapp (2005) page 157

27. Craft (1996) pages 73-74

28. ibid

29. Keel (2002) page 107

30. Harpur (2003) page 77

31. More can be found in see e.g. the Bords' *The Bigfoot Casebook* the first version summarised online: http://home.clara.net/rfthomas/cb/chrono.html

32. (2005) *Vanishing Bigfoot and Anecdotal Accounts: Implications and Challenges for Researchers.* http://www.unifiedworlds.com/BFvanishing.htm

33. http://www.unifiedworlds.com/desertapes.htm#threerivers

34. http://www.unifiedworlds.com/desertapes.htm#Horizon%20Montanez

35. *Fortean Times #208* page 40

36. Kelleher and Knapp (2005) page 45

37. Kelleher and Knapp (2005) page 149

38. *Desert News* 1997

39. Kelleher and Knapp (2005) pages 46-47

40. Kelleher and Knapp (2005) page 48

41. Redfern (2004)

42. Where the local paper described me as three angry Americans – a description I fail on every point

43. I am suspicious of some of the local press coverage of which pet-eating troglodytes is the most prominent, alongside "Bigfoot nearly made me loose my baby." My concerns about the latter leading to their claims about me mentioned in the previous footnote.

44. (2006) *Bigfoot almost made me lose my baby.*. http://tinyurl.com/3dlvzk
45. Murdie and Halliday (2005)
46. Redfern (2004) chapter 12.
47. Redfern (2004) pages 18-19
48. Dongo & Bradshaw (1995) pages 11-14
49. Dongo & Bradshaw (1995) pages 22-23
50. Analysis needn't cost a penny either – I have been contacted by one major lab eager to test cryptid hair samples. I've also been in touch with another who will do metallurgic analysis of any metal from UFOs.
51. Good (1993) Chapter 3
52. Good (1993) page 68
53. Sutherly (1996) page 152
54. http://www.ncbuy.com/news/2004-02-18/1008952.html
55. Vallee and Davis
56. Loren Coleman's comments on the UFO UpDates mailing list (4th February, 2002): http://www.virtuallystrange.net/ufo/updates/2002/feb/m04-022.shtml

Michael Grosso – *The Beatific Vision (p. 255)*

1. Ernesto Bozzano, "Apparitions of Deceased Persons at Deathbeds," *The Annals of Psychical Science 3* (1906), pp. 67-100
2. William Barrett, *Deathbed Visions* (London: Methuen, 1926), p. 2.
3. Barrett, ibid., p. 25.
4. George Gallup Jr. with William Proctor, *Adventures in Immortality* (New York: McGraw Hill, 1985), p. 85.
5. Barrett, ibid., pp. 72-74
6. Karlis Osis, *Deathbed Observations by Physicians and Nurses* (New York: Parapsychology Foundation, 1961).
7. Ibid., p. 23.
8. Karlis Osis and Erlendur Haraldsson, *At the Hour of Death* (New York: Avon, 1977).
9. Walter Cannon, "'Voodoo' Death," *American Anthropologist 44, no. 2* (1942), pp. 169-181.
10. Paul Edwards, *Immortality* (New York: Prometheus Books, 1997).
11. Brierre de Boisement, *On Hallucinations* (London: Henry Renshaw, 1859).

Lightning Source UK Ltd.
Milton Keynes UK
UKOW02f1127130914

238540UK00001B/100/P